Rethinking Social Policy

Rethinking Social Policy

Race, Poverty, and the Underclass

CHRISTOPHER JENCKS

 HarperPerennial

A Division of HarperCollins*Publishers*

A hardcover edition of this book was published in 1992 by Harvard University Press. It is here reprinted by arrangement with Harvard University Press.

RETHINKING SOCIAL POLICY. Copyright © 1992 by Christopher Jencks. All rights reserved. Printed in the United States of America. No part of this book may be used or reproduced in any manner whatsoever without written permission except in the case of brief quotations embodied in critical articles and reviews. For information address HarperCollins Publishers, Inc., 10 East 53rd Street, New York, NY 10022.

HarperCollins books may be purchased for educational, business, or sales promotional use. For information please write: Special Markets Department, HarperCollins Publishers, Inc., 10 East 53rd Street, New York, NY 10022.

First HarperPerennial edition published 1993.

Library of Congress Cataloging-in-Publication Data

Jencks, Christopher.
    Rethinking social policy: race, poverty, and the underclass/
Christopher Jencks.—1st HarperPerennial ed.
        p.   cm.
    Originally published: Cambridge, Mass.: Harvard University Press, 1992.
    Includes bibliographical references and index.
    ISBN 0-06-097534-2 (pbk.)
        1. United States—Social conditions—1980– . 2. United States—Social policy.
3. Public welfare—United States. 4. United States—Race relations. 5. Urban poor—
Government policy—United States.   I. Title
[HN59.2.J46   1993]
361.6'1'0973—dc20   92-53407

97 RRD 10

Acknowledgments

When I was a journalist in the early 1960s I learned that I could save myself weeks of library work by using the telephone to exploit the substantive and bibliographic expertise of social scientists around the country. As long-distance rates fell and my Rolodex grew fatter, this habit became an addiction. As a result, I have accumulated intellectual debts so numerous and so complex that I cannot hope to remember and acknowledge them all. I have tried to acknowledge some of those who helped me write this book in the notes for specific chapters, but in four cases the debts are more general and require special comment.

Like most authors, I tend to resent my editors, but there are occasional exceptions. Robert Silvers of the *New York Review* is in my judgment the best editor in America. His editorial and substantive suggestions greatly improved the chapters on discrimination, the safety net, and crime, which first appeared in his journal.

My wife, Jane Mansbridge, also read every line that appears here, often more than once and often at unusually inconvenient times. She improved the prose with judicious editing, restrained my impulse to give needless offense in order to achieve dramatic effect, stimulated my thinking with helpful suggestions and sensible objections, and forced me to deal with contradictions that I had ignored.

Susan Mayer, who now teaches at the University of Chicago's Graduate School of Public Policy Studies, worked with me throughout the 1980s on studies of material hardship and well-being. Years of conversation covering nearly all the issues raised in this volume have exerted an immense effect on my thinking.

Kathryn Edin, with whom I wrote Chapter 6, convinced Mayer and me that we could resolve many of the puzzles posed by the surveys we were analyzing if we would recognize that our respondents had no reason to trust our interviewers and often failed to report much of their income. She also convinced me that a less "scientific" approach to collecting data could often yield far more accurate results.

While all these friends have made invaluable suggestions, an author cannot expect even his best friends to spend more than a few hours looking for flaws in his arguments or data. If you want to do first-rate work you must pray for good enemies as well as friends. With luck, a good enemy will devote weeks or even months to looking for mistakes that a friend would miss. I did not have any truly dedicated enemies when writing these essays, but Thomas Sowell, Charles Murray, Richard Herrnstein, and Elliott Currie all wrote thoughtful responses to my reviews. Each of their responses advanced my understanding of issues about which we disagreed, and I am grateful to them all.

I have been lucky in my institutional affiliations as well as my colleagues. The Center for Urban Affairs and Policy Research at Northwestern has given me free time for writing of a kind that few American social scientists enjoy. In addition, I had a sabbatical leave in 1982–83 supported jointly by the John Simon Guggenheim Memorial Foundation and Northwestern University, and another in 1985–86 supported by the Institute for Advanced Study in Princeton. During the late 1980s the Ford Foundation, the Sloan Foundation, and the Russell Sage Foundation supported my research with Susan Mayer on changes in poor families' material standard of living and thereby became unwitting supporters of the last three essays in this volume. Needless to say, none of these organizations is responsible for my cantankerous views or my technical errors. Nonetheless, without their help my views would have been even more cantankerous and my errors even more numerous than they are.

Contents

Introduction 1

1. Affirmative Action 24

2. The Safety Net 70

3. Crime 92

4. The Ghetto 120

5. The Underclass 143

6. Welfare 204

Notes 237

Index 277

Introduction

When I arrived in Washington as a very junior editor at the *New Republic* in 1961, the term "social policy" was not part of America's political vocabulary. This linguistic gap reflected the legislative realities of the time. Except for the Social Security Act, the federal government had almost no policies or programs for solving social problems. It was not trying to reduce poverty or end discrimination against minorities. It did not play a significant role in educating the young, caring for the sick, or preventing violent crime. Nor was it doing anything to discourage teenage parenthood, to encourage couples to marry before they had children, or to keep couples with children together. Congress did provide money for urban renewal, but this was a bricks-and-mortar program that dealt with poor neighborhoods by tearing them down and moving the residents elsewhere, not by trying to improve poor people's lives.

Then as now, most northern Democrats wanted Washington to take a more active role in solving social problems, but a coalition of conservative southern Democrats and Republicans consistently blocked such proposals. The conservatives rightly feared that if the federal government moved beyond financing bombers, highways, and slum clearance, it would begin to pass laws and make regulations that limited the discretion of conservative local leaders back home.

The only important exception to the general rule that Washington did not make social policy, the Social Security Act, was a legacy of the Great Depression and the New Deal. As its name implies, social security was supposed to reduce the risk that individuals who had become used to life in a particular economic niche would suddenly find themselves pushed out of it. Its two most important components were Unemployment Insurance (UI) and Old Age and Survivors Insurance (OASI, known in the vernacular simply as "social security"). UI was supposed to protect workers against the effects of business downturns. OASI was supposed to protect families against destitution when the breadwinner died or became too old to work.

Like private insurance, these two social-insurance programs reinforced the existing social and moral order. Neither program gave people money unless they or a member of their family worked for it. Both programs gave more money to those who worked in well-paid jobs than to those who worked in poorly paid jobs. As a result, both programs reinforced not only the work ethic but the social hierarchy that America had created on the bedrock of wage inequality.

Along with these two social-insurance schemes, the Social Security Act also authorized "public assistance" for single mothers, the blind, the elderly, and the disabled. Individuals could qualify for these programs even if they had never worked. Nonetheless, public assistance for the elderly, blind, and disabled was widely accepted, because few Americans thought these programs rewarded immoral or foolish behavior. The one truly controversial form of public assistance was for single mothers. It was initially called Aid to Dependent Chidren (ADC), later renamed Aid to Families with Dependent Children (AFDC), but always known colloquially (and pejoratively) as "welfare."

Because support for single mothers has long been the federal government's most unpopular policy, it is important to ask why Congress authorized such support in the first place. When Congress established ADC in 1935, it thought it was subsidizing a set of state programs known as "mothers' pensions." These programs had been established to ensure that indigent widows of good character did not have to place their children in orphanages. Not all states explicitly restricted benefits to widows, but most states did limit benefits to mothers who could provide their children with a "suitable" home. Local officials usually interpreted this requirement as excluding unwed, separated, and divorced mothers, on the grounds that such women set a poor moral example for their children. In any event, Congress thought it was underwriting programs that deferred to local prejudices about who deserved help and who did not.

Yet as soon as the act was passed, federal officials began chipping away at local restrictions designed to keep unwed, separated, and divorced mothers off the rolls.[1] In 1939, moreover, Congress made widows with children eligible for social security benefits if their husbands had contributed to the system. As a result, ADC became mainly a program for unwed, separated, and divorced mothers.[2] Since most Americans were still strongly opposed to both unwed motherhood and divorce, a program that sanctioned and even rewarded such behavior was bound to be unpopular. No serious effort was ever made to eliminate ADC, but it seems safe to say that Congress would never have voted to create such a program had it not already existed. In an important sense, therefore, ADC was an historical accident.

In light of the endless controversy over ADC, congressional reluctance to make other kinds of social policy was easy to understand. Nonetheless, John Kennedy's narrow electoral victory in 1960 reflected widespread public feeling that America needed more national leadership to deal with its domestic problems. Sputnik had convinced many Americans that their schools needed improvement, and most liberals felt that this would only happen if the federal government provided both money and direction. Persistently high rates of unemployment in depressed areas like Appalachia and among the poorly educated workers almost everywhere were also a national concern, and many thought that the federal government should take the lead in fashioning a solution. Perhaps most important, blacks had begun to challenge de jure segregation in the south, evoking a violent response from white supremacists. As a result, a growing number of northern whites wanted the federal government to outlaw overt racial discrimination. Congress refused to act on President Kennedy's proposals for dealing with these matters, but after Kennedy was shot and Lyndon Johnson became president, it passed a flood of new social legislation.

Liberal Reform, Equal Opportunity, and Social Science

Unlike the New Deal, whose enduring legacy was a set of programs designed to prevent the nonpoor from falling into poverty, Johnson's Great Society programs were mainly concerned with helping the poor rise in the world. This shift in emphasis led to a shift in rhetoric. Whereas New Deal speechwriters had talked about economic "security," Great Society speechwriters talked about economic "opportunity." Indeed, they called the enabling legislation for the war on poverty the Economic Opportunity Act of 1964.[3] The provisions of the Civil Rights Act of 1964 that barred racial discrimination in employment were also meant to help equalize economic opportunity. And when the Johnson administration finally persuaded Congress to authorize new forms of federal aid to education in 1965, most of the new programs were aimed at equalizing educational opportunity.

Political enthusiasm for equal opportunity rested on two factual assumptions. First, everyone assumed that almost all poor adults had grown up in poverty. Americans therefore saw poverty as a byproduct of the fact that poor children had a hard time moving up in the world, not of the fact that working-class children had a significant chance of moving down. Second, everyone assumed that "getting an education" more or less guaranteed a poverty-free life. Taken together, these assumptions implied that if only poor children could get the kind of education that middle-class children already got, no one would end up poor.

Yet at the very moment when the federal government was investing unprecedented sums in equalizing opportunity, social scientists were collecting data that cast doubt on the assumptions behind this effort. Two studies, one directed by James Coleman and the other by Peter Blau and Otis Dudley Duncan, were especially relevant. Both were sponsored by the federal government, both involved enormous national surveys, and both exploited recent advances in computer technology to address questions that would have been almost unanswerable a decade earlier.

The "Coleman Report," published in 1966, investigated the reasons why some schoolchildren did better than others on tests of verbal fluency, reading comprehension, and math skills.[4] Coleman and his colleagues found that test performance depended far more on students' family background and the background of their classmates than on the resources that school boards devoted to the students' education. Coleman found little evidence that students learned more in newer buildings, in smaller classes, or from teachers who had more experience or more training than the average teacher.[5] These widely publicized findings raised serious questions about America's ability to move poor children out of poverty by redistributing educational resources. At a minimum, such findings suggested that extra resources would help poor children only if educators used the resources in novel ways.

Blau and Duncan's research, which also began to appear in 1966, had even more far-reaching implications.[6] They showed that a man's occupation in adulthood was only moderately related to his family background.[7] At first glance, this finding may seem inconsistent with

Coleman's findings about school performance, but the inconsistency is more apparent than real. Coleman and his colleagues did not find a strong relationship between children's family background and their test performance. Family background accounted for only 12 to 18 percent of the variation in children's verbal skills and even less of the variation in their reading and math skills.[8] The effect of background on test scores looked strong only when Coleman contrasted it to the even weaker effects of school characteristics on test scores.

Blau and Duncan's findings should have raised serious questions about the widespread assumption that poverty was largely inherited. Their work clearly implied that while many people were poor because they had trouble climbing out of poverty, many others were poor because they had slipped down the social ladder into poverty. But Blau and Duncan's focus was on men's occupations rather than incomes, and they did not emphasize their findings' implications for the war on poverty. As a result, their research got less public attention than Coleman's.[9]

Blau and Duncan's work did not imply, of course, that rich children were as likely as poor children to become poor adults. Millionaires' sons and daughters seldom fall all the way to skid row. But a lot of men and women do end up poorer than their parents. As a result, significant numbers of poor people have grown up in families that were not poor, at least by the standards of their time. This finding suggests that even if we could eliminate poverty in one generation, an economic and social system such as ours would allow a fair number of people to fall into poverty in the next generation. So long as equal opportunity includes the opportunity to be poor, some people will take advantage of that opportunity (or have it thrust upon them).

When the Coleman Report appeared in 1966, I was working at a left-of-center Washington think tank called the Institute for Policy Studies, where hardly anyone paid much attention to quantitative research. I myself was a former English major, whose only training in such matters had been a one-semester undergraduate course in statistics. Nonetheless, Coleman's work made a strong impression on me, because it seemed to provide objective support for many of my long-standing prejudices. I had always thought, for example, that my schoolmates influenced me more than my teachers did. Coleman seemed to show that this experience was very general. Having taught high school briefly after graduating from college, I also thought it absurd to expect that teachers could ever fully compensate children for having been born into the wrong family. So far as I could see, the only way to equalize opportunity was to remove all children from their homes and raise them communally, as the Israeli kibbutzim did. Since that was inconceivable in America, I thought talk of equalizing educational opportunity was just another form of pie-in-the-sky. Coleman seemed to confirm my suspicions.

But Coleman's work was important to me for another reason as well. Until 1966 I had assumed that exerting political influence depended on organization, money, and luck, usually in that order. After watching the public reaction to the Coleman Report, I became convinced that new evidence could also change some people's minds about political questions. This opened up possibilities I had never seriously contemplated before.

When Blau and Duncan's research came to my attention later in 1966, my thinking about equal opportunity underwent an even more profound change.[10] Their finding that American society was quite fluid reinforced my assumption that even if we could equalize opportunity, this would not suffice to eliminate poverty. In other important respects, however, their work challenged my previous beliefs. I had always assumed, for example, that education was becoming steadily more important in determining economic success. I had also assumed that this meant family background was becoming less important. Blau and Duncan showed that, while education had been quite important for a long time, there was little evidence that its importance was growing. Nor did they find evidence that the influence of family background had declined over the course of the twentieth century. My assumption that America was becoming more meritocratic—a notion implicit in almost everything I had read up to that point in my life—therefore appeared to be wrong.

Reading these two studies changed my career. From 1961 to 1966 I saw myself as a journalist and political activist. By 1967 I had become convinced that the war on poverty would fail even if it got as much money as the war in Vietnam was getting. I saw no prospect that the radical egalitarianism of the student movement would ever be acceptable to most American adults, perhaps because it was not acceptable to me. I therefore decided to embark on what proved to be a lengthy and only partially successful effort to rethink the liberal approach to social policy. Sobered by the fact that Blau and Duncan had failed to confirm many of my prejudices, I also decided that the only way to rethink liberal egalitarianism was to start by getting the facts more or less right. At a minimum, that meant familiarizing myself with the findings of quantitative social science.

In the summer of 1967 I returned to Harvard, where I had been an undergraduate from 1954 to 1958. There I found that one of my new colleagues in the Graduate School of Education, Marshall Smith, was willing to teach me how to analyze survey data. I also found a number of other colleagues who shared my interest in the relationship between schooling, equal opportunity, and economic success. In due course I persuaded them to join me in writing a book about the subject, which was published in 1972 under the title *Inequality: A Reassessment of the Effect of Family and Schooling in America.*[11]

Inequality argued that, contrary to what most economists assumed, we could not eliminate poverty simply by doubling or tripling everyone's income. This strategy would not work, we argued, because people need more goods and services when their society gets richer. Needs increase not just because people think they need more when their neighbors have more, but also for practical reasons.

In 1900, for example, America was organized on the assumption that city residents would get around on foot or by streetcar. Outside the cities, Americans traveled by foot or horse. In such a world an automobile was clearly a luxury. Over the course of the twentieth century, however, most Americans acquired cars. This had two effects. First, public transportation atrophied. Second, most employers and shops moved to areas that were accessible only by car, and most families did the same. Outside a few major cities, therefore, not having a car meant not being able to get to work, to shops, or to friends' homes, making a car a necessity for most Americans.

Many other consumer goods have followed the same trajectory, starting as luxuries but gradually becoming necessities. Telephones were a luxury in 1900, when hardly anyone had one. Today, when almost everyone has a telephone, those without service are cut off from family and friends, who no longer write letters. Indeed, those without telephones often have trouble even keeping a job, both because employers now expect workers to call in when they are sick and because workers without telephones cannot make hasty changes in their childcare or transportation arrangements.

Because changes in the way the average family lives require changes in the way poor families live, economic growth alone cannot eliminate poverty. If a rich country wants to rid itself of poverty, *Inequality* argued, it must keep the economic gap between those at the bottom of the economic hierarchy and those in the middle relatively small. This argument implied that if America wanted to win its war on poverty, it would have to reduce economic inequality.[12]

If income inequality among adults were largely traceable to differences in their experiences as children, equalizing the conditions in which children were raised would in due course reduce inequality among adults. *Inequality* argued, however, that since family background explained only a modest fraction of the variation in men's incomes, equalizing the conditions in which children grew up would not greatly reduce economic inequality in the next generation of adults. Indeed, we took this claim a step further, arguing that even if everyone got exactly the same amount of schooling—a goal more far-reaching than anything envisioned by the architects of the war on poverty—some people would end up with incomes far below the average and would not be able to afford the basic necessities of life. We concluded that, if America wanted to eliminate poverty, it would have to redistribute money rather than just redistributing school resources or childhood experiences.

From Equal Opportunity to the Safety Net

The idea that we needed a safety net for those who could not compete successfully in the labor market was hardly new, even in 1972. In America, however, the federal government had traditionally been very reluctant to create such a safety net. Able-bodied adults with low-wage jobs got almost no government help, even if they earned far less than the government said they needed to support their family. Those with no job at all fared a little better, but not much. They could collect unemployment insurance for a few months. After their UI ran out, those without children got no further federal benefits. Most states had a general assistance program for childless adults, but these programs paid almost nothing. Jobless adults with children were eligible for AFDC if they had no spouse, but jobless couples were eligible in only half the states, and even these states usually administered the program for jobless couples (known as AFDC-UP, for "unemployed parent") in such a way as to ensure that very few collected anything.

In 1969 Richard Nixon had proposed a Family Assistance Plan
(FAP) that would have provided a guaranteed income for all parents if
they were willing to work. And in 1972 the Democratic nominee for
president, George McGovern, had endorsed a guaranteed income for
everyone. But Congress rejected FAP in the fall of 1972, as *Inequality*
was going to press, and the voters rejected McGovern a few weeks
later. The closest Congress was willing to come to a guaranteed income
was the Supplemental Security Income (SSI) program, which provided
a small guaranteed income for the elderly, blind, and disabled. Congress passed SSI at the end of 1972, after rejecting FAP. Since then,
Congress has shown little interest in extending the principle of a guaranteed income to able-bodied adults under sixty-five or to children.

Nonetheless, Congress did move beyond the Johnson administration's equal-opportunity strategy for fighting poverty, by establishing a
set of programs that gave the nonelderly poor certain basic necessities
either free or at very low cost. In 1965 Congress established Medicaid,
which provided many (though not all) poor people with free medical
care. In 1970 it federalized the food-stamp program and set a minimum benefit level, making the program almost indistinguishable in
practice from a guaranteed income. Later in the decade Congress went
even further, broadening eligibility for food stamps and increasing
their value. Throughout the 1970s Congress also expanded federal rent
subsidies for the poor, largely through "Section 8" subsidies to private
developers who set aside apartments for low-income families.

Unlike Lyndon Johnson's war on poverty, the growth of means-
tested transfers during the Nixon and Ford administrations was largely
a product of congressional initiative. Each piece of legislation was
shaped by a different set of committees, preoccupied with different
problems and eager to please different interest groups. Because there
was little presidential leadership, there was no central planning mechanism to ensure that the cumulative result was a safety net that helped
everyone the average legislator wanted to help. Some groups, such as
the working poor, got almost no help. Others, such as the mentally ill,
got far less than they needed. So while these programs provided the
beginnings of a safety net, it was a net full of gaping holes.

Because the new safety net was not a byproduct of presidential politics or White House leadership, it also got less public attention than
Johnson's antipoverty programs had. Nonetheless, by the mid-1970s
the federal government was spending far more on these new programs

than it had ever spent on its equal-opportunity programs. This change in priorities profoundly altered public debate about social policy.

So long as liberal social-policy initiatives were aimed at equalizing opportunity, few conservatives challenged the goal. Instead they quarreled with liberals' tactics for achieving the goal. Some conservatives doubted that the money spent on compensatory education was helping much. Others raised analogous questions about job-training programs. Many conservatives argued that affirmative-action programs designed to equalize opportunity were promoting reverse discrimination. At least on the surface, however, this was a debate about means, not ends.[13]

Unlike programs aimed at equalizing opportunity, the safety net was relatively immune to this kind of tactical criticism. When Congress gave money to the elderly and the disabled, the recipients almost all cashed the checks, and most lived better as a result. When Congress gave welfare mothers and their children free medical care, they saw doctors more often. When it created a national food-stamp program, recipients ate somewhat more and had a lot more money to spend on other things. When it subsidized Section 8 housing, those families lucky enough to get a certificate lived in somewhat nicer apartments and paid far less rent.

The conservative complaint about the safety net was not that it failed but that it succeeded. By design, the safety net drew no distinction between those who had brought their troubles on themselves (the "undeserving" poor) and those who were victims of circumstances beyond their control (the "deserving" poor). A single mother could collect welfare regardless of whether she deliberately chose to have her children out of wedlock or was abandoned by an alcoholic husband. A family could get food stamps if its income was low, regardless of whether the head worked fifty hours a week at a low-wage job or spent the day in front of a television set. Indeed, the safety net actually punished people for working harder, by cutting their benefits when they earned more. This meant, in effect, that the safety net lowered the economic cost of both indolence and folly. So when male joblessness and single motherhood began to increase, conservatives were quick to blame these increases on the safety net.

Conservative politics in America revolve around two basic ideas. First, most conservatives think hierarchy natural and equality dangerous. Second, most conservatives are deeply suspicious of government. As the 1970s wore on, conservative writers began to weave these two themes into a sweeping critique of liberal social policy. On the moral level, philosophers like Robert Nozick revived the old argument that governmental redistribution was unjust because it took wealth created by competent, industrious individuals and gave it to others who had no legitimate claim on it.[14] On the practical level, conservative economists argued that redistribution reduced people's incentive to acquire skills and work hard, leaving less to distribute. Some conservatives went even further, asserting that the welfare state actually made the poor worse off.

The conservatives who exerted the most influence on public debate during these years were as prone to oversimplification as the liberals who had dominated debate a decade earlier. It is easy to see why this was so. Persistent invocation of a few widely accepted ideas is a powerful rhetorical tool, especially in a political system dominated by television. But thinking in sound bites does not lead to sensible policy choices, no matter what principles you espouse.

Some ideological differences are simply a matter of conflicting values. (Is redistribution just or unjust? Is out-of-wedlock childbearing immoral?) In cases of this kind, making the same value judgment in every situation, regardless of the context, seems to make sense. But most ideological arguments depend on facts as well as values. (Will socialism raise economic output faster than capitalism? Will raising the minimum wage increase unskilled workers' standard of living, or will the benefits of higher wages be offset by declines in employment? Will higher AFDC benefits increase the incidence of single parenthood so much that children as a group end up worse off?) When facts matter, applying the same principles to every situation leads to foolishness.

If we look across the broad sweep of economic history, for example, government intervention in the marketplace has almost certainly done more harm than good. But that general conclusion would not have told the Swedes in 1945 whether government intervention would do their country more harm than good over the next forty years. (In fact, massive government intervention probably helped the Swedes in this instance, because their government was unusually honest and competent.) The general principle that government regulation does more harm than good is even less useful if we want to predict the effect of a specific intervention at a particular moment in history. A sensible judgment about the minimum wage in the United States today, for example, depends on precisely how many low-wage jobs would disappear if the minimum wage were raised, not on the average impact of government regulation in all the times and places about which we have information.

Or consider another example. We know that many people respond to economic incentives. All else equal, therefore, sensible people expect that raising AFDC benefits will encourage both out-of-wedlock births and family breakups. But that general conclusion is of no use in a debate over welfare policy. In such a debate the important question is *how many* additional fatherless families we will have if we raise AFDC by, say, $100 a month. If the number is very small, we can afford to ignore the problem. If it is very large, even hard-core liberals will want to consider other approaches to helping such families. We cannot resolve quantitative questions of this kind by invoking general principles.

Sorting Out the Debate

After Ronald Reagan's election in 1980, the conservative critique of egalitarian social policy began to dominate the mass media, and liberals were on the defensive everywhere. Yet few liberals seemed to feel that their political difficulties stemmed from real weaknesses in the policies they advocated. Instead they felt that the public had been hoodwinked by a group of well-financed bigots. In time, they thought, the fever would pass, the diverse members of the old New Deal coalition would again recognize that they had common interests, and we would be able to get on with the business of constructing a humane welfare state.

I was less sanguine. I thought broad public acceptance of the liberal agenda unlikely unless the content of that agenda changed in significant ways. In due course I decided to do a series of essays on what I took to be the central questions dividing liberals from conservatives. Since the *New York Review of Books* was both the best and the most widely read serious journal in the country, it seemed the natural place to write about such matters. To accommodate its needs, I decided to turn my observations into a series of long book reviews. I wrote three of these review-essays between 1983 and 1986. With some revisions, they constitute the first three chapters of this book.[15]

Equal opportunity. The first chapter, which focuses on two books by the laissez-faire economist Thomas Sowell, discusses attempts to offset the effects of racial discrimination through various forms of "affirmative action." I started with this topic because it dramatized the limitations of both liberal and conservative ideology. The persistence of widespread racial discrimination illustrates conservatives' inability to reconcile the workings of a free market with most Americans' conception of equal opportunity (or even fairness). The controversy surrounding affirmative action also illustrates liberals' inability to find a politically workable definition of equal opportunity. I try to show that, without some kind of numerical targets, profit-oriented firms will often deny qualified blacks jobs that they deserve. But I also argue that black activists and white liberals often manipulate such targets or quotas to ensure that blacks get jobs even when better-qualified whites are available. Both outcomes perpetuate racial conflict.

The safety net. Chapter 2 turns to the effects of the safety net, focusing on Charles Murray's influential book *Losing Ground*. Murray's most publicized claim was that the growth of transfer programs had impoverished the poor rather than enriching them. As I try to show, that claim has little factual basis. But Murray made another argument that I take more seriously, namely that building a safety net for single mothers who do not work undermines traditional social norms about work and marriage—norms for which we currently have no politically viable alternative. I conclude that until liberals transform AFDC, so that it reinforces rather than subverts American ideals about work and marriage, our efforts to build a humane welfare state will never succeed.

The politics of heredity. Chapter 3 takes up a more traditional conservative argument, namely that inequality is at least partly due to heredity. I had been concerned with such arguments since 1959, when I first read Michael Young's remarkable book *The Rise of the Meritocracy*. During the late 1960s I reviewed the research on heredity and IQ fairly carefully, concluding that children's genes did, in fact, exert considerable influence on their test performance. *Inequality* had endorsed that conclusion, outraging many liberals.

But *Inequality* had also argued that, contrary to what both liberals and conservatives assumed, a correlation between genotype and school performance had no clear political implications. Knowing that migraine headaches are often inherited does not tell us whether they are treatable. The same holds for learning problems. There is no evidence that genetically based learning problems are harder to treat than environmentally based problems. The opposite could equally well be true. At present, as *Inequality* emphasized, we are not very good at treating either sort of problem.

In 1985 James Q. Wilson and Richard Herrnstein revived the nature-nurture controversy in a slightly different form. In *Crime and Human Nature* they argued that an individual's propensity to commit violent crimes depended partly on his or her genetic makeup. Chapter 3 examines this argument. Just as with test scores, I conclude that genes do influence criminal behavior. But just as with test scores, I also conclude that this fact is politically neutral. Knowing that a mugger has an extra Y chromosome does not tell us whether the judge should lock him up and throw the key away, as conservatives claim, or give him a suspended sentence and a job, as liberals claim. Nor would knowing that the mugger's father beat him as a child tell us which of these strategies to follow.

The last part of Chapter 3 turns briefly from conservative to liberal theories about crime, discussing Elliott Currie's book *Confronting Crime*. Currie argued that crime was often a byproduct of economic inequality. I conclude that, while economic inequality may sometimes contribute to violent crime, the available evidence does not suggest that it plays a major role.

The Underclass Debate

After 1986 the political climate began to change. In the early Reagan years many middle-of-the-road Americans wanted to reduce inflation and encourage economic growth, no matter what the short-term cost to the poor. Many also thought that if we could get the economy back on track this would do more for the poor in the long run than any amount of government spending. By the late 1980s this assumption was no longer defensible. Inflation had come down, unemployment had declined, personal income was up, and the economy was growing. But for the first time in living memory, long-term growth had not helped the poor, even in absolute terms.

The poor were clearly better off in the late 1980s than in the depths of the 1982–83 recession. But even in 1989, with the business cycle near its peak and real per capita income at an all-time high, the official poverty rate was higher than it had been in 1979.[16] Poverty was also more visible. New York City, where a large fraction of the nation's opinion leaders live, felt increasingly like a third-world city. Its posh restaurants were full of Wall Street traders who spent money like Indian rajahs, but its public places were full of the homeless.

The failure of the trickle-down theory made Americans more attentive to liberal arguments for helping the poor, but it did not bring consensus about what policies the government should pursue. If legislators had still been mainly concerned with reducing material hardship, the solution would have been obvious: improve the safety net. But by the late 1980s even liberal legislators were worried that improving the safety net might make the nation's problems worse rather than better.

Legislative anxiety about the social costs of improving the safety net was, of course, partly self-serving. At the administration's behest, Congress cut taxes in 1981. The government then borrowed staggering sums to finance a military buildup. Since raising taxes again was politically unacceptable, improving the safety net meant either cutting back military expenditures or borrowing more. Centrist legislators were unwilling to do either, so they found it convenient to argue that new programs might not really help the poor.

But legislative anxiety about the dangers of making social problems worse also stemmed from a change in legislators' ideas about the causes of poverty. One measure of this change was widespread adoption of the term "underclass." During the late 1960s and early 1970s, liberals and radicals argued against the traditional sociological view that different classes had different values and norms of behavior. At least in cultural terms, the left saw America as a classless society whose members all shared common values and aspirations. People were poor only because they had not had sufficient opportunity to realize their middle-class aspirations. By the late 1980s only a few hard-core liberals still clung to a pure version of this "blocked opportunities" hypothesis. Few Americans thought that the poor enjoyed the same opportunities as the rich, but most thought that poor people's own choices contributed to their economic troubles.

Middle-class attitudes toward the poor changed partly because America had once again become a Mecca for unskilled immigrants, some of whom did better here than the native-born poor. Those with the worst problems were mostly Afro-Americans and Puerto Ricans. Immigrants from other parts of Latin America tended to do somewhat better, while those from Asia, who usually came from more privileged backgrounds, did much better. Conservatives saw these ethnic differences as a byproduct of cultural differences—an umbrella term that subsumed everything from whether ethnic tradition assumed that effort would be rewarded to ethnic norms regarding sex, marriage, and childbearing. Some liberals argued that talking about culture was just another way of "blaming the victim" and continued to emphasize the effects of discrimination. But after two decades of affirmative action, even liberals had begun to doubt that racial discrimination alone could account for all the problems of American blacks and Puerto Ricans.

At first, most liberals also objected to the word "underclass," because of its cultural overtones. Eventually, however, many began using the term. Some simply ignored its cultural implications. Others conceded that there were cultural differences between the poor and the nonpoor, but argued that these differences were a consequence of poverty rather than its cause. Chapters 4 and 5 deal with different aspects of this underclass debate.

Ghetto culture. Chapter 4 discusses William Julius Wilson's book, *The Truly Disadvantaged,* which played a central role in persuading liberals that the term "underclass" was not just a racist slur. Unlike many liberals, Wilson accepted the conservative view that antisocial and self-destructive behavior had increased in poor black neighborhoods. But unlike most conservatives, Wilson saw these changes in ghetto residents' behavior as a byproduct of economic and demographic changes over which the ghetto had almost no control. On the economic side, Wilson argued that the decline of urban manufacturing made it much harder for unskilled and semiskilled black men to support a family. On the demographic side, he argued that as successful blacks moved out of ghetto neighborhoods in the 1970s, those left behind became socially isolated from mainstream society. As a result, they created what Wilson called a "ghetto culture," in which joblessness, illegitimacy, welfare receipt, and crime were accepted as normal. Wilson labeled these ghetto residents the "underclass."

The decline of urban manufacturing and the increased chance that poor urban blacks would have poor neighbors almost certainly contributed something to the increase in black joblessness, illegitimacy, and welfare use between 1965 and 1985. Chapter 4 argues, however, that these economic and demographic shifts cannot possibly explain the entire change in black Americans' behavior since 1965. At least two other factors probably played an important role. First, the white middle class, whose cultural norms dominate the mass media, became far more tolerant of "deviant" behavior. Second, the civil-rights movement made young blacks less willing to accept subservient roles, especially in settings dominated by whites.

Chapter 4 raises difficult questions about the relationship of black to white culture that I do not discuss in detail. Until the mid-1960s, most liberal whites assumed that American blacks wanted to become just like whites. It seemed to follow that once the United States eliminated de jure segregation and overt discrimination, blacks would climb the same economic and social ladder that European immigrants had climbed between 1840 and 1960. The first step would be for blacks to get as much education as whites. Then blacks would enter the same occupations and earn the same incomes as whites. Blacks and whites would begin living in the same neighborhoods. Eventually, the optimists thought, blacks and whites would intermarry, creating a single café-au-lait society and a single deracinated culture.

By 1980 young blacks and whites were spending almost the same number of years in school, but the rest of the story was not unfolding the way liberal whites had hoped.[17] To begin with, while black-white differences in academic performance were narrowing, black students still learned considerably less than whites during any given year of school.[18] Perhaps for this reason, blacks were substantially less likely than whites to earn college or graduate degrees (see Table 5.7), even though they spent almost as many years in school as whites. Young black men also earned lower wages and worked less regularly than young whites with the same educational credentials.[19] And even when black families earned above-average incomes, they mostly lived in black neighborhoods.[20]

Black and white liberals blame these differences on whites, arguing that white-controlled school systems assign blacks to worse schools, that teachers expect less of black students, that white employers discriminate against black workers in hiring and promotion decisions, and that realtors steer blacks and whites to different neighborhoods. Black and white conservatives argue that such discrimination is not sufficiently pervasive or influential to explain all the differences we see between blacks and whites. Such conservatives usually claim that blacks' behavior is also a byproduct of their unique cultural heritage, which prepares blacks for failure rather than success. That heritage is clearly a byproduct of white oppression, but conservatives argue that it now has a life of its own, independent of how whites behave today.

So long as we focus on how much children learn in school or how much adults earn when they work, it is almost impossible to separate the effects of past and current discrimination. There are, however, some other forms of behavior on which the larger society exerts less direct influence. If we give standardized tests to preschool children, for example, we cannot invoke differences in school quality to explain the results. Black children score lower on such tests than white children, even when they come from superficially similar socioeconomic backgrounds (see Table 4.3). This fact suggests that even when black and white families have similar resources, they raise their children quite differently, and these differences have an adverse effect on black children's school performance.[21]

There is also fairly strong evidence that mainstream American norms of behavior exert less influence on blacks than on whites with the same amount of schooling. Blacks are more likely than whites with the same amount of schooling to have their babies out of wedlock (see Table 5.15). Young blacks also commit more violent crimes than young whites with the same amount of schooling.[22] Such differences can, of course, be seen as part of racism's appalling historical legacy. But if all whites were suddenly struck color-blind, we would not expect these differences to disappear overnight—indeed, they would probably persist for several generations. That is what it means to invoke "culture" as an explanation of such differences.

Most whites see racial differences in crime and illegitimacy as evidence that the black community does not accept—or at least does not enforce—the same norms of behavior as the white community. Most whites also assume that differences of this kind contribute to blacks' economic troubles. As a result, most whites think white culture is superior to black culture. It is easy to see why such views infuriate blacks, who know that their culture has extraordinary strengths as well as weaknesses. But to outsiders, the failures of black culture are far more visible than the successes. One inevitable result is that while many whites are prepared to treat blacks as equals if they "act white," few are prepared to treat blacks as equals if they "act black." Because I can see no good way of resolving this kind of cultural conflict, Chapter 4 is by far the most pessimistic in the book.

Is the black underclass growing? The average American worker's real hourly earnings grew steadily from 1947 to 1972. After that, wage growth stopped. The poverty rate also stopped falling, and male joblessness became more common. All these economic changes hit blacks especially hard. Chapter 5 investigates the extent to which they were associated with other forms of social breakdown, as the underclass story implies they were.

Among blacks, only one of the half-dozen social indicators that I examine follows the same trajectory as the economic indicators. From 1960 to around 1975, the illegitimacy rate was such that the average black woman could expect to have one baby out of wedlock during her lifetime. After 1975 that figure began to rise. This is consistent with the underclass story.

No other measure of social breakdown among blacks rose and fell in tandem with economic conditions. Births to teenagers and high-school dropout rates fell steadily among blacks from 1960 to 1985, despite the ups and downs of the economy. Black seventeen-year-olds' reading scores also rose steadily. And while blacks were more likely to depend on welfare and to commit violent crimes in 1985 than in 1960, the big increases in these problems occurred in the late 1960s and early 1970s, when black poverty was falling and black male joblessness had not yet risen appreciably. After 1974, when economic conditions got worse, black welfare use leveled off and black crime actually declined. It is hard to argue, therefore, that economic change had any consistent effect on black teenage fertility, dropout rates, reading skills, crime, or welfare use.

None of this means there is no underclass (or as I would prefer to say, no lower class). But if we want to understand why the incidence of social problems is changing, we need to look at each problem separately and examine its distinctive etiology. Changes in the frequency of these social problems are not closely linked to economic changes—or to one another.

The *welfare problem*. Chapter 6, which I wrote with Kathryn Edin, looks in more detail at what I regard as America's most serious social-policy error, namely the way in which we try to help single mothers. Edin and I argue that America does not provide most unskilled single mothers with a socially acceptable strategy for supporting their families. As a result, most have adopted socially unacceptable strategies.

In interviews with fifty Chicago welfare recipients, Edin found none who were subsisting on what they got from the welfare department. All fifty supplemented their AFDC checks with income from other sources, which they concealed from the welfare department. Consumer-expenditure surveys strongly suggest that the same pattern occurs elsewhere. Edin's interviews with Chicago mothers who work at low-wage jobs show that they cannot live on their wages alone either.[23] In order to make ends meet, unskilled single mothers must combine income from several sources. Some illegally combine welfare with work. Some illegally combine welfare with help from boyfriends or relatives. A few combine work with help from friends and relatives. While this strategy is legal, it is not practical for most single mothers unless their earnings are above average or they get a lot of help from others.

If we want to reduce the prevalence of fraud, encourage single mothers to work, and be sure their children's basic physical needs are met, both liberals and conservatives will have to give ground. Conservatives will have to abandon the pretense that all single mothers could get along without government help if only they had jobs. Liberals will have to abandon the idea that single mothers have a right to government help even if they are not willing to take a low-wage job. Both sides have begun to make the required concessions, but both have a long way to go.

If we could overcome these ideological problems, designing sensible policies for helping single mothers would become much easier. Instead of trying to make the lot of welfare recipients better, liberals could concentrate on helping families in which the head worked but earned so little that the family was still poor. These families need a more generous Earned Income Tax Credit to cover their childcare costs, guaranteed eligibility for Section 8 housing certificates, a more generous food-stamp allowance, and a Medicaid system they can join by paying, say, 5 percent of their monthly income. When parents cannot find work, we also need to offer them public employment at the minimum wage. Congress has taken some steps along these lines since 1988. At its current rate of progress, however, Congress could easily take another fifty years to undo the damage it inadvertently did when it created ADC in 1935.

Ideology and Prejudice in Social Criticism

This book addresses questions that have divided liberals from conservatives for many years. It includes many arguments that will offend orthodox liberals and others that will offend orthodox conservatives. The reader who infers that I am neither is correct. But the book does not propose a coherent alternative to traditional liberalism or conservatism. If it has a single consistent message, it is that all such ideologies lead to bad social policy.

Any successful ideology, be it radical, liberal, or conservative, must combine a small number of assumptions about how the world ought to work with a large number of assumptions about how the world really does work. It must select these moral and empirical assumptions so that they appear internally consistent. No successful ideology can afford to assume that the real-world costs of achieving its moral goals are high. The ongoing quest for internal consistency that I see as the hallmark of any successful ideology makes realism extremely difficult.

My aim in this book has been to unbundle the empirical and moral assumptions that traditional ideologies tie together, making the reader's picture of the world more complicated (and making my arguments harder to remember). Nonetheless, while I have tried to disentangle assumptions that most ideologies tie together, I have not been able to dispense with such moral and factual assumptions altogether. I have simply tried to make my assumptions more tentative, looking for evidence that they are wrong as well as evidence that they are right.

My distinctive combination of prejudices may also confuse readers who have learned to expect ideological consistency in what they read. Oversimplifying, I would say my prejudices favor cultural conservatism, economic egalitarianism, and incremental reform. Because this is a somewhat unusual combination of views, it deserves a word of explanation.

My cultural conservatism makes me favor traditional social norms about how people ought to behave until I am convinced that new norms really work better. Having been divorced twice, for example, I am quite aware that marriage is an imperfect and fragile institution. Still I see no evidence that having children out of wedlock does a better job of ensuring that children get the economic, social, and moral support they need. So I cling to the old-fashioned view that couples who have children without marrying are putting their children's welfare in jeopardy. Single parenthood sometimes works out well, of course. But because I think it risky, I do not think society should view prospective parents' failure to marry with indifference, any more than it views failure to buckle a child's seatbelt with indifference. This prejudice makes me willing to use morally loaded terms like "illegitimacy" that many liberals regard as antiquated and intolerant.

I also know how awful many jobs are, and I favor public employment schemes that offer every willing worker a job that meets certain basic standards. Nonetheless, so long as some people have to work at awful jobs, I do not think others should have a right to refuse such jobs and demand public assistance, sponge off their parents, or prey on their neighbors. This feeling makes me describe young men who will not take a job at Burger King as "idle" rather than just "unemployed."

I recognize that such judgments about other people's responsibilities are controversial. But I do not think the dangers of controversy are as great as the dangers of moral neutrality. These are not the kinds of questions on which citizens can simply agree to disagree. If a society cannot create broad consensus about who is responsible for raising children and supporting them economically, it will soon have a lot of children for whom nobody takes much responsibility. Likewise, if we cannot maintain political consensus about who is obligated to work and at what kinds of jobs, we will not be able to agree on a system for helping those we do not expect to work. Public debate about such matters will not lead to complete agreement, especially in a nation as diverse as America, but without such debate agreement will become even more elusive than it is now.

My economic egalitarianism is in some ways a byproduct of my cultural conservatism. I do not believe that a culture built on undiluted individualism can survive very long. Indeed, my distaste for what Wilson calls "ghetto culture" derives from my sense that it tolerates a degree of selfishness and irresponsibility, especially on the part of males, that is extremely destructive in any community, but especially in poor communities. My even stronger distaste for the white yuppie culture of the 1980s derives from a similar judgment. Because I believe we must all take a fair amount of responsibility both for one another and for the society of which we are a part, I think we in America have a moral obligation to distribute our material goods and services more equally. I also think we could do this without undermining most people's motivation to work at socially useful tasks.

My commitment to achieving such goals through incremental reform hardly warrants discussion in 1991, when events in Eastern Europe and the Soviet Union have made everyone conscious of how much revolutionary change can cost. (This clearly holds for the initial effort to destroy capitalism overnight, which was a human catastrophe. The human costs of trying to destroy communism overnight are not yet clear, but I fear they may be nearly as high, at least in the Soviet Union.)

I should emphasize, however, that what I mean by incremental reform is not just political opportunism. For me, incremental reform implies a long-term strategy, which is then implemented through a sequence of small steps. These steps must relate to one another politically as well as economically, so that each step helps make the next seem desirable. The best example of such a strategy is probably the way Swedish socialists transformed their country after World War II. I have no illusions that Swedish socialism would work in the United States. The Swedish system requires far more social solidarity, legislative responsibility, and governmental competence than the United States has ever had. But the Swedish socialists' approach to reform did embody two principles that seem to me essential in any democracy, including America's. On the one hand, they sought to shape public opinion rather than just follow it. On the other hand, they made no legislative changes until they had created a political consensus that the changes were needed. Thus even if the next election went against them, their reforms were seldom undone.

In the end, however, this is not a book about political principles or prejudices. Quite the contrary. These six essays all try to show that, if we want to make better social policies in the United States, we should pay less attention to generalities and more to examples. Instead of arguing about affirmative action, for instance, we should think about how a firm fills a particular job. Instead of trying to generalize about the overall effect of the welfare state, we should look at the diverse effects of particular social programs. Instead of debating nature versus nurture, we should try to understand how a particular gene or set of genes influences some specific form of behavior. Instead of asking whether the underclass has grown, we should ask whether specific social problems have become more common among particular groups and, if so, when and why the change occurred. Instead of agonizing about welfare dependency, we should ask where welfare recipients really get their money. If this book encourages readers to think about social policy more concretely, it will have served its primary purpose.

= 1 =

Affirmative Action

The 1980 elections marked the end of an era in American race relations.[1] Between 1964 and 1980 federal officials had argued about the moral legitimacy and practical benefits of particular strategies for helping blacks catch up with whites economically, but few questioned the basic assumption that the government ought to promote this goal in one way or another. The quest for racial equality had led to three kinds of federal activity. First, the government pressured private employers to hire blacks for jobs that had traditionally been reserved for whites. Second, in order to help blacks qualify for these jobs, the government spent a lot of money on education and job training, and spent it so that blacks received a substantial fraction of the benefits. Third, for families without a breadwinner, nearly half of which were black, Congress provided food stamps, Medicaid, and more housing subsidies.

Public support for all these policies diminished fairly steadily from 1964 to 1980. Even in the mid-1960s many Americans felt that supporting families without a breadwinner encouraged both promiscuity and idleness. As more mothers entered the labor force, the idea that the government should pay those without husbands to stay home became even less popular. Federal spending on education and job training for the disadvantaged had been seen in the mid-1960s as an economically efficient and socially painless device for reducing racial inequality, but when negative evaluations of these programs began rolling in, enthusiasm waned somewhat, especially among legislators. Federal pressure on private employers to eliminate discrimination against blacks was also widely accepted in the mid-1960s, at least in the north. But when efforts to offset the effects of past discrimination forced some firms to adopt rules that favored less qualified blacks over more qualified whites, most whites turned hostile.

After Ronald Reagan took office in 1981, top federal officials stopped assuming that the federal government had a special obligation to help blacks become as rich as whites. Reagan won congressional support for cutting back most of the major federal programs designed to accomplish this goal. Real federal spending on education and job training was cut, eligibility for AFDC, food stamps, and Medicaid was narrowed, and federal pressure on private employers to hire more blacks was reduced. Liberal Democrats in Congress challenged these policy changes throughout the 1980s, but with limited success. By 1990 America was, if anything, even more divided than it had been in 1980 about whether the government should make special efforts to help blacks. Many blacks and whites felt they needed a new strategy for dealing with racial inequality, but there was no consensus about what this strategy should be.

Thomas Sowell, a black economist trained by Milton Friedman and his colleagues at the University of Chicago, has been campaigning against special treatment for blacks since the early 1970s. In two influential books, *Ethnic America* and *Markets and Minorities,* he argues that ethnic minorities do better in laissez-faire economic systems than in systems subject to government regulation.[2] *Ethnic America* describes how the Irish, Germans, Jews, Italians, Chinese, Japanese, Africans, Puerto Ricans, and Mexicans came to America, how they dealt with the discrimination they all encountered, and how they progressed economically despite the absence of government help and sometimes in the face of government opposition. *Markets and Minorities* uses standard economic logic to analyze the effects of government programs aimed at eliminating discrimination and its presumed consequences. Both books are briefs for Sowell's view that governments should pursue color-blind policies and let different ethnic groups look out for themselves.

Sowell's political argument rests on three factual claims, all of which liberals question. First, Sowell shows that although racial and ethnic discrimination have been common throughout American history, the victims of such discrimination have often ended up more affluent than their former oppressors. While most liberals agree that many other victims of discrimination eventually prospered in America, they still see discrimination as the most important reason for black Americans' persistent economic problems.

Second, Sowell argues that in a competitive economy discrimination against racial and ethnic minorities is expensive to those who engage in it. Competition therefore tends to eliminate discriminatory practices unless they are backed up by legal sanctions. Liberals, in contrast, assume that the costs of racial discrimination fall largely on the victims, not their oppressors. Most liberals therefore believe that discrimination can persist more or less indefinitely unless the government takes an active role in preventing it.

Third, Sowell insists that government efforts to eliminate private discrimination do more harm than good, mainly serving the interests of white liberals and middle-class blacks, not the interests of poor blacks. Almost all liberals reject this view, arguing that government efforts to eliminate racial discrimination played a major part in reducing economic inequality between blacks and whites during the 1960s and 1970s, and that further government effort will be required to achieve full equality.

This chapter will argue that reality is more complex than either liberals or conservatives assume. My argument will have three themes. First, I will try to show that the economic consequences of discrimination depend to a great extent on its pervasiveness. Sporadic discrimination of the kind many European immigrants encountered in America is unlikely to do its victims much economic harm, though it may well harm them in other important ways. Nearly universal discrimination, which is what blacks encountered in America at least until the 1960s, can have much more serious economic effects.

My second theme is that the economic consequences of discrimination depend to a great extent on how it affects the victim's behavior. If discrimination spurs its victims to greater effort ("we have to be twice as good as they are in order to do equally well"), it may actually help them economically. If discrimination convinces its victims that effort is never rewarded, or if it makes them so angry or resentful that they are unable to work with their oppressors, it can have catastrophic economic consequences. The negative stereotypes that employers use to justify discrimination can thus become self-fulfilling prophecies, although this does not always happen.

My third theme will be that while some kinds of discrimination are costly to employers, as Sowell claims, other kinds of discrimination are economically efficient. When discrimination is economically efficient, it will persist indefinitely unless the government stamps it out, just as liberals claim.

Empirically, I will argue that government efforts to eliminate discrimination played a significant role in narrowing the wage gap between blacks and whites from 1964 to 1980. But I will also argue that affirmative-action programs have had substantial political and psychological costs, and that these costs have increased over time. I conclude that we still need affirmative action, but not the kind we have had over the past generation.

Economic Differences among Ethnic Groups

In order to assess Sowell's claim that many ethnic minorities overcame discrimination and achieved a high level of affluence in America, we need to identify the descendants of these minorities. This is no simple matter, since the hallmarks of ethnic identity—language, religion, and physical appearance—change from one generation to the next. The best source of recent data on ethnicity is the National Opinion Research Center's General Social Survey (GSS), which has asked roughly 1500 people questions about their ancestry in almost every year since 1972.[3] Table 1.1 divides America's adult population into ethnic groups using three criteria: physical appearance (black or nonblack), religion (Jewish or gentile), and geographic origins ("From what country or part of the world did your ancestors come?"). I have tried to define groups the way American society as a whole defines them, which means that I have not been able to make my criteria logically consistent. I distinguish Irish Catholics from Irish Protestants, for example, but lump together German Catholics and Protestants. I classify people as Jews if they report their religion as Jewish, regardless of their national origin, but I do not apply this principle to Catholics, Methodists, or other religious groups. I define people as black if their appearance led the interviewer to classify them as black, but I define people as Native Americans or Asians only if they told the interviewer that their ancestors were all Native Americans or all came from an Asian country.

The problem of deciding who is black deserves particular attention, because it dramatizes the way in which Africans' experience in America has differed from that of other ethnic minorities. Both black and white

Table 1.1 Household Income as Percent of U.S. Average, by Ethnic Group, 1972–1989

Ethnic group	Percent of all households	Household income as percent of U.S. average[a]
European groups		
Jews[b]	2.2	155
Irish Catholics	1.8	118
French	.9	113
Italians	3.5	107
British	7.4	106
French Canadians	.6	104
Poles	1.9	101
Germans	10.3	101
Czechs	.8	98
Dutch	1.0	95
Irish Protestants[c]	3.1	94
Scandinavians	2.5	93
Other Europeans	2.4	112
Non-European groups		
Asians	.7	127
Native Americans	.9	71
African Americans[d]	11.4	68
Mexicans[e]	1.7	64
Puerto Ricans[e]	.6	62
Other Hispanics[e]	.7	94
Unclassifiable		
Mixed background[f]	36.2	112
Unknown background[g]	9.5	77
Total	100.0	100

Source: National Opinion Research Center, Cumulative General Social Survey, 1972–1989 (N=24, 893). The data cover all adult respondents who reported their income (91.8 percent of the cumulative sample). Household income is not adjusted for household size. National-origin groups include only those who said their ancestors came from a single country.

a. Sampling errors for percentages in column 2 are approximately equal to (.046) (column 2)/ (column 1)$^{.5}$. For Jews, for example, the standard error of the estimate in column 2 is (.046)(155)/ 2.2$^{.5}$ = 4.8 points.

b. Includes all respondents who answered "Jewish" when asked "What is your religious preference?" The count therefore excludes some Jewish nonbelievers.

c. Includes a few Irish respondents who described their religion as "none."

d. Includes all respondents whom interviewers classified as "black," regardless of their national origin.

e. Excludes blacks, non-English speakers, and individuals of mixed geographic origins. The category "other Hispanic" includes respondents who said their ancestors came from either Spain or a Latin American country other than Mexico.

f. Includes all nonblack gentiles whose ancestors came from two or more countries.

g. Includes nonblack, gentile respondents who could not name the part of the world from which their ancestors came or who named only "America" and did not say they were Native Americans.

Americans classify individuals as black if their appearance suggests even a small amount of African blood. This rule yields a high degree of consensus about who is black. When the GSS telephones individuals whom its interviewers classified as black and asks them their race, 98 percent describe themselves as black.[4] Our approach to racial classification also means that when racially mixed couples have children, these children almost always describe themselves as black and are seen that way by others.

Americans are far less sensitive to physical differences among non-Africans. The GSS, for example, asks its interviewers to note every respondent's race and tells them to ask if there is any doubt whatever. Even when respondents say all their ancestors were Native Americans, GSS interviewers classify half of these individuals as white and most of the rest as black. They classify only a handful as "other." Indirect evidence suggests that most Americans of mixed European and Native American ancestry also tell the Census Bureau that they are white.[5] Interviewers also classify almost all Mexican Americans as white, even though many appear to have a lot of Native American ancestors. Mexicans mostly classify themselves as white too.[6] The relatively low saliency of physical differences among nonblacks has many important social consequences. Native Americans and Mexicans are far more likely than blacks to marry Europeans, for example.

Table 1.1 shows the mean household income of different American ethnic groups as a percentage of the national average. Sowell's claim that many ethnic minorities overcame discrimination and achieved extraordinary affluence in America is clearly correct. There is room for controversy about which European groups encountered the most discrimination in America, but few would argue that European gentiles had a harder time than their Jewish counterparts, that Irish Catholics were able to exclude Americans of British origin from top jobs, or that social stereotypes helped Italians get jobs that the Scandinavians and Dutch deserved. Yet Jews are far better off than any other major American ethnic group, Irish Catholics are now more affluent than the WASPS who were once said to run the country, and Italian Americans are doing better than their Dutch and Scandinavian competitors.

While Table 1.1 supports Sowell's view that discrimination seldom led to persistent poverty among European minorities, it offers less support for another of his arguments, namely that an ethnic group's success in America depended to a great extent on the values, skills, and traditions it brought from the old country. If cultural legacies were of critical importance, groups that prospered in Europe should have done the same in America. I have not been able to find statistics comparing the incomes of Jews and gentiles in Europe. Within the gentile population, however, the European economic order has been almost completely reversed in America. Germans and Scandinavians are richer than Italians in Europe but poorer in America. Protestants are richer than Catholics in Ireland but poorer in America. Indeed, the whole tradition of Protestant affluence and Catholic poverty that inspired Max Weber's reflections on the economic impact of religious ideas has been stood on its head here. Catholics from almost every European country are now better off in America than Protestants from the same country, although the differences are seldom as large as those between Irish Catholics and Protestants.

How did this happen? The short answer is that nobody really knows. Consider the Irish. Irish Protestants (often known as "Scotch Irish" to distinguish them from Irish Catholics) blended so easily with their British cousins that few Americans even think of them as a separate ethnic group. Because they did not establish their own churches, political machines, or voluntary associations, they never entered American consciousness in the way Irish Catholics did. The absence of organizations for mutual aid may, in turn, help explain why Irish Protestants are now worse off economically than Irish Catholics. But then again it may not.

None of this means that Sowell is wrong when he suggests that a group's initial economic position was heavily influenced by its skills and traditions. But ethnic traditions that led to affluence in Europe did not always have the same effect in America, and in many cases a group's skills and outlook changed rapidly once it arrived in the New World. (Such changes can, of course, occur even in the absence of migration. In 1850 the English were the richest people in Europe, while the Italians were among the poorest. Today, for reasons no economist can explain, the Italians are richer than the English.)

Variations among non-European groups are equally puzzling. Asians are doing better than any European group except the Jews. Blacks, Mexicans, Puerto Ricans, and Native Americans are worse off than any European group. Once we exclude Mexicans and Puerto Ricans, other Hispanics are doing almost as well as the average American. It is easy to see why Mexicans and Puerto Ricans, many of whom are recent immigrants with limited English and little education, are doing worse than Europeans. The persistence of black poverty is more difficult to explain. Blacks have spoken English longer than most Americans, and most blacks have now lived in cities for at least a generation. In addition, young blacks now spend almost as much time in school as young whites. What, then, has gone wrong?

Africans' experience in America differed from that of Europeans in three closely related ways. First, almost all European immigrants came to America voluntarily, saw it as a land of opportunity, and assumed that their task was to adapt to the new society they had chosen to make their own. Those who disliked America often returned home. Africans, in contrast, almost all arrived here as slaves. This inevitably made them far more ambivalent than most whites about the legitimacy of the social and legal system they encountered here. It also helped create a culture in which resistance to those in authority was widely tolerated and often admired.

A second major difference between Europeans and Africans was that the descendants of European immigrants almost all had the option of shedding their ethnic identity and becoming just plain Americans. For Africans, physical differences usually made "passing" impractical. Individual African Americans therefore had less incentive than European Americans to adopt "mainstream" American ways.

A third crucial difference between blacks and other minorities, to which I have already alluded, is that while economic discrimination against European minorities was common, it was never anything like universal. For blacks, in contrast, economic discrimination was almost universal until the 1960s.

While these historical, cultural, biological, social, and legal differences between blacks and other minorities have all contributed to blacks' current economic problems, it is not obvious which factors have played the largest role. Liberals almost always blame blacks' economic problems on employers' discriminatory practices. Conservatives rightly argue that there are other possible explanations. One popular theory holds that black family income is artificially depressed by the fact that so many black families have no male breadwinner. Another theory holds that black men work less regularly than whites because they are less committed to the work ethic. If black men were in fact less eager than whites to work, they would end up with less income even if employers were completely color-blind.[7]

Does Black Family Structure Distort Black Income Statistics?

The Census Bureau defines a family as any group of two or more related persons living together. If relatives do not live together or if people who live together are not related, they do not constitute a family. Ethnic differences in living arrangements can therefore produce significant differences in family income even when groups have precisely the same income per person. Asians, for example, are more likely than Europeans to live in extended families with many potential earners. As a result, Americans of Asian descent have higher family incomes than those of European descent, even though the Asians' income per person is lower.[8]

Blacks are more likely than either Asians or whites to live in single-parent families composed of a mother and her children. Since single mothers report only a third as much income as married couples, many observers have concluded that black poverty must be at least partly attributable to black living arrangements.[9] Plausible as this explanation seems, it is basically wrong. Few single mothers, black or white, could triple their family income by marrying, because most men with high incomes are already married. In 1987, for example, 2.5 million unmarried black women between the ages of twenty-five and sixty-four headed families. There were fewer than 600,000 unmarried black men in this age range with incomes as high as the average married black man.[10] Thus even if all black women who headed families had married the richest available black man, their families would still have been poorer than most. Furthermore, many unmarried black men live with their mother or sister. Had they married, their departure might have made their wife somewhat better off, but at the expense of making their sister or mother worse off.

If we want to assess the impact of family structure on black Americans' economic position, we need a measure that compares the economic resources available to blacks and whites in a way that is independent of family structure and living arrangements. The most obvious possibility is to focus on income per person. Table 1.2 compares blacks to whites on both income per family and income per person.

Table 1.2 Measures of Change in the Economic Position of Nonwhites, 1954–1989

Measure	Nonwhite/white ratio				Black/white ratio				
	1954	1959	1964	1969	1969	1974	1979	1984	1989
Income per family	.563	.555	.620	.662	.636	.633	.624	.610	.609
Income per person	–	–	–	.572	.555	.581	.587	.574	.587
Income per adult[a]	.559	.551	.624	.647	.629	.649	.648	.629	.643
Weeks worked per adult[b]	1.051	1.029	1.027	1.001	.995	.918	.888	.864	.892

Sources: Rows 1 to 3 are from U.S. Bureau of the Census, *Current Population Reports*, Series P-60 (Washington: U.S. Government Printing Office), no. 162 (tables 12 and 29) and no. 168 (tables 7, 13, and 17). Row 4 is from *Economic Report of the President, 1990* (Government Printing Office, 1990), table C-38.

a. Includes all individuals over the age of 14 prior to 1984 and all those over the age of 15 thereafter.

b. Estimated from the percentage of the civilian noninstitutional population aged 16 or over employed in an average week. In 1954, for example, 55.2 percent of white adults worked in an average week, compared to 58.0 percent of nonwhites. The ratio of weeks worked by the average nonwhite adult to weeks worked by the average white adult was therefore .580/.552 = 1.051.

Substituting income per capita for income per family makes blacks look worse off, not better off. This is largely because blacks have more children than whites. As a result, black families not only have less money than white families but also have more mouths to feed.

If we want a measure of economic resources that does not depend on either living arrangements or fertility, we must restrict our attention to those adults who are old enough to have income of their own. Row 3 of Table 1.2 compares blacks to whites on this measure. During the 1950s and 1960s racial disparities in income per adult and income per family were almost identical. In 1969, for example, the average black adult had 37 percent less income than the average white adult, while the average black family had 36 percent less income than the average white family. It follows that even if black adults had had precisely the same marriage patterns and living arrangements as white adults, the average black family's economic situation would hardly have changed.

The distinction between family income and individual income does, however, take on at least symbolic importance when we look at trends since 1969. The ratio of black to white family income fell slightly during the 1970s and 1980s, convincing many observers that blacks were losing ground relative to whites. Yet black adults' share of personal income did not fall after 1969; it rose slightly. The modest lag in black family income after 1969 was thus a statistical artifact, caused by changes in black family structure rather than a decline in black adults' share of personal income.

Nonetheless, the main message of Table 1.2 is that blacks fare almost as poorly on measures that ignore family structure as on measures that take family structure as given. This does not necessarily mean that family structure has no long-term impact on black incomes. Growing up in a single-parent household may have some adverse effect on blacks' potential earnings when they grow up. Remaining unmarried may also reduce a black man's incentive to work long hours. But the basic reason why blacks are poorer than whites is not that they organize their families the wrong way but that individual blacks earn less money.

Racial Differences in Employment

Some ethnic groups work more than others. In 1979, for example, 66 percent of Asian women over the age of sixteen worked for pay, compared to only 55 percent of white women.[11] High rates of employment inevitably boost Asians' family income, even when their wages are low. Historically, black women were also more likely than white women to have paid jobs. In the 1960s, however, this pattern began to change. By the mid-1970s white women were as likely as black women to work for pay. This remained true throughout the 1980s. Meanwhile, black men were leaving the labor force in large numbers. As a result, black adults are now considerably less likely than white adults to hold paid jobs (see row 4 of Table 1.2).

The character of black male joblessness has also changed. In the 1950s black men experienced considerably more short-term unemployment than white men but were only marginally more likely to withdraw from the labor force. Between 1963–1965 and 1985–1987 the proportion of black men aged twenty-five to fifty-four who did no paid work for an entire calendar year rose from 5 to 14 percent. Among whites, it increased only from 3 to 5 percent.[12]

Conservatives tend to blame black men's withdrawal from the labor force on the growth of the welfare state and a concomitant decline in the work ethic. Liberals usually blame the economy for not generating enough jobs. Because conservatives tend to see joblessness as voluntary, they think disparities in hourly wages are a better measure of economic inequality than disparities in annual earnings. Since liberals think joblessness is involuntary, they emphasize disparities in annual earnings or income. This disagreement has important political consequences, because racial differences in annual income are much larger than racial differences in weekly or hourly wages.

To see why this conflict is hard to resolve empirically, a hypothetical example is helpful. Suppose a town's labor force is half black and half white and that the town's sole employer has two kinds of jobs, one paying $10 an hour and one paying $4 a hour. Suppose the employer prefers white to black workers and offers $10 jobs to every white but to only half the blacks. The employer offers the remaining blacks jobs at $4 an hour. On the average, therefore, the employer offers whites $10 and blacks $7 an hour. Most people would presumably agree that being black in such a community lowered a worker's potential economic welfare by 30 percent.

Now suppose that the town's blacks refuse to take $4 jobs because they think they deserve at least as much as whites. A census survey would then show that employed blacks earned exactly the same amount as whites, and observers who focused exclusively on hourly wages would conclude that discrimination was a thing of the past. If the local employer also had a permanent sign outside his plant saying "Help Wanted," many whites would also assume that the high rate of joblessness among blacks was evidence that they were enmeshed in a culture of poverty that had sapped their will to work.

The real world is more complex than this, but the example does illustrate the way data on hourly or weekly earnings can mislead us. When workers can only find jobs that pay badly, many work irregularly and some leave the labor force altogether.[13] Such workers are disproportionately black. The wage disparity between blacks and whites who work therefore underestimates the disparity we would observe if everyone worked.

Liberals often try to solve this problem by including nonworkers in their statistics and then calculating the racial disparity in annual earnings or income. This strategy can, however, be as misleading as emphasizing weekly earnings. In my hypothetical town blacks were offered 70 percent of what whites are offered, but blacks' actual earnings were only 50 percent of the white average, because blacks did not take the low-wage jobs they were offered. By looking only at annual earnings we implicitly assume that those who do not work in a given week could not have found a job at any wage in that week. This assumption is sometimes realistic, but not always. In an effort to steer a middle course between these two sorts of error, I will try to discuss both weekly and annual earnings. In many cases, however, I have data on only one or the other, not both.

Comparing Men with the Same Amount of Schooling

Perhaps the most astonishing single assertion in *Markets and Minorities* is Sowell's claim that "the data do not show current employers' discrimination in pay among black or Hispanic male, full-time workers."[14] Table 1.3 shows the ratio of black to white income in 1987 for men and women with varying amounts of schooling. Looking first at men, which almost everyone concerned with racial inequality habitually does, we see that black college graduates who worked full-time throughout 1987 ended up with 25 percent less money than their white counterparts. The picture for men with less education was broadly similar. Because fewer black than white men worked full-time throughout 1987, the gap is even wider when we compare all blacks to all whites than when we compare those with steady jobs.

Table 1.3 Black Income as a Percent of White Income in 1987 among Persons Aged 25 or Over, by Sex, Education, and Employment Status

	No high school	Some high school	High school graduate	Some college	College graduate	Total
All persons						
Men	74.0	68.9	63.8	72.3	69.8	58.7
Women	84.1	84.9	98.3	98.9	100.9	85.8
Full-time, year-round workers						
Men	81.9	77.1	71.7	76.8	75.4	67.8
Women	91.4	87.3	91.9	86.2	86.2	85.5

Source: "Money Income of Households, Families, and Persons in the United States, 1987," *Current Population Reports,* Series P-60, no. 162 (1989), table 35. The means for all persons aged 25 and over exclude those persons who were residents of institutions or members of the armed forces in March 1988, but include all other persons enumerated by the CPS regardless of whether they had any income.

The fact that employers pay a black college graduate less than a white college graduate does not necessarily mean that they discriminate on the basis of race per se. Black and white college graduates differ in ways that might lead even a color-blind employer to pay whites more. When black and white students take tests that measure vocabulary, reading comprehension, mathematical skill, or scientific information, for example, blacks do much worse than whites (see Chapters 4 and 5). If employers valued educated workers mainly for their skills in these areas, whites would almost inevitably earn more than blacks with the same amount of schooling.

In reality, however, employers do not put much weight on cognitive skills when they decide how much to pay a worker. The best evidence on this point comes from research using the Armed Forces Qualification Test (AFQT), which was designed to predict men's success in the military. The AFQT measures verbal fluency, arithmetic reasoning, familiarity with tools, and ability to understand spatial relationships. One can scale AFQT scores using the familiar IQ metric, in which the average person scores 100, one person in six scores above 115, one in forty scores above 130, one in six scores below 85, and one in forty scores below 70. Using this metric, blacks typically score nine to twelve points below whites with the same amount of schooling.[15]

A 1964 survey found that when men in their early thirties had the same amount of schooling, a twelve-point advantage on the AFQT typically led to an earnings differential of only 9 percent. A 1987 survey that covered both veterans and nonveterans in their twenties found that a twelve-point AFQT advantage was associated with a 9 percent wage advantage among blacks and a 6 percent advantage among whites.[16] Since black men actually earned 20 to 30 percent less than whites with the same amount of schooling in 1987, other factors must also have been at work.

Folklore suggests that test performance may have more impact on earnings today than it had in 1964–1972, but folklore is a notoriously unreliable guide to changes of this kind, and I know no hard evidence that would support such claims. Furthermore, racial differences in test performance have diminished since the early 1970s (see Chapter 5). Thus when we see that black men still have incomes 25 or 30 percent lower than white men with the same amount of schooling, we cannot plausibly attribute much of this difference to the skills that conventional cognitive tests measure.

Black workers may, however, differ from white workers in other ways that affect the value of their services. Employers are at least as likely to complain about their black employees' work habits and motivation as about their technical skills. I know no objective data on racial differences in work habits and motivation, but I have been struck in my own research by the fact that blacks say they are less satisfied with their jobs than whites who make the same amount of money. This remains true even when one holds constant differences in occupational status, fringe benefits, job security, hours, unionization, and the like.[17] If dissatisfaction is linked to job performance, as countless organizational theorists claim, the fact that blacks are less satisfied could mean that they perform worse than whites with similar skills. Were that the case, even unprejudiced employers would end up paying blacks less than whites with similar credentials. This would remain true even if blacks had good reasons for being dissatisfied. If, through no fault of their own, blacks had worse relations with their supervisors or fellow workers, and if this led to poor performance, it would make economic sense for employers to pay blacks less than whites, even though this would violate most people's sense of fairness.

Other indirect evidence also suggests that black men behave in ways that lower their value to their employers. Black men commit far more violent crimes than white men, for example.[18] Many employers are reluctant to hire men with criminal records. Black men's propensity to break the law may also indicate that they are more likely to break company rules, although I know no hard data on this point.

Young black men are also more likely than white men with the same amount of schooling to father children whom they do not live with or support. This situation is not a matter of direct concern to employers. But if young black men were to approach their work in the same way that they approach contraception and parenthood, employers would have good reason to avoid hiring them for responsible jobs.

Before accepting explanations of this kind, however, the reader should pause to consider Table 1.4, which compares the incomes of white college graduates to those of many different nonwhite groups. It shows that in 1969 even Chinese and Japanese Americans with B.A.'s earned less than their white counterparts, although the gap was only half as large as that between blacks and whites. Tabulations based on smaller samples suggest that this was still true in 1979.[19] Chinese and Japanese Americans have generally attended good schools, do very well on standardized tests, and live in affluent parts of the country. Almost all observers, including Sowell, describe them as hard-working and highly motivated. There is no obvious explanation for their low earnings other than discrimination. But if we allow for the possibility that discrimination significantly reduced Chinese and Japanese Americans'

Table 1.4   Income of Non-European Male
College Graduates as a Percent
of the U.S. Average for Male
College Graduates, 1969

Filipinos	59
Blacks	61
American Indians	64
West Indians	65
Chinese	80
Hispanics	84
Puerto Ricans	80
Japanese	86

Sources: Data on Hispanics and the United States as a whole are from Bureau of the Census, *1970 Census of Population, United States Summary, Detailed Characteristics,* PC(1)-D1, (Government Printing Office, 1974), tables 249 and 250. All other estimates are from Thomas Sowell, ed., *Essays and Data on American Ethnic Groups,* (Washington: Urban Institute Press, 1978).

incomes, then surely we must allow for the possibility that it played an even larger role for blacks.

Yet if discrimination is really crucial, as liberal doctrine claims it is, how are we to explain the other striking fact in Table 1.3, namely that black women with college degrees had as much income as their white counterparts in 1987? One answer is that black women with college degrees were more likely to work than their white counterparts. When white women worked full-time throughout 1987, they earned 9 to 16 percent more than their black counterparts. A disparity of this size could, however, be largely explained by the fact that white women do better on standardized tests. Whatever the explanation, it seems clear that black women's economic problems derive mainly from being women, not from being black.

Five Kinds of Economic Discrimination

Conservative suggestions that employers have sound economic reasons for not paying black men as much as white men suggest that liberals need to think more carefully about the causes and meaning of discrimination. The first step is to distinguish between economically rational and irrational reasons for discrimination.

The economically irrational reasons for discrimination fall into two broad classes, which I will call "principled" and "myopic." Principled discrimination is rooted in ethnic solidarity. In the 1950s, for example, one would sometimes encounter southern employers who believed that one of their black workers was as valuable as any of their white workers, but nonetheless felt that paying a black worker as much as a white would undermine white supremacy. As a result, some of the most talented black workers moved north, leaving their former employers worse off. I call this principled discrimination because the employer's commitment to white supremacy takes precedence over his economic self-interest. Discrimination of this kind is no longer common in America.[20]

What I call myopic discrimination often originates in a commitment to white supremacy, but its immediate motive is a set of ethnic stereotypes that leads employers to underestimate the skill or reliability of black workers. An employer who does not notice that a black worker is as good as a white worker is an obvious example. An employer who will not consider a highly recommended black job applicant because he believes that all blacks are lazy is another example.

Both principled and myopic discrimination reduce the quality of a firm's labor force without reducing its wage bill. If all competing firms engage in such discrimination, they can pass its cost on to their customers through higher prices or inferior services. But if some employers stop engaging in such discrimination, those who continue to discriminate will find themselves at a competitive disadvantage. When firms face intense competition, as many American firms now do, they will normally turn to any available pool of cheap, competent workers. Once a few firms do this, price competition will force others to do the same. As this happens, firms will bid up the wages of the previously excluded group until all equally productive workers earn about the same amount.

So long as no major-league baseball team hired blacks, for example, the costs of discrimination fell on promising black players, who could not play in the major leagues, and on fans, who saw worse games than they would have seen in the absence of discrimination. Once a few clubs hired blacks, however, all other clubs had an incentive to do the same in order to assemble winning teams. Owners who persisted in hiring only white players when they could get better black ones at the same price had to pay for their prejudice by losing games, which usually meant losing revenue as well. The same logic applied when banks first began to hire female tellers.

These examples suggest that neither principled nor myopic discrimination is likely to persist unless all competing firms can somehow collude with one another to discriminate equally. Such collusion seldom works unless the conspirators can impose significant economic or social costs on anyone who breaks ranks. Sometimes the government helps them out by making discrimination legally obligatory. Sometimes unions force all competitors to hire union members and restrict membership to whites. In small towns, informal social sanctions often suffice to enforce such rules. But without some enforcement mechanism, either formal or informal, there will sooner or later be an entrepreneur who puts short-term profits ahead of white supremacy, or who figures out that he can get better workers than his competitors by ignoring traditional racial stereotypes.

While competitive pressures tend to eliminate those forms of discrimination that are economically irrational, firms also have economically rational reasons for discriminating. These reasons fall into three broad classes, which I label consumer-driven, worker-driven, and statistical.

What I call consumer-driven discrimination occurs when a firm believes that a black worker could perform a given job satisfactorily but also believes it would lose business if it assigned a black worker to the job in question. When the owners of major-league baseball teams refused to hire blacks, for example, this was seldom because they were principled white supremacists or unable to see that some black ballplayers were as good as many whites they hired. Most owners refused to hire black players because they believed that their predominantly white fans preferred all-white teams. If the owners were right, the fans were engaged in principled discrimination. The owners, in contrast, were behaving in an economically rational manner.

Employers may also think that their customers engage in myopic discrimination. Some airline passengers still believe that blacks cannot master complex technical skills, for instance. Some of these passengers might well avoid airlines that hired a lot of black pilots. If such passengers were numerous, airlines would have a sound economic reason for not hiring black pilots, even if they knew the pilots in question were as good as whites.

What I call worker-driven discrimination is probably even more common than consumer-driven discrimination. Most work requires cooperative effort. This means that a worker's value to a firm depends partly on how well he or she gets along both with other workers and with supervisors. If most of the workers in a group are white, and if some of these whites have trouble getting along with blacks, black workers will be less valuable as a result. Blaming this entirely on blacks is obviously unjust. But from the employer's viewpoint justice is irrelevant. If an employer needs a work force capable of collaborative effort, and if this means that all his workers must be the same color (or that he can only hire blacks with an unusual talent for getting along with whites), he must either accept this fact or spend a lot of money dealing with racial conflict. The same logic applies if a firm has a lot of white supervisors who cannot work well with black subordinates.

What I call statistical discrimination (a term invented by the economist Edmund Phelps) resembles what I have called myopic discrimination in that it is based on ethnic stereotypes.[21] In this case, however, the stereotypes are accurate. Suppose a bank has found over the years that its black tellers make slightly more mistakes than its white tellers. Suppose that when all else is equal blacks with four years of college perform as well as whites with two years of college, while blacks with two years of college perform as well as white high-school graduates. If this were the bank's experience, an economically rational policy would be to hire blacks only if they had at least two more years of schooling than otherwise similar whites. Statistical discrimination of this kind would be illegal, but it might nonetheless make economic sense from the bank's viewpoint.

In theory, the bank has an alternative. It can ignore race when hiring, set high performance standards, and fire every teller who falls below these standards, regardless of race. This approach will yield a higher level of performance than relying on any proxy for performance, be it educational credentials, test scores, or skin color. This approach will also protect the bank from lawsuits, at least if it can demonstrate that its performance criteria make sense and are administered in a color-blind way. The "if" is important, however. In practice, a firm may well be sued if it hires color-blind and then fires more blacks than whites. It is unlikely to be sued if it hires relatively few blacks and never fires anyone.

In general, telling a personnel manager to hire everyone and then fire the least competent is efficient when incompetents are easy to identify, easy to fire, and unlikely to do much damage before they are fired. But few jobs meet all these requirements. In some jobs it is hard to tell whether workers are performing unsatisfactorily until they make a serious mistake. In other jobs it is hard to fire workers even when they perform unsatisfactorily, because the firm is committed to rules that make poor performance very hard to prove or because firing people upsets those who remain on the payroll. When a firm is filling jobs of this kind, it must try to screen out unsatisfactory applicants in advance.

The screening devices available for predicting workers' probable performance are seldom very reliable. This is true not just when firms rely on skin color but when they rely on education, references, interviews, or tests. As a result, screening devices always raise serious questions about procedural justice. Suppose, to take a real example, that a hospital is looking for an anesthesiologist and that the applicant with the best medical credentials is a former alcoholic. If the hospital is concerned only with minimizing risks to patients, and if it examines statistics on the proportion of former alcoholics who take up drinking again, it may decide not to hire an ex-alcoholic for such a job. If the hospital consults its attorney, however, it will be told that statistical discrimination of this kind violates federal regulations governing the employment of individuals with medical handicaps. The hospital can discriminate against an applicant because of *current* alcohol abuse, presumably because current abuse is a good predictor of future abuse. The hospital cannot discriminate against an applicant because of *past* alcohol abuse, even though past abuse is also a statistically useful predictor of future abuse. It is easy to see why former alcoholics favor such rules. It is equally easy to see why a hospital would oppose them.

Similar dilemmas arise if job performance is correlated with race. Suppose that a bus company wants to screen out drivers who drink too much, and that its records show a somewhat higher rate of alcohol abuse among whites and blacks than among Asians. Because it is illegal to use race as a criterion for hiring drivers, the company's lawyers urge it to look for other ways of screening out drinkers. If the company tries to do this, however, it soon learns that there is no reliable way of predicting who will drink on the job. Thus if there were a correlation between race and alcohol abuse, this association would probably persist even among individuals who had identical letters from former employers and who said exactly the same things in interviews.

This situation puts the bus company in a moral dilemma. If it wants to distribute jobs in the fairest possible way, it should ignore race when hiring drivers, even though it knows race is correlated with alcohol abuse. If it wants to minimize accidents and lawsuits, it should favor Asian applicants when all else is equal. Statistical discrimination of this kind would obviously be unfair to the great majority of black and white applicants, who do not drink on the job. It would also be illegal, since it would penalize abstemious blacks and whites for the fact that others of their race broke the rules. But if the bus company wanted to maximize either its profits or its customers' safety, it would not be swayed by worries about procedural justice.

Racial differences in job performance need not always drive an economically rational employer to engage in statistical discrimination. Consider a large firm that has caught slightly more black than white cashiers with their hands in the till. If the firm knows it has a lot of undetected theft, and if the amount of money involved is substantial, it may conclude that it would be better off hiring only white cashiers. But whether such a policy makes economic sense depends on the alternatives. If a new accounting system could detect thefts quickly and reliably, the firm might be able to save money by cutting wages, hiring on a color-blind basis, and then firing the handful of cashiers who stole. If persuading managers not to make racist remarks reduced thefts by black cashiers, and if changing managers' behavior were relatively easy, that too would be cheaper than refusing to hire blacks. But when there are statistical differences in average performance, when these differences persist even after a firm has screened applicants using all the readily available evidence, when these differences cannot be eliminated by easily implemented changes in managers' behavior, and when the cost of hiring the wrong person is high, failure to engage in statistical discrimination can cost firms a lot of money.

Confronted with arguments of this sort, liberals usually challenge the factual premise that blacks perform worse than whites. In a society pervaded by racist stereotypes, skepticism about alleged racial differences certainly makes sense. If a firm detects more thefts by blacks than by whites, for example, this need not mean that blacks steal more. It may just mean that white (or even black) supervisors watch blacks more carefully than whites. But it is folly to assume that careful inquiry will always prove that blacks are indistinguishable from whites. Even if a firm treats black and white workers even-handedly, it cannot change the fact that its black workers are likely to be exposed to an extraordinary amount of white hostility, abuse, and humiliation in public places.[22] Such treatment, when combined with the historical legacy of racism, leaves scars that are not easily healed.

My argument up to this point suggests that the conservative case against affirmative action contains an internal contradiction. Conservatives argue that we cannot infer the presence of discrimination from the fact that blacks earn less than whites with the same paper qualifications, because paper qualifications are a poor proxy for actual performance. This argument is correct. But because it is correct, employers often engage in statistical discrimination. Competition also encourages many firms to discriminate if their customers, their workers, or their supervisors are racially prejudiced. It follows that the temptation to discriminate will never disappear entirely in a truly laissez-faire economy. If we want firms to resist such temptations, the government must raise the cost of succumbing by harassing firms that do so.

Free-market enthusiasts sometimes respond to this argument by suggesting that if blacks perform worse than whites with comparable credentials, employers who refuse to hire blacks are not really discriminating after all. That argument seriously distorts the everyday meaning of discrimination. Consider cashiers again and assume for the moment that 5 percent of white cashiers with good references steal, compared to 3 percent of Asian cashiers with similar references. Refusing to hire white cashiers may make economic sense under these circumstances, but it is still discriminatory. After all, 95 percent of white cashiers are honest. Refusing to hire them because a handful of cashiers who happen to be the same color have been caught stealing is a classic case of guilt by association. The fact that such behavior is economically rational does not make it socially or legally desirable. Such practices are illegal because allowing them has social costs we do not want to pay.

Racial discrimination of this kind is also illegal because, unlike discrimination against high-school dropouts or people who cannot read, it penalizes people for traits they cannot alter. When the army refuses to let high-school dropouts enlist, it is clearly penalizing many competent dropouts for the sins of other incompetent dropouts. But victims of such discrimination can solve their problem by returning to school. Blacks have no comparable recourse when firms use skin color to predict performance.

My analysis of discrimination raises equally serious questions about the internal logic of liberal arguments for affirmative action. Proponents of affirmative action almost always deny the existence of economically relevant differences between black and white workers with the same formal credentials. Since consumer-driven and worker-driven discrimination can only affect a limited range of jobs, the traditional liberal view implies that most labor-market discrimination is based on some combination of principle and myopia. If that were the case, discrimination would lower profits. But if discrimination lowered profits, competition would soon eliminate it. Government action might be needed to accelerate the required change, but once the transition was complete, the need for government action would largely disappear. Few liberals accept this conclusion, because few really believe that American firms could hire more black workers without incurring significant costs. Instead, most liberals believe that firms ought to hire more black workers no matter what the cost, because refusal to do so is unjust. If that is what we believe, we should say so. Then we should try to devise ways of spreading the cost of justice more evenly across the entire society.

When Is Discrimination Costly to Its Victims?

Almost every American, liberal or conservative, seems to believe that when employers discriminate, the victims end up poorer as a result. This view is far too simple. Consider major-league baseball again. Suppose the American League had remained completely white while the National League hired on a color-blind basis. Suppose too that a third of the nation's best baseball players are black. Intuitively, most people expect that excluding blacks from the American League would drive down black players' salaries. In fact, this should not happen. In the world I have described, National League teams would pay blacks as much as whites and would be two-thirds black. American League teams would be completely white, but since blacks would not play for them, their salaries would not suffer. Nor would the American League have any reason to pay whites more than the National League did.

Now imagine a somewhat more realistic world. All teams hire both blacks and whites, but all owners also believe that white stars draw slightly more fans than equally skilled black stars. Whites therefore command slightly higher salaries than blacks. Because this form of discrimination is less conspicuous, most people expect it to have less economic effect than keeping one league entirely white. But because this form of discrimination is universal, black players cannot escape it. As a result, it costs blacks more than complete exclusion from one league would.

We can see the same principle at work if we look at the options open to Jews and blacks who graduated from good law schools in the 1930s. If a Jew sought a job with a leading New York firm at that time, he (it would almost always have been "he") soon discovered that most of these firms hired only gentiles. But he also discovered some exceptions. His job search was therefore likely to have two results. First, he would conclude that there was a great deal of discrimination against Jews and would probably become a supporter of both fair-employment legislation and the Anti-Defamation League. Second, he would get a job that allowed him to contribute generously to these causes. Indeed, Table 1.1 suggests that if he compared his earnings to the earnings of his gentile classmates thirty years later, he would probably find no evidence that discrimination had hurt him economically. This would not mean no discrimination had occurred. It would just mean he had been able to find a niche in which his ethnicity was not a handicap. For him, the cost of discrimination would have been psychological, not monetary.

A young black lawyer's experience would have been quite different. No good New York firm hired blacks in the 1930s. Even liberal firms assumed that their clients would never accept a black attorney. Blacks therefore looked elsewhere for work, sometimes entering government, sometimes joining a civil-rights organization, sometimes establishing their own practice dealing with black clients. As a result, even a leading black lawyer was likely to earn far less than his white classmates.

By the late 1970s young black lawyers appeared to confront a situation more like the one Jews had confronted in the 1930s than like the one blacks had confronted then. A number of good law firms hired blacks. Indeed, many seemed eager to hire blacks so long as they talked, thought, and acted like the firm's white recruits. But young black lawyers still faced one major problem that Jews had never faced to the same degree. Even in the 1930s young Jewish lawyers could join firms whose senior partners were also Jewish. These firms got a lot of business from successful Jews. Some also developed areas of specialized expertise that attracted a lot of non-Jewish clients. As a result, many of these firms paid their partners very well. For Jews who did not want to act like WASPS or did not know how to, joining a Jewish firm was an attractive option.

Young black lawyers seldom have analogous opportunities even today. Prosperous black law firms are rare, partly because they get less work from black businesses than Jewish firms get from Jewish businesses and partly because black firms have not attracted much business from whites. This means that in most cases ambitious black lawyers must still enter firms in which the senior partners are white. Once hired, they must worry about the possibility that their superiors undervalue their services simply because they are black. When a more senior lawyer criticizes their performance, they are likely to wonder about the critic's motives. Anxiety of this kind can breed anger and even paranoia.

The subjective consequences of discrimination, both real and imagined, depend on an individual's temperament and past experience. These traits vary in systematic ways. Black women, for example, seem to me to have developed strategies for dealing with discrimination that do them less harm than the strategies many black men use. When a black man thinks someone has shown him disrespect or treated him unfairly, he is likely to show his anger, perhaps because this is the only way he can maintain his self-respect. Women are less likely to feel that their self-respect requires them to challenge their boss when they think he has mistreated them or when they suspect him of racism. They tell one another stories about how unfair their boss's behavior is, or why they deserved the promotion someone else got, but they do not tell their boss off. This is, I think, one reason why employers take a more benign view of black women than black men.[23]

Racism and discrimination also seem to me to affect black immigrants differently from native-born blacks. Blacks from Africa and the West Indies encounter plenty of discrimination when they come to America, but they do not seem to take it to heart in quite the same way that native-born blacks do. Perhaps this is because their sense of themselves as foreigners allows them to take a more instrumental view of such matters. White expatriates in black Africa are also barred from many jobs because they are white, but they seldom take this personally. They simply ask whether the opportunities open to them in Africa are better or worse than those back home. If they can do better in Africa, they soldier on. Black immigrants in the United States seem to do the same.

These examples suggest that if we want to understand the economic costs of discrimination we need to think more than we usually do about the way different individuals and groups react to it. In particular, we need to think more about how people's reactions vary from one historical and political context to another. Careful thinking about this issue might well help the victims of discrimination devise more effective political strategies for dealing with it.

The Economic Effects of Affirmative Action

Title VII of the 1964 Civil Rights Act outlawed employer discrimination against blacks and other minorities. Executive Order 11246, issued in 1965, required federal contractors to establish affirmative-action plans for complying with Title VII. By the late 1960s most large American firms had such plans, and at least in principle their progress was being monitored by the Office of Federal Contract Compliance (OFCC). Narrowly construed, affirmative action refers only to these plans. In everyday usage, however, it embraces all efforts to improve black job opportunities that go beyond eliminating formal discrimination, regardless of whether these efforts are mandated by federal law.

In the mid-1960s, when these programs first took shape, most federal officials hoped that a combination of corporate conscience, private pressure, and the threat of lawsuits by aggrieved workers would cut racial disparities in employment and earnings quite rapidly. As we shall see, racial disparities in weekly earnings did narrow during the 1960s, but not as fast as either blacks or white liberals hoped they would. Furthermore, while unemployment rates fell in the late 1960s, the black rate remained roughly twice the white rate. Partly because progress seemed so slow relative to the standards of that optimistic era, government policy changed in two important ways during 1971. First, in *Griggs v. Duke Power Company* the Supreme Court held that Title VII barred a wide range of nominally color-blind employment practices that had put blacks at a disadvantage. Second, Congress authorized the Equal Employment Opportunity Commission (EEOC) to begin suing private employers when they appeared to have violated Title VII's requirements.

Because of these changes, employers had to take Title VII more seriously in the 1970s than in the 1960s. The EEOC and OFCC monitored firms more carefully, and they interpreted Title VII as requiring firms to do far more.[24] Almost all big firms began to hire at least a few blacks in low- and middle-level positions. Some firms hired and promoted blacks whom they would not have hired or promoted if they had been white.

When the Reagan administration took office in 1981, one of its avowed objectives was to make federal requirements less "burdensome." It exempted some firms from affirmative-action requirements, loosened the standards a firm had to meet for its program to be acceptable, and quietly reduced the threat of sanctions if firms failed to make good on their promises. Budgets were cut at both EEOC and the Office of Federal Contract Compliance Program (which incorporated OFCC in 1978). Nonetheless, many of the rules put in place during the 1970s remained in force, and both EEOC and OFCCP remained more active than they had been in the late 1960s.

It is hard to assess the effects of these changes in federal policy, because they reflected changes in public opinion that also exerted a direct effect on firms' hiring and promotion practices. In addition, the labor market was also changing throughout this period for reasons that had nothing to do with race. Tight labor markets have traditionally helped blacks more than whites, while slack labor markets have hurt blacks more than whites. The labor market tightened steadily during the middle and late 1960s, weakened in the early 1970s, collapsed after the first oil shock in 1974, recovered somewhat in the late 1970s, suffered its worst setback in half a century during the early 1980s, and then gradually recovered in the late 1980s. Weak demand for labor during the 1970s probably reduced whatever benefits blacks reaped from more stringent affirmative-action requirements, and the deep recession of the early 1980s probably hurt blacks far more than the Reagan administration's attitude toward affirmative action.

Sowell claims that the principal black beneficiaries of affirmative action were college graduates. One simple way to test this claim is to ask whether the ratio of black to white earnings narrowed more for college graduates than for other groups during the years when EEOC and OFCC were most active and employers were most concerned with improving the racial mix of their workforce. Table 1.5, which is based on work by James Smith and Finis Welch, shows how the ratio of black to white weekly earnings changed for men with different amounts of schooling between 1949 and 1979.

Looking first at the 1950s, we see a dramatic improvement in the

Table 1.5   Black Male Weekly Earnings as a Percent of White Male Weekly Earnings, by Education and Experience, 1949–1979

Experience and education	1949	1959	1969	1979
Men with 1–40 years' experience				
College graduate or more	50	60	73	76
Some college	56	63	75	80
High school graduate	67	66	72	79
Some high school	71	70	79	75
No high school	64	67	74	83
Men with 1–10 years' experience				
College graduate or more	68	69	85	88
Some college	84	75	91	89
High school graduate	82	73	81	83
Some high school	76	71	84	87
No high school	67	66	74	84

Source: Adapted from James P. Smith and Finis R. Welch, "Black Economic Progress after Myrdal," *Journal of Economic Literature,* 27 (June 1989), table 11. The sample includes U.S. citizens who were not in the armed forces, not living in group quarters, had between 1 and 40 years of work experience, worked at least 26 weeks during the previous year, were not enrolled in school, and whose estimated weekly earnings (based on annual earnings divided by weeks worked) fell between $19.80 and $1,875 in 1980 dollars.

relative earnings of college-educated blacks, but not in the relative earnings of blacks without any higher education. Among men with less than ten years of work experience, there is hardly any improvement even among the college-educated. The record from 1949 to 1959 does not offer much support for Sowell's contention that minorities do best when government intervention is least.

In 1949 and 1959, when Jim Crow rules were still widely accepted, the ratio of black to white weekly earnings was lower among college graduates than among men without any college education. By 1969 the black-white wage gap no longer showed any systematic relationship to educational attainment. This change suggests that highly educated blacks were indeed the greatest beneficiaries of increased demand for black workers during the 1960s, just as Sowell claims.

In the early 1970s, when federal pressure to hire blacks became intense, young black college graduates briefly commanded higher salaries than their white counterparts.[25] This situation was very short-lived, however. The estimates for men with less than ten years of experience in Table 1.5 show that by the end of the 1970s black-white differences in weekly earnings were only a little smaller than they had been in 1969, and black college graduates had gained no more than less-educated blacks. This was true for older black men as well.

John Bound and Richard Freeman have extended this story down to 1988 for men with less than ten years of experience.[26] Their estimates focus on hourly rather than weekly wages, and they include statistical adjustments for the effects of age, geographic location, and the exact number of years of school a man had completed. Among men without higher education, the racial gap grew by 2 or 3 percent between 1979 and 1988.[27] This change is too small to be of much practical importance, but it again demonstrates that, contrary to what Sowell sometimes suggests, reduced government intervention does not guarantee black progress.

For college graduates, Bound and Freeman tell an even more disturbing story. They estimate that the typical young black male B.A. earned 4 percent less than his white counterpart in 1973, 8 percent *more* in 1975–76, 4 percent less in 1979–80, and 15 percent less in 1987–88. The fact that this reversal of fortune began in the late 1970s suggests that we cannot blame it entirely on Reaganism. The rapid increase in black college enrollments in the late 1960s may have been a more important factor. By the late 1970s the supply of young black

B.A.s was much larger than it had been a decade earlier, so firms did not have to pay as well in order to get black faces in their front offices.

Up to this point I have concentrated on weekly earnings. Many economists have suggested that civil-rights legislation, like minimum-wage legislation, is likely to have two contradictory effects on black workers' earnings. On the one hand, Title VII should encourage a firm with black workers to make sure that it pays these workers as well as it pays whites with equivalent qualifications. On the other hand, any change that suddenly raises the cost of black labor without raising its productivity is likely to reduce demand for black workers, making it harder for the least desirable black workers to find jobs.

In theory, this danger was dealt with by rules requiring employers to treat black and white job applicants more even-handedly than they had before 1964. In practice, however, laws and regulations that bar discrimination in hiring are harder to enforce than those that bar discrimination against workers who are already on a firm's payroll. Blacks who already work for a firm are in a good position to monitor the way it distributes pay and promotions. If they think their employer is mistreating them, they may well take legal action. This possibility gives their employer a strong incentive to treat them fairly. Indeed, firms have an incentive to treat their black employees somewhat better than their white employees, because blacks who think they have been mistreated can sue more easily than whites with similar grievances.

Blacks who apply for jobs from outside a firm have much greater difficulty knowing whether they are being treated fairly. They seldom know much about a firm's other applicants, so if a firm does not hire them, they cannot tell whether they have been victims of discrimination. Nor does OFCCP review firms because they do not hire enough black workers. It reviews large firms, regardless of whether they have a lot of black workers or only a few.[28] A rational firm could easily conclude that it is more likely to be sued if it hires a lot of blacks with marginal qualifications, some of whom will have to be fired (or at least not promoted), than if it hires fewer blacks, takes only those with outstanding records, and treats them extremely well.

If a firm has to pay black workers more than in the past, and if it also has to be more cautious about disciplining them or passing them over for promotion, it is likely to ask itself whether blacks are worth what they now cost. If its answer is no, it will look for ways of reducing the number of blacks on its payroll. The safest way of doing this is to relocate in an area where few blacks live: a remote white suburb, a rural area with few black residents, a southwestern state where most unskilled workers are Mexicans rather than blacks, or perhaps even Taiwan or Mexico. Thousands of firms have made such moves over the past generation. These moves have had many motives, but the search for cheap, skilled, easily disciplined workers has usually been near the top of the list. In practice, firms that move seem to favor places where their workers will not be black and will not be sympathetic to unions. Title VII does not—and probably cannot—regulate such moves. Yet their adverse effect on black employment could easily offset all the positive effects of affirmative action.

These possibilities suggest that liberals should ask whether affirmative-action requirements have contributed to the decline in black men's chances of finding work. One crude way to answer this question is to ask when the ratio of weeks worked by blacks to weeks worked by whites began to decline. Figure 1.1 addresses this question using data

Figure 1.1

Ratio of Blacks' to Whites' Weeks Worked among Men with 1–40 Years of Experience, by Educational Attainment, 1963–1987

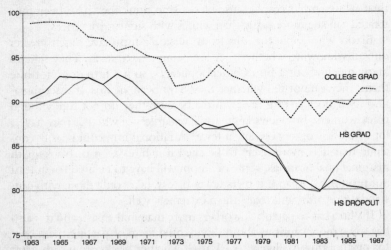

Source: Three-year moving averages from annual files of the March Current Population Survey assembled by Robert Mare and Christopher Winship. Tabulations by Christine Kidd, Rich Mrizek, and David Rhodes.

Figure 1.2

Ratio of Blacks' to Whites' Weeks Worked among Men with 1–10 Years of Experience, by Eduational Attainment, 1963–1987

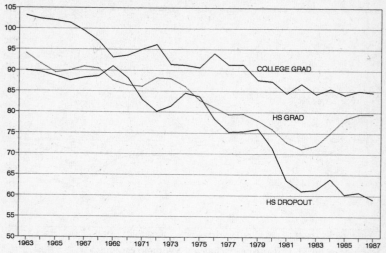

Source: See Fig. 1.1

on men with one to forty years of experience. Figure 1.2 presents data on men with one to ten years of experience.[29]

Among college graduates, the ratio of black to white employment declined fairly steadily from 1965 to 1981. These dates coincide almost exactly with the period when employers worried most about meeting federal affirmative-action requirements. In the late 1980s, when affirmative-action rules were less of a threat and the relative cost of hiring black B.A.s was lower than it had been a decade earlier, their employment prospects began to improve relative to whites, although the trend is so weak and irregular that it may not turn out to have much significance.

Among men without higher education, Figures 1.1 and 1.2 tell a more ambiguous story. The black-white disparity in rates of employment narrowed somewhat in the late 1960s, which is what we would expect in a tight labor market. After 1969, blacks lost ground faster than whites, but this could be because aggregate demand for unskilled and semiskilled workers was not keeping up with the supply. We see

Figure 1.3

Ratio of Blacks' to Whites' Annual Earnings among Men with 1–40 Years of Experience, by Educational Attainment, 1963–1987

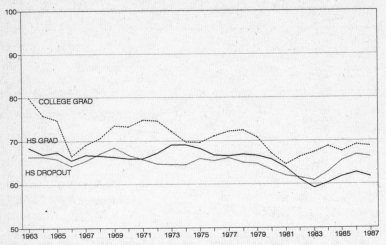

Source: See Fig. 1.1. Estimates include men with no earnings.

these trends in even more dramatic form among men with less than ten years of experience. After 1981, when affirmative-action pressures diminish, the ratio of black to white employment begins to rise among high-school graduates. Among high-school dropouts, however, the ratio continues to decline.

For most of the period that concerns us, black men's wages were improving relative to the white average, while their chances of having any job at all were deteriorating relative to the white average. This raises the question of whether, on balance, blacks gained or lost. One way to assess the net effect of these contradictory trends is to compare blacks' annual earnings to the annual earnings of whites with the same amount of schooling. Figure 1.3 shows how this ratio changed between 1963 and 1987. Unlike most data on earnings, Figure 1.3 takes account of men with no earnings whatever. Partly for this reason it tells a somewhat surprising and deeply troubling story.

- If we compare 1987 to 1963, the ratio of black to white earnings never changes by more than a couple of percentage points. Judging by their mean annual earnings, therefore, black men have made almost no progress relative to whites with the same amount of schooling. This fact seems to support Sowell's claim that affirmative action had little net effect.

- Among college graduates, black gains in weekly earnings more than offset their losses in employment in the late 1960s and early 1970s. After that, black college graduates began losing ground.[30]

- Among men without any higher education, trends in weeks worked and weekly earnings offset each other even in the 1960s and 1970s.

One might argue that Figure 1.3 underestimates the economic benefits of affirmative action, because things would have been even worse in its absence. To make this case one needs direct evidence that affirmative action helped blacks. The strongest evidence for this view comes from comparisons between firms with federal contracts, which are subject to monitoring by OFCCP, and firms without such contracts, which are monitored only by EEOC. This comparison shows that while federal contractors had disproportionately white workforces in 1966, their workforces had become disproportionately black by 1970, and there was a further shift between 1970 and 1974. This change was even more pronounced for black women than for black men. Black representation in professional and managerial jobs also improved more among federal contractors than among noncontractors.[31]

If we couple the fact that federal contractors hired more blacks with the fact that employers generally hired fewer (relative to the available supply), one can infer that the civil-rights movement and Title VII have probably had two consequences. On the one hand, they made firms more cautious about hiring blacks, because they knew black workers had more rights than their white counterparts, and firms prefer workers with as few rights as possible. On the other hand, affirmative action also put strong pressure on federal contractors to hire blacks anyway. The result seems to have been that noncontractors hired fewer blacks, while contractors hired more. Overall, however, demand for black workers failed to keep up with the supply, so joblessness among black men increased.

The historical record also suggests that affirmative action created both winners and losers within the black male workforce. Black men who found steady jobs were better off than ever before, because their wages rose relative to white norms. But a growing minority of black men could not find steady jobs. They were worse off than before. This does not mean, as Sowell sometimes implies, that black college graduates were necessarily winners or that less-educated blacks were necessarily losers. There seem to have been both winners and losers at every educational level. Joblessness increased among young black college graduates, so some black college graduates were among the losers. Weekly earnings increased among black dropouts, so those who found steady work were among the winners. Nonetheless, Sowell seems to be right in claiming that affirmative action had economic costs as well as benefits for blacks.

The Political Costs of Affirmative Action

While there is no general agreement about the economic consequences of affirmative action, almost everyone agrees that it has had important political costs. These costs derive from the fact that federal policies have not led employers to adopt color-blind employment practices. Instead, employers now have a mix of practices, some of which favor whites and some of which favor blacks. As a result, both whites and blacks now see themselves as victims of discrimination.

In order to understand how this happened, one must remember that the ground rules for interpreting Title VII were established in the 1960s, when cities were burning and racial warfare seemed a real possibility. Public officials, judges, civil-rights leaders, and business leaders all assumed that racial conflict was rooted partly in blacks' economic troubles and that these troubles derived partly from past discrimination. A consensus therefore developed that ending racial violence required policies that would not only treat black workers fairly in the future but would eliminate the effects of past discrimination as quickly as possible.

Eliminating the legacy of past discrimination was hard to reconcile with color-blind hiring for two reasons. First, in order to acquire the information, skills, personal contacts, and judgment that employers seek when they fill a good job, a worker must usually have held other jobs that are almost equally good or must at least have spent a lot of time around the sorts of people who hold such jobs. Since blacks had very limited access to such jobs before 1964, and since they had almost no social contact with the whites who held such jobs, color-blind hiring rules seemed likely to exclude most older blacks from good jobs for the rest of their working lives. Second, most good jobs carried an implicit guarantee of tenure if the jobholder continued to perform at whatever level an employer had judged acceptable in the past. Since turnover in good jobs was low, rules that merely guaranteed blacks equal access to such jobs when a white retired would have kept blacks from getting their fair share of such jobs for at least a generation.

The federal officials and judges charged with implementing Title VII resolved the conflict between color-blind hiring and improving blacks' economic position in a way that protected most but not all white privileges. Firms were allowed to retain all their old employees, no matter what procedures had been used to hire them. Firms were also allowed to consider education and work experience when filling new vacancies, so long as they could demonstrate that these considerations were relevant to job performance. But in some cases firms also had to estimate the proportion of blacks they would hire if fair rules prevailed and then make a good-faith effort to achieve this goal promptly. Firms sometimes had to hire disproportionate numbers of blacks until they reached their hiring goals.

Suppose, for example, that a police department had hired only white officers prior to 1964 but after much litigation agreed that the force ought to be 25 percent black. To achieve this goal expeditiously the department might also agree that half of its new hires would be black until it reached its target of a 25 percent black force. But if fairness dictates a 25 percent black force, reserving half of all vacancies for blacks will almost inevitably be unfair to white applicants in the short run. Suppose, for example, that the department has three times as many applicants as places, that it ranks applicants on the basis of education, test scores, references, and the like, and that a quarter of those who rank in the top third of the pool are black. If the department reserves half its vacancies for blacks, it will have to hire some blacks who do not rank in the top third of the pool while rejecting some whites who do. It will, in short, have to set a lower cutoff point for blacks than for whites. (If half of the department's top applicants were blacks, black plaintiffs would never have agreed to a 25 percent black force as the ultimate goal.)

For those who worry only about achieving a fair allocation of jobs between races, discriminating against today's white applicants in order to offset the consequences of having discriminated against yesterday's black applicants may seem fair enough. But most Americans are concerned with allocating jobs fairly between individuals as well as groups. If your main concern is justice for individuals, penalizing young whites for the fact that older whites benefited from discrimination in the past seems unjust. Such a policy therefore has substantial political costs. Young whites who are refused jobs for such reasons do not blame older whites who got jobs they did not deserve a decade or two earlier. They blame blacks for their role in creating rules that are unfair today.

In some cases, moreover, employers have adopted policies that do not even pretend to be racially neutral. A police department, for example, might agree that half of its officers should be black because half of the city's residents are black, ignoring the fact that only a quarter of the applicants who meet its traditional hiring criteria are black. Having reached such an agreement, the department will have to fiddle its traditional system for ranking applicants, creating a lot of ill will among white officers and applicants.

Agreements of this kind are often denounced as "political," but they also rest on practical considerations much like those that lead shopkeepers to hire white rather than black salesworkers or make baseball teams pay white stars more than black stars. No sensible police chief wants to deploy an overwhelmingly white force in overwhelmingly black neighborhoods, no matter how high the white officers' scores were on the qualifying exam. Most police chiefs believe that a racially mixed force is less likely to start riots and better able to keep order than an overwhelmingly white force. Since that is what the police are supposed to do, black skin becomes, in the language of EEOC, a "bona fide occupational qualification."

This line of argument raises difficult legal and political problems, however. If an urban police chief can favor applicants with black skins because black officers cause less trouble when policing black neighborhoods, should a suburban chief be able to favor white applicants on the grounds that white skin is an asset when policing a white neighborhood? And if skin color is a legitimate job qualification for a police officer, why should it be illegitimate for others who work in all-black or all-white communities? Once we admit that the public is not color-blind, pragmatism and efficiency provide a rationale for all sorts of practices that are currently illegal and should almost certainly remain so. It makes sense to me that a police force should be somewhat representative of the community it polices, just as a jury should. But I have not been able to find a principle for adjudicating conflicts between the claims of efficiency and the claims of fairness that strikes me as either intellectually or morally satisfying.

Twenty years ago many liberals felt uncomfortable with reverse discrimination but were willing to accept it as a temporary device for eliminating the legacy of Jim Crow. Few imagined that such policies would be permanent. Instead, they assumed that as young blacks entered the labor force they would get their fair share of good jobs. As older blacks retired, racial inequality would gradually disappear. Once that happened, it would become possible to distribute new openings entirely on the basis of performance rather than skin color.

The young blacks who entered the labor force in the mid-1960s have now reached middle age. Their children, who began entering the labor force in the 1980s, have spent their entire lives in a post-civil-rights society. Nonetheless, these children still earn far less than their white counterparts, especially if they are males. This situation has convinced many liberals that affirmative-action policies established in the mid-1960s, including policies that overtly or covertly discriminate in favor of blacks, are still essential. But the case for such policies can no longer rest on the claim that they are just transitional and will soon give way to color-blind policies. If we think affirmative action must continue until blacks earn as much as whites, it now seems clear that we will need it for many decades to come.

The most plausible argument for reverse discrimination today is, I think, that we need formal discrimination in favor of blacks to offset the effects of persistent informal discrimination against them. Suppose, for example, that you are the "equal opportunity" officer in a large corporation. You know that some of the company's supervisors are old-fashioned racists, who prefer white to black workers for reasons that have nothing to do with job performance. You are not in a position to fire these supervisors because they are hard to identify, the case against them is extremely difficult to prove, and even when the case is clear, their superiors often want to keep them because they are outstanding in other respects. What are you to do?

If some supervisors discriminate against blacks while the rest are color-blind, blacks will get less than their fair share of job offers and promotions. If you want to ensure that the company as a whole treats blacks even-handedly, and if some supervisors discriminate against blacks, one obvious response is to ensure that other supervisors discriminate in favor of blacks. To achieve this goal you set numerical hiring goals for each division of the company and allow divisional managers to achieve these goals however they want. If you can make division managers take these goals seriously, they will begin to reward their subordinates for hiring and promoting blacks. This will have uneven results. Some supervisors will drag their feet, continuing to favor whites. Some will be even-handed. Some will try to curry favor with their boss by favoring blacks. With luck, antiblack and problack bias may roughly offset one another.

Unfortunately, a firm that pursues policies of this kind cannot expect either black or white workers to think they have been treated fairly. Blacks who work for old-fashioned racists will feel ill treated. Whites who work for supervisors who lean over backwards to help blacks will also feel ill treated. Nor can the firm really claim that its policies are just, since as every child knows "two wrongs don't make a right." In the long run, moreover, this strategy will lead to internal segregation, since blacks will transfer to departments where they do well and whites will do the same. Nonetheless, this approach to racial equality may often do less harm than any feasible alternative.

When reverse discrimination leads to conspicuous racial differences in job performance, however, its social cost becomes substantial. The example I know best is the college classroom. Most selective colleges want more black students. They therefore favor academically marginal black applicants over comparable whites. Since almost all colleges pursue such policies, a black student usually gains admission to a more selective college than an academically comparable white. Since most students attend the most selective college that admits them, black students are likely to end up in colleges where their predicted grades put them in the bottom half of the entering class.

Some black students defy the odds and do well academically. On the average, however, blacks earn lower grades than their white classmates in almost every college. Both black and white students notice this fact. They see that relatively few blacks choose hard majors, such as chemistry or engineering, and that few end up with high grades even if they choose "soft" majors like sociology and education. Students also notice that the black students in their own classes are less likely to know what the professor expects them to know. These experiences inevitably reenforce traditional prejudices about blacks' academic abilities.

The same thing happens to athletes. Athletic ability and grades are almost uncorrelated among high-school students. But because college admissions offices discriminate in favor of athletes, they usually end up in places where they are outclassed academically. Both students and faculty then notice that athletes are usually poor students. Jokes about slow-witted jocks become a staple of undergraduate humor. There is one crucial differences between athletes and blacks, however. Encouraging the nation's future professional and managerial elite to think that athletes are dimwits does no serious social harm, because very few undergraduates remain athletes after they graduate, and those who make a career out of sports reap such spectacular rewards that they can survive jokes about their academic skills. A policy that encourages the nation's future leaders to believe that blacks are slow learners will, in contrast, do incalculable harm over the long run, because blacks cannot shed their skin after graduation.

Policies that put blacks in situations where they cannot perform as well as most whites may also have significant psychological costs for blacks. Most of us will do almost anything to preserve our self-respect. This means we avoid competitions in which we expect to do badly. If we are poor athletes, we avoid sports. If we are poor students, we often quit school. If we stay in school, we usually do as little work as possible, because we find it easier to maintain our self-respect if we get a C− after doing very little work than if we get a C+ after weeks of hard work. Colleges that admit large numbers of academically marginal black students should not, therefore, be surprised when these students create a subculture in which working hard is devalued. Athletes do the same thing.

For all these reasons I have come to the reluctant—and still hesitant—conclusion that, when reverse discrimination leads to visible racial differences in job performance, its political costs outweigh its economic benefits. When reverse discrimination does *not* lead to visible differences in performance, the clear implication is that the selection criteria on which blacks ranked lower than whites were inappropriate to begin with and should be abandoned. I therefore favor interpreting Title VII as requiring employers to justify any selection criterion that eliminates disproportionate numbers of blacks. But I also favor interpreting Title VII as forbidding reverse discrimination once valid selection criteria have been established.

Many conservatives, including Sowell, want to go much further than this. They believe that the government should not regulate private employers' hiring and promotion policies at all. For reasons I have already discussed, an unregulated labor market is unlikely to produce color-blind hiring and promotion policies. If Title VII were repealed, firms in competitive industries would have to engage in worker-driven, consumer-driven, and statistical discrimination against blacks in order to stay competitive. This means that if we want to move the country toward color-blind employment policies, we cannot repeal Title VII or even leave it unenforced. Instead, we need to rethink what Title VII should require of employers.

Numerical Goals and Quotas

The Supreme Court's 1989 decision in *Ward's Cove Packing Co. v. Frank Atonio* reinterpreted Title VII in such a way as to put a substantially greater burden of proof on individuals who claimed they had been victims of discrimination. Liberals in Congress responded by proposing new legislation designed to reverse *Ward's Cove*. The Bush administration opposed this effort, on the grounds that the proposed legislation would force companies to establish racial quotas in order to avoid being sued. At the time this chapter was completed, the outcome of the struggle remained uncertain.

By the end of the 1980s quotas had acquired such a bad name that even liberals usually felt obliged to disavow them. This was because inflexible quotas often lead to a double standard for hiring. But quotas need not be inflexible. In most situations quotas are "soft." They constitute targets that a firm or department tries to reach, but which it need not reach if it can show it made a good-faith effort. These soft quotas are often known as "numerical goals" or "targets." Conservatives claim that they too are undesirable. Most liberals, including myself, disagree.

Hiring decisions inevitably depend on a multitude of complicated factors. Proving that racial bias affected any one decision is therefore almost impossible. It follows that monitoring hiring decisions on a case-by-case basis is also impossible. Attempting to do so creates a mountain of useless paper and serves mainly to enrich lawyers. The only practical way to prove discrimination in most settings is to use statistical evidence. The traditional legal approach was to define the pool of workers from which a firm could plausibly fill certain positions and calculate the percentage of blacks in this pool. If a firm's workforce was significantly whiter than the pool from which it could have drawn, a plaintiff could argue that the firm must have been discriminating. This was, of course, a rebutable presumption. But at least until recently such a statistical case put a strong burden of proof on the defendant.

This approach to defining and eliminating discrimination is, I believe, perfectly reasonable as long as we realistically define the pool of workers from which a firm can draw. In practice, however, we seldom do this. Instead, plaintiffs deliberately define the pool of available workers as broadly as possible, so as to justify their claim that the defendant should have hired more blacks. Once a numerical goal is set at an unrealistically high level, the only way it can be met is through reverse discrimination. That gives numerical goals a bad name—as indeed it should.

In leading universities, for example, appointments of senior faculty depend largely on the quantity and influence of a candidate's scholarly publications. If those who set hiring goals for such universities wanted to ensure color-blind decisions, they would try to devise racially neutral methods for determining what fraction of the most productive and influential scholars in each field were black. There is, of course, no completely objective system for ranking a scholar's contribution to knowledge, especially when he or she is still young and the record is skimpy. It seems fair to assume that those who publish nothing have contributed little, but some scholars who publish a lot also contribute little.

Nonetheless, universities have devised a variety of objective criteria for checking departmental recommendations about hiring and promotion. University review committees and administrators rely fairly heavily on the prestige of the journals in which a candidate has published, since they know that most scholars send their work to the best place that will accept it. Many universities also check to see how often a candidate's work has been cited by others. These measures are far from perfect, but if one allows for differences among specialties within each discipline, such methods probably suffice to construct a demographic profile of the most influential scholars in a discipline. Such data could provide a rough estimate of how many black scholars a top department would hire if it made decisions on a color-blind basis.

No particular department is likely to conform precisely to averages derived in this way. I would expect my own university, which is located just outside Chicago in a racially mixed community, to recruit more black scholars than the University of Wisconsin in Madison, where blacks are less likely to want to live. A department's success in recruiting black faculty is also likely to depend on its areas of specialization, the character of its student body, and so on. But if one starts with realistic estimates of the size of the pool from which a department is recruiting, it is possible to adjust numerical targets to take account of such factors.

Officials charged with formulating affirmative-action plans do not set their goals in the way I have described, because they do not actually want departments to engage in color-blind hiring. Instead, they want to hire more black faculty, even if this means bending traditional standards a bit. To promote this goal they define the pool of potentially available black faculty more broadly—by including all recent Ph.D.s who are black, for example. This measure exaggerates the number of black scholars a top academic department could hire without using a double standard. But for that very reason such a measure appeals to both blacks and white liberals, since it implies that departments could easily do more if they set their minds to the task.

No one involved in this process actually favors setting lower standards for black than white faculty. Those who claim that departments have done too little simply assert that qualified black scholars exist and that departments could find them by looking harder. When applied to any one department, this claim is presumably correct. If my department tries harder than your department to recruit Nobel laureates, then if all else is equal my department will end up with more laureates than yours. The same logic applies to black scholars. In the aggregate, however, persuading more departments to try harder will not increase the number of Nobel prizewinners. Nor will it increase the number of distinguished black scholars, except perhaps in the very long run.

While academic organizations have often used a double standard to increase the proportion of black students and faculty, nonacademic organizations have sometimes abandoned their traditional selection system altogether. Many traditional job requirements, such as educational credentials and high scores on multiple-choice tests, exclude more black than white applicants. The 1971 *Griggs* decision held that when a requirement excluded more blacks than whites, an employer had to show that the requirement was really related to job performance. Many large employers responded by hiring consultants to evaluate their hiring and promotion requirements. These consultants were often unable to find a statistically reliable relationship between job performance and the firm's traditional selection criteria. Indeed, they were often unable to find a statistically reliable relationship between job performance and *any* selection criterion. As a result, some firms dropped their old screening systems and began hiring in such a way as to get a larger number of black workers.

But the fact that psychologists cannot find a statistically reliable relationship between job performance and traditional selection standards does not prove that no such relationship exists. In many cases the relationship is merely obscured by some combination of sampling and measurement errors. When job performance is hard to evaluate, as it often is, there is bound to be a lot of measurement error. When the number of workers holding a given position is small, as it is in most small firms, there is also a high risk of sampling error.

By placing the burden of proof on employers, *Griggs* forced them—and ultimately their customers—to pay for the limitations of social science. In *Ward's Cove,* the court appears to have shifted the burden of proof from employers to black job applicants. This will presumably make it easier for firms to use selection standards of uncertain validity even when these standards exclude more blacks than whites. In effect, this will force blacks to pay for the limitations of social science. Such a change will make life easier for employers and will sometimes allow firms to hire slightly better workers. But no one should suppose that forcing blacks to pay for the limitations of social science constitutes a step toward justice.

The Future of Affirmative Action

Where should we go from here? We clearly need to reappraise both racial quotas and traditional schemes for selecting promising workers. In order to win broad political support, such a reappraisal will have to embody three principles. First, competence is always a legitimate job requirement. Second, a record of past competence is almost always the best predictor of future competence. Third, while skin color is sometimes a legitimate job qualification, those who want to treat it this way must base their case on what a specific worker does (counseling black students, for example), not on the assertion that hiring more blacks will help the organization meet its affirmative-action goals. The purpose of such goals should be to discourage discrimination against blacks, not to encourage discrimination in their favor.

Few advocates of affirmative action deny the importance of competence, but they often challenge traditional (white) definitions of what particular jobs require. Why, for example, should a professor in a rich private university be judged solely by the quantity and influence of his publications? Why not take seriously the teaching, the committee work, and the hand-holding that are also part of a college professor's job? These are legitimate questions. But if universities answer them by changing their traditional criteria for judging faculty, they must change their criteria for hiring whites as well as blacks. Otherwise they create an environment in which whites constantly say of job candidates that they are "very good for a black," or "the best black we can get." Hiring policies that encourage this kind of thinking seem likely to perpetuate racism rather than reduce it.

In the 1960s and 1970s enthusiasts of affirmative action also denied that past performance was the best predictor of future performance. Many argued that blacks who had learned little in school, left school young, or compiled spotty employment records were simply the victims of past discrimination, and that they would do better if given another opportunity. This was sometimes true, just as it was for whites. In general, however, experience has shown that damaged lives are hard to make whole, regardless of whether the victim is black or white. This means that, even in a drastically unequal and frequently unjust society such as ours, past failures usually imply future failures for blacks as well as for whites. Employers who operate on this assumption are reasonable people, not closet racists.

If we start with the principle that competence is always a legitimate job requirement, the next question is what we should do when we cannot predict who will perform competently. Here we confront a true conflict between the claims of procedural justice and the claims of economic efficiency. Given our deplorable history in racial matters, and given the grave risk that racial conflict may still unravel the fragile fabric of our society in the years ahead, we cannot afford to let employers do as they please. We need to keep reiterating that statistical, consumer-driven, and worker-driven discrimination are wrong even when they are efficient, and we need to keep making such behavior both risky and costly.

This said, I think the time has come to declare that reverse discrimination is also bad social policy. That means we need to conduct a case-by-case reexamination of hiring goals for minorities in specific firms, aimed at ensuring that these goals are consistent with setting uniform performance standards for blacks and whites.

Along with more realistic hiring goals, we need a more realistic approach to nonracial job requirements. The *Griggs* decision, especially as implemented by EEOC, placed an enormous burden of proof on employers who wanted to use test scores, educational credentials, or similar criteria for choosing workers. Rather than shifting this burden to jobless black workers, as the Supreme Court seems intent on doing, we should shift it to society as a whole. Congress should support a large-scale program of research to determine which tests and credentials predict performance in various broad classes of jobs. A program of this kind would almost certainly show that the haphazard way in which consultants have evaluated traditional hiring standards led us to abandon many practices that made sense.[32] When several criteria for selecting workers are almost equally reliable, we also need to know which one is least likely to exclude blacks. Using information of this kind, the Labor Department should issue regulations that tell firms which credentials and tests they can legally use in various kinds of jobs. Firms that follow these rules should be immune from lawsuits.

My argument is not, then, that we should abandon our efforts to stamp out discrimination or that we should abandon affirmative action. To do so would make a bad racial problem even worse. For the forseeable future, many different firms will stand to gain economically from discrimination, and unless the government is active in discouraging such practices, they will persist. Nonetheless, our criteria for identifying discrimination do need to change. We need numerical goals, but they must be based on realistic assessments of how many blacks a firm can recruit without establishing a double standard. We must, in other words, keep affirmative action, but we must also give it a new meaning that is consistent with color-blind performance standards.

= 2 =

The Safety Net

From 1946 until 1964 the conservative politicians who dominated Congress thought that the federal government might be capable of transforming American society, but they saw this as a danger to be avoided at almost any cost.[1] For the next twelve years the liberals who dominated Congress thought that the federal government should try to cure almost every ill Americans were heir to. After 1976 the political climate in Congress changed again. The idea that government action could solve—or even ameliorate—social problems became unfashionable, and federal spending was increasingly seen as waste. As a result, federal social-welfare spending, which had grown from 5 percent of the nation's gross national product in 1964 to 11 percent in 1976, has remained stuck at 11 percent since 1976.

In the early 1980s conservative writers began trying to shift the prevailing view again, by arguing that federal programs were not just ineffective but positively harmful. The "problem," in this emerging view, was not only that federal programs cost a great deal of money that the citizenry would rather spend on video recorders and Caribbean vacations, but that such programs hurt the very people they were intended to help.

Losing Ground, by Charles Murray, is still the most persuasive statement so far of this new variation on Social Darwinism.[2] Murray's name has been invoked repeatedly in Washington's debates over the budget—not because he has provided new evidence on the effects of particular government programs, but because he is widely presumed to have proven that federal-social policy as a whole made the poor worse off after 1964. Murray's popularity is easy to understand. He writes

70

clearly and eloquently. He cites many statistics, and he makes his statistics seem easy to understand. Most important of all, his argument provides moral legitimacy for budget cuts that many politicians want to make in order to reduce the federal deficit.

Murray summarizes his argument as follows:

> The complex story we shall unravel comes down to this:
> Basic indicators of well-being took a turn for the worse in the 1960s, most consistently and most drastically for the poor. In some cases, earlier progress slowed; in other cases mild deterioration accelerated; in a few instances advance turned into retreat. The trendlines on many of the indicators are—literally—unbelievable to people who do not make a profession of following them.
> The question is why . . .
> The easy hypotheses—the economy, changes in demographics, the effects of Vietnam or Watergate or racism—fail as explanations. As often as not, taking them into account only increases the mystery.
> Nor does the explanation lie in idiosyncratic failures of craft. It is not just that we sometimes administered good programs improperly, or that sound concepts sometimes were converted to operations incorrectly. It is not that a specific program, or a specific court ruling or act of Congress, was especially destructive. The error was strategic . . .
> The most compelling explanation for the marked shift in the fortunes of the poor is that they continued to respond, as they always had, to the world as they found it, but that we—meaning the not-poor and undisadvantaged—had changed the rules of their world. Not of our world, just of theirs. The first effect of the new rules was to make it profitable for the poor to behave in the short term in ways that were destructive in the long term. Their second effect was to mask these long-term losses—to subsidize irretrievable mistakes. We tried to provide more for the poor and produced more poor instead. We tried to remove the barriers to escape from poverty, and inadvertently built a trap.

In appraising this argument we must, I believe, draw a sharp distinction between the material condition of the poor and their social, cultural, and moral condition. If we look at material conditions we find that, Murray notwithstanding, the position of poor people showed marked improvement after 1965, which is the year Murray selects as his "turning point."[3] If we look at social, cultural, and moral indicators, the picture is far less encouraging. But since most federal programs are aimed at improving the material conditions of life, it is best to start with them.

The Poverty Rate

In making his case that "basic social indicators took a turn for the worse in the 1960s," Murray begins with the official poverty rate. The income level, or "threshold," that officially qualifies a family as poor varies according to the number and age of its members and rises every year with the Consumer Price Index, so in theory it represents the same level of material comfort year after year.[4] If a family's total money income is below its poverty threshold, all its members are counted as poor. The official definition of the poverty level is to a large extent arbitrary. When a 1983 Gallup survey asked how much money a couple with two children needed to "get along in this community," for example, the typical respondent said $15,000. The "poverty" threshold for such a family was only $10,000 in 1983. But few would deny that people with incomes below the poverty threshold are poor.

Table 2.1 shows that the official poverty rate fell from 30 to 22 percent of the population during the 1950s and from 22 to 13 percent during the 1960s. This hardly seems to fit Murray's argument that social indicators took a turn for the worse in the 1960s. The official rate was still 13 percent in 1980, but even this was not exactly a "turn for the worse." At most, we could say that "earlier progress stopped."

Furthermore, the official poverty statistics underestimate actual progress since 1965. To begin with, the Consumer Price Index (CPI), which the Census Bureau uses to correct the poverty thresholds for inflation, exaggerated the amount of inflation between 1965 and 1980 by about 13 percent, because of a flaw in the way it measured housing costs. The official poverty line therefore represented a higher standard of living in 1980 than in 1965. If we use the Personal Consumption Expenditure (PCE) deflator from the National Income Accounts to adjust the poverty line for inflation, Table 2.1 shows that poverty fell from 19 percent in 1965 to 13 percent in 1980.

A more fundamental problem with the official poverty statistics is that they do not take account of changes in families' *need* for money. They make no adjustment for the fact that Medicare and Medicaid now provide many families with low-cost medical care, or for the fact

Table 2.1 The Condition of the Poor, 1950–1980

Category	1950	1960	1965	1970	1980
Poverty rate					
Official[a]	30	22	17	13	13
Corrected official[b]	31	25	19	15	13
"Net"	30	–	18	–	10
Infant mortality as a percent of live births[c]					
White	2.7	2.3	2.2	1.8	1.1
Black	4.4	4.4	4.2	3.3	2.2
Gap	1.7	2.1	2.0	1.5	1.1
Life expectancy in years[c]					
White	69.1	70.6	71.0	71.7	74.4
Nonwhite	60.8	63.9	64.1	65.3	69.5
Gap	8.3	6.7	6.9	6.4	4.9
Median family income (in 1980 dollars)[d]	$10,500	$14,000	$16,200	$19,200	$21,000
Gross national product[e] (in 1980 dollars)					
Per worker	$15,300	$18,900	$22,300	$23,400	$24,600
Per household	$21,900	$24,900	$28,900	$30,600	$32,600

a. From Murray, pp. 65 and 245. The 1950 value is approximate. Corrected for inflation using the Consumer Price Index.

b. Corrected for inflation using the Personal Consumption Expenditure deflator and for measurement changes in 1966, 1974, and 1979.

c. *Statistical Abstract of the United States, 1984.*

d. US Bureau of the Census, *Current Population Reports,* Series P-60, no. 132, corrected for inflation using the PCE deflator, not the CPI.

e. *Economic Report of the President, 1984.*

that food stamps have reduced families' need for cash, or for the fact that more families now live in government-subsidized housing.

Experts on poverty have devised a number of different methods for estimating the value of noncash benefits. Most conservatives prefer the "market value" approach, which values noncash benefits according to what it would cost to buy them on the open market and adds this amount to recipients' incomes. To see what this implies, consider Mrs. Smith, an elderly widow living alone in Indiana, who is covered by both Medicare and Medicaid. Private insurance comparable to Medicare-Medicaid would have cost Mrs. Smith $4000 in 1979.[5] To get Mrs.

Smith's "true" income, advocates of the market-value approach simply add $4000 to her money income. Since, by the official standard, Mrs. Smith's poverty threshold was only $3472 in 1979, the market-value approach would put her above the poverty line even if she had no cash income whatever. This is plainly absurd. Mrs. Smith cannot eat her Medicaid card or trade it for a place to live or even use it for transportation to her doctor's office.

If we want a more realistic picture of how Medicare and Medicaid have affected Mrs. Smith's life, we must answer two distinct questions: how it affected her ability to obtain medical care and whether it cut her medical bills.

When the Census Bureau values noncash benefits according to what they save the recipient, it finds that they lowered the 1980 poverty rate from 13 to 10 percent.[6] The Census has not made comparable estimates for the 1950s or 1960s, but we can make informed guesses about 1950 and 1965. In 1965, Medicare and Medicaid did not exist, food stamps reached fewer than 2 percent of the poor, and there were 600,000 public housing units for 33 million poor people. In 1950 food stamps did not exist at all and there were 200,000 public housing units for 45 million poor people. Taken together, these programs could hardly have cut the poverty rate by more than one point in either year. On this assumption Table 2.1 estimates the "net" poverty rate at 10 percent in 1980, 18 percent in 1965, and 29 percent in 1950.[7]

It should go without saying that since the original poverty threshold was arbitrary, these statistics do not prove that only 10 percent of the population was "really" poor in 1980. The figure could be either higher or lower, depending on how you define poverty. The figures do, however, tell us that the proportion of the population living below our arbitrary threshold was almost twice as high in 1965 as in 1980, and almost three times as high in 1950 as in 1980. At least in economic terms, therefore, Murray is wrong: the poor made a lot of progress after 1965.

Furthermore, even these "net" poverty statistics underestimate the improvement in poor people's material circumstances. Mrs. Smith's $4000 Medicaid card may not lift her out of poverty, but it has dramatically improved her access to doctors and hospitals. In 1964, before Medicare and Medicaid, middle-income families typically saw doctors five times a year, whereas the poor saw doctors four times a year. By 1981, middle-income families were seeing doctors only four times a year, while the poor were seeing them almost six times a year. Since the poor still spent twice as many days in bed as the middle classes, and were three times as likely to describe their health as "fair" or "poor," this redistribution of medical care still fell short of what one would expect if access depended solely on need.[8] But it was a big step in the right direction.

Increased access to medical care seems to have improved poor people's health. The most widely cited health measure is infant mortality. The United States does not collect statistics on infant mortality by parental income, but it does collect these statistics by race, and it seems reasonable to assume that differences between whites and blacks parallel those between rich and poor. Table 2.1 shows that the gap between blacks and whites, which had widened during the 1950s and narrowed only trivially during the early 1960s, narrowed very rapidly after 1965. The table tells a similar story about overall life expectancy. Life expectancy rose more from 1965 to 1980 than it had from 1950 to 1965, and the disparity between whites and nonwhites narrowed faster after 1965 than before. Nobody knows how much Medicare and Medicaid contributed to these changes, but notwithstanding all the defects in the American medical care system, it is hard to believe they were not important.[9]

Nonetheless, despite all the improvements since 1965, Murray is right that, apart from health, the material condition of the poor improved faster from 1950 to 1965 than from 1965 to 1980. The most obvious explanation is that the economy turned sour after 1970. Inflation was rampant, output per worker increased very little, and unemployment began to edge upward. The real income of the median American family, which had risen by an average of 2.9 percent a year between 1950 and 1965, rose only 1.7 percent a year between 1965 and 1980. From 1950 to 1965 it took a 4.0 percent increase in median family income to lower net poverty by one percentage point. From 1965 to 1980, because of expanding social-welfare spending, a 4.0 percent increase in median income lowered net poverty by 1.2 percent. Nonetheless, median income grew so much more slowly after 1965 that the decline in net poverty also slowed.[10]

Murray rejects this argument. In his version of economic history the nation as a whole continued to prosper during the 1970s. The only problem, he claims, was that "the benefits of economic growth stopped trickling down to the poor." He supports this version of economic history with statistics showing that gross national product grew by 3.2 percent a year during the 1970s compared to 2.7 percent a year between 1953 and 1959. This is true, but irrelevant. The economy grew during the 1950s because output per worker was growing. It grew during the 1970s because the labor force was growing. The growth of the labor force reflected a rapid rise in the number of families dividing up the nation's economic output. GNP per household hardly grew at all after 1970 (see Table 2.1).[11]

But a question remains. As Table 2.2 shows, total government spending on social-welfare programs grew from 11.2 to 18.7 percent of GNP between 1965 and 1980. If all this money had been spent on the poor, poverty should have fallen to virtually zero. But social-welfare spending is not mostly for the poor. Although it includes programs aimed primarily at the poor, such as Medicaid and food stamps, it also includes programs aimed primarily at the middle classes, such as college loans and military pensions, and programs aimed at almost everybody, such as medical research, public schools, and social security. In 1980, only a fifth of all social-welfare spending was explicitly aimed at low-income families, and only a tenth was for programs providing cash, food, or housing to such families.[12] Table 2.2 shows that cash, food, and housing for the poor grew from 1.0 percent of GNP in 1965 to 2.0 percent in 1980.[13] This was a large increase in absolute terms. But redistributing an extra 1.0 percent of GNP could hardly be expected to reduce poverty to zero.

A realistic assessment of what social policy accomplished between 1965 and 1980 must also take account of the fact that if all else had remained equal, demographic changes would have pushed the poverty rate up during these years, not down. Table 2.2 shows that both the number of people over sixty-five and the number living in families headed by women grew steadily from 1950 to 1980. We do not have poverty rates for these groups in 1950, but in 1960 the official rates were roughly 33 percent for the elderly and 45 percent for families headed by women. Since neither group includes many jobholders, economic growth does not move either group out of poverty very fast. From 1960 to 1965, for example, economic growth lowered official poverty from 22 to 17 percent for the nation as a whole, but only lowered it from 33 to 31 percent among the elderly and from 45 to 42 percent among households headed by women.

When poverty became a major social issue during the mid-1960s,

Table 2.2 Social-Welfare Spending and Need, 1950–1980

Category	1950	1960	1965	1970	1980
Percent of GNP spent on					
"Social welfare"	8.2	10.3	11.2	14.7	18.7
Means-tested cash benefits, food stamps, and housing subsidies[a]	0.9	0.8	1.0	1.2	2.0
Percent of persons who were					
Over 65	8	9	9	10	11
In families headed by women	6[b]	7	9	10	12
In AFDC families	1.5	1.7	2.3	4.7	4.9
Illegitimate births as a percent of all births	4	5	8	11	19
Percent of personal income derived from					
Social Security and SSI	0.4	2.8	3.3	3.9	5.9
AFDC	0.3	0.3	0.3	0.6	0.6
Mean monthly payment (in 1980 dollars) to					
Retired workers	$138	$184	$195	$228	$341
AFDC family of four[c]	NA	$396	$388	$435	$350
Official poverty rate[d]					
Persons over 65	NA	33[e]	31[e]	25	16
Persons in families headed by women	NA	45	42	38	37
Percent of all poor people who were					
In families headed by women	NA	18	23	30	35
Over 65	NA	14	18	19	13

Sources: *Statistical Abstract, 1984; Economic Report of the President, 1984; Historical Statistics of the United States;* and *Current Population Reports,* Series P-60, no. 145. Pre-1980 dollars are converted to 1980 dollars using the PCE deflator.

a. Includes all "Public Aid" and "Housing" expenditures, less Medicaid. "Public Aid" includes some social services.

b. Estimated from data on percent of families headed by women in 1950 and 1960, and percent of persons in such families in 1960.

c. Benefit level for a family with no other income. (For source, see Table 5.5 in Chapter 5.)

d. Corrected for measurement change in 1966.

e. Estimated from the total poverty rates in 1960 and 1965 and from the poverty rates for the elderly in 1959 and 1966.

government assistance to the elderly and to families headed by women was quite modest. In 1965 the typical retired person got only $184 a month from social security in 1980 dollars, and a large minority got nothing whatever. Only about a quarter of all families headed by women got benefits from Aid to Families with Dependent Children (AFDC), and benefits for a family of four averaged only $388 a month in 1980 dollars (see Table 2.2).

From 1965 to 1970 the AFDC system changed drastically. Welfare offices had to drop a wide range of restrictive regulations that had kept many women and children off the rolls. It became much easier to combine AFDC with employment, and benefit levels rose appreciably. As a result of these changes something like half of all persons in families headed by women appear to have been receiving AFDC by 1970.[14]

But as the economy floundered in the 1970s legislators began to draw an increasingly sharp distinction between the "deserving" and the "undeserving" poor. The deserving poor were those whom legislators judged incapable of working, namely the elderly and the disabled. Despite their growing numbers, they got more and more help. By 1980 the average social-security retirement check bought 50 percent more than it had in 1970, and official poverty among the elderly had fallen from 25 to 16 percent. Taking noncash benefits into account, the net poverty rate was lower for those over sixty-five than for those under sixty-five in 1980.[15]

We have less precise data on the disabled, but we know their monthly benefits grew at the same rate as benefits for the elderly, and the percentage of the population receiving disability benefits also grew rapidly during the 1970s. Since we have no reason to suppose that the percentage of workers actually suffering from serious disabilities grew, it seems reasonable to suppose that a larger fraction of the disabled were getting benefits, and that poverty among the disabled fell as a result.

While legislators were increasingly generous to the "deserving" poor during the 1970s, they showed no such concern for the "undeserving" poor. The undeserving poor were those who "ought" to work but did not do so. They were mainly single mothers and marginally employable men whose unemployment benefits had run out—or who had never been eligible in the first place. Single men whose unemployment benefits have run out seldom get federal benefits. Most states offer them token "general assistance," but it is seldom enough to live on. Data on this group are scanty.

Single mothers do better than unemployable men because legislators are reluctant to let their children starve and cannot find a way of cutting benefits for mothers without cutting them for children as well. As Table 2.2 shows, the purchasing power (in 1980 dollars) of AFDC benefits for a family of four rose from $388 a month in 1965 to $435 in 1970. In addition, Congress made food stamps available to all low-income families after 1971. These were worth another $150 to a typical family of four.[16] By 1972, the AFDC-food stamp package for a family of four was worth about $577 a month. Benefits did not keep up with inflation after 1972, however, and by 1980 the AFDC-food stamp package was worth only $495 a month.[17] As a result, the welfare rolls grew no faster than the population after 1975, though the number of families headed by women continued to increase.[18]

According to Murray, keeping women off the welfare rolls should have raised their incomes in the long run, since it should have pushed them into jobs where they would acquire the skills they needed to better themselves. This did not happen. The official poverty rate in households headed by women remained essentially constant throughout the 1970s, at around 37 percent. Since the group at risk was growing, families headed by women accounted for a rising fraction of the poor.

Taken together, Tables 2.1 and 2.2 tell a story very different from the one Murray tells in *Losing Ground*. First, contrary to what Murray claims, net poverty declined almost as fast from 1965 to 1980 as before. Second, the decline in poverty after 1965, unlike the decline before 1965, occurred despite unfavorable economic conditions and depended to a great extent on government efforts to help the poor. Third, the groups that benefited from this "generous revolution," as Murray rightly calls it, were precisely the groups that legislators hoped would benefit, notably the aged and the disabled. The groups that did not benefit were the ones that legislators did not especially want to help. Fourth, these improvements took place despite demographic changes that would ordinarily have made things worse. Given the difficulties, legislators should, I think, look back on their efforts to improve the material conditions of poor people's lives with some pride.

Social Policy and Single Motherhood

Up to this point I have treated demographic change as if it were entirely beyond human control, like the weather. According to Murray, however, what I have labeled "demographic change" was a predictable byproduct of government policy. Murray does not, it is true, address the role of government in keeping old people alive longer. But he does argue that changes in social policy, particularly the welfare system, were responsible for the increase in families headed by women after 1965. Since this argument recurs in all conservative attacks on the welfare system, and since scholarly research supports it in certain respects, it deserves a fair hearing.

Murray illustrates his argument with an imaginary Pennsylvania couple called Harold and Phyllis. They are young, poorly educated, and unmarried. Phyllis is also pregnant. The question is whether she will marry Harold. Murray first examines her situation in 1960. If Phyllis does not marry Harold, she can get the equivalent of about $70 a week in 1984 money from AFDC. She cannot supplement her welfare benefits by working, and on $70 a week she cannot live by herself. Nor can she live with Harold, since the welfare agency checks up on her living arrangements, and if she is living with a man she is no longer eligible for AFDC. Thus if Phyllis doesn't marry Harold she will have to live with her parents or put her baby up for adoption. If Phyllis does marry Harold, and if he gets a minimum-wage job, they will have the equivalent of $124 a week (in 1984 dollars). This isn't much, but it is better than $70. Furthermore, if Phyllis is not on AFDC she may be able to work herself, particularly if her mother will help look after the baby. Unless Harold is a complete loser, Phyllis is likely to marry Harold—if he asks.

Now the scene shifts to 1970. The Supreme Court has struck down the "man in the house" rule, so Phyllis no longer has to choose between Harold and AFDC. She can have both. According to Murray, if Phyllis does not marry Harold and he does not acknowledge that he is the father of their child, Harold's income will not count when the local welfare department decides whether Phyllis is eligible for AFDC, food stamps, and Medicaid. This means she can get paid to stay home with her child while Harold goes out to work, but only so long as she doesn't marry Harold. Furthermore, the value of her welfare package is now roughly the same as what Harold or she could earn at a minimum-wage job. Remaining eligible for welfare is thus more important than it was in 1960, as well as being easier. From Phyllis's viewpoint, marrying Harold is now quite costly.

While the story of Harold and Phyllis makes persuasive reading, it is misleading in several respects. First, it is not quite true, as Murray claims, that "any money that Harold makes is added to their income without affecting her benefits as long as they remain unmarried." If Phyllis is living with Harold, and Harold is helping to support her and the child, the law requires her to report Harold's contributions when she fills out her "need assessment" form. What has changed since 1960 is not Phyllis' legal obligation to report Harold's contribution but the likelihood that she will be caught if she lies. Federal guidelines issued in 1965 now prohibit "midnight raids" to determine whether Phyllis is living with Harold. Furthermore, even if Phyllis concedes that she lives with Harold, she can deny that he pays the bills and the welfare department must then prove her a liar. Still, Phyllis must perjure herself, and there is always some chance she will be caught.

A more serious problem with the Harold and Phyllis story is that Murray's account of Harold's motives is not plausible. In 1960, according to Murray, Harold marries Phyllis and takes a job paying the minimum wage because he "has no choice." But the Harolds of this world have always had a choice. Harold can announce that Phyllis is a slut and that the baby is not his. He can tell Phyllis to get an illegal abortion. He can join the army. Harold's parents may insist that he do his duty by Phyllis, but then again they may blame her for leading him astray. If Harold cared only about improving his standard of living, as Murray suggests, he would not have married Phyllis in 1960.

According to Murray, Harold is less likely to marry Phyllis in 1970 than in 1960 because, with the demise of the "man in the house" rule and with higher benefits, Harold can get Phyllis to support him. But unless Harold works, Phyllis has no incentive either to marry him or to let him live off her meager check, even if she shares her bed with him occasionally. If Harold *does* work, and all he cares about is having money in his pocket, he is better off on his own than he is sharing his check with Phyllis and their baby. From an economic viewpoint, in short, Harold's calculations are much the same in 1970 as in 1960. Marrying Phyllis will still lower his standard of living. The main thing that has changed since 1960 is that Harold's friends and relatives are less likely to think he "ought" to marry Phyllis.

This brings us to the central difficulty in Murray's story. Since Harold is unlikely to want to support Phyllis and their child, and since Phyllis is equally unlikely to want to support Harold, the usual outcome is that they go their separate ways. At this point Phyllis has three choices: get rid of the baby (through adoption or abortion), keep the baby and continue to live with her parents, or keep the baby and set up housekeeping on her own. If she keeps the baby she usually decides to stay with her parents. In 1975 three-quarters of all first-time unwed mothers lived with their parents during the first year after the birth of their baby. (No room for Harold here.) Indeed, half of all unmarried mothers under twenty-four lived with their parents in 1975—and this included divorced and separated mothers as well as those who had never been married.[19]

If Phyllis expects to go on living with her parents, she is not likely to worry much about how big her AFDC check will be. Phyllis has never had a child and she has never had any money. She is used to her mother's paying the rent and putting food on the table. Like most children she is likely to assume that this arrangement can continue until she finds an arrangement she prefers. In the short run, having a child will allow her to leave school (if she has not done so already) without having to work. It will also mean changing a lot of diapers, but Phyllis may well expect her mother to help with that. Indeed, from Phyllis' viewpoint having a child may look rather like having another little brother or sister. If it brings in some money, so much the better, but if she expects to live with her parents, money is likely to be far less important to her than her parents' attitude toward illegitimacy. This is the main thing that changed for her between 1960 and 1970.

Systematic efforts at assessing the impact of AFDC benefits on illegitimacy rates support my version of the Harold and Phyllis story rather than Murray's. The level of a state's AFDC benefits has no measurable effect on its rate of illegitimacy. In 1984, AFDC benefits for a family of four ranged from $120 a month in Mississippi to $676 a month in New York. David Ellwood and Mary Jo Bane have done a meticulous analysis of the way such variation affects illegitimate births.[20] In general, states with high benefits have *less* illegitimacy than states with low ones, even after we adjust for differences in race, region, education, income, urbanization, and the like. This may be because high illegitimacy rates make legislators reluctant to raise welfare benefits.

To get around this difficulty, Ellwood and Bane asked whether a change in a state's AFDC benefits led to a change in its illegitimacy rate. They found no consistent effect. Nor did high benefits widen the disparity in illegitimate births between women with a high probability of getting AFDC—teenagers, nonwhites, high-school dropouts—and women with a low probability of getting AFDC.

What about the fact that Phyllis can now live with Harold (or at least sleep with him) without losing her benefits? Doesn't this discourage marriage and thus increase illegitimacy? Perhaps. But Table 2.2 shows that illegitimacy has risen at a steadily accelerating rate since 1950. There is no special blip in the late 1960s, when midnight raids stopped and the man-in-the-house rule passed into history. Nor is there consistent evidence that illegitimacy increased faster among probable AFDC recipients than among women in general.

Murray's explanation of the rise in illegitimacy thus seems to have at least three flaws. First, most mothers of illegitimate children initially live with their parents, not their lovers, so AFDC rules are not very relevant. Second, the trend in illegitimacy is not well-correlated with the trend in AFDC benefits or with rule changes. Third, illegitimacy rose among movie stars and college graduates as well as welfare mothers.[21] All this suggests that both the rise of illegitimacy and the liberalization of AFDC reflect broader changes in attitudes toward sex, law, and privacy, and that they had little direct effect on one another.

But while AFDC does not seem to affect the number of unwed mothers, as Murray claims, it does affect family arrangements in other ways. Ellwood and Bane found, for example, that benefit levels had a dramatic effect on the living arrangements of single mothers. If benefits are low, single mothers have trouble maintaining a separate household and are likely to live with their relatives—usually their parents. If benefits rise, single mothers are more likely to maintain their own households.

Higher AFDC benefits also appear to increase the divorce rate. Ellwood and Bane's work suggests that if the typical state had paid a family of four only $180 a month in 1980 instead of $350, the number of divorced women would have fallen by a tenth. This might be partly because divorced women remarry more hastily in states with very low benefits. But if AFDC pays enough for a woman to live on, she is also more likely to leave her husband. The Seattle-Denver "income maintenance" experiments, which Murray discusses at length, found the same pattern.

The fact that high benefits lead to high divorce rates is obviously embarrassing for liberals, since most people view divorce as undesirable. But it has no bearing on Murray's basic thesis, which is that changes in social policy after 1965 made it "profitable for the poor to behave in the short term in ways that are destructive in the long term." If changes in the welfare system were encouraging teenagers to quit school, have children, and not take steady jobs, as Murray contends, he would clearly be right about the long-term costs. But if changes in the welfare system have merely encouraged women who were unhappy in their marriages to divorce their husbands, or have discouraged divorced mothers from marrying lovers about whom they feel ambivalent, what makes Murray think this is destructive in the long term?

Are we to suppose that Phyllis is better off in the long run married to Harold if he drinks or beats her or molests their teenage daughter? Surely Phyllis is a better judge of this than we are. Or are we to suppose that Phyllis's children will be better off if she sticks with Harold? That depends on how good a father Harold is. The children may do better in a household with two parents, even if the parents are constantly at each other's throats, but then again they may not. Certainly Murray offers no evidence that unhappy marriages are better for children than divorces, and I know of none.

Shorn of rhetoric, then, the "empirical" case against the welfare system comes to this. First, high AFDC benefits encourage single mothers to set up their own households. Second, high AFDC benefits encourage mothers to end bad marriages. Third, high benefits may make divorced mothers more cautious about remarrying. All these "costs" strike me as benefits.

Consider Harold and Phyllis again, but this time imagine that they married in 1960 and that it is now 1970. They have three children, Harold still has the deadend job in a laundry that Murray says he took in 1960, and he has now taken both to drinking and to beating Phyllis. Harold still has two choices. He can leave Phyllis or he can stay. If he leaves, Phyllis can try to collect child support for him, but her chances of success are low. So Harold can do as he pleases.

Phyllis is not so fortunate. She is unable to earn much more than the minimum wage, so she cannot support herself and three children without help. If she is lucky she can go to her parents. Otherwise, if she lives in a state with low benefits, she has two choices: stick with Harold or abandon her children. Since she has been taught to stick with her children, she has to stick with Harold. If she lives in a state with high benefits, she has a third choice: she can leave Harold and take her children with her. In a sense, AFDC is the price we pay for Phyllis's commitment to her children. At 0.6 percent of total personal income, it does not seem a high price.

Giving Phyllis more choices has obvious political drawbacks. So long as Phyllis lives with Harold, her troubles are her own. We may shake our heads when we hear about them, but we can tell ourselves that all marriages have problems and that that is the way of the world. If Phyllis leaves Harold—or Harold leaves Phyllis—and she comes to depend on AFDC, her problems become public instead of private. Now if she cannot pay the rent or does not feed her children milk, this could be because her monthly check is too small, not because she doesn't know or care about the benefits of milk or because Harold spends the money on drink. Taking collective responsibility for Phyllis' problems is not a trivial price to pay for liberating her from Harold. Most of her problems will, after all, remain intractable. But our impulse to drive her back into Harold's arms so that we no longer have to think about her is the kind of impulse we should resist.

Does Helping Hurt?

The idea that Phyllis will be the loser in the long run if society gives her more choices exemplifies a habit of mind that seems as common among conservatives as among liberals. First you figure out what kind of behavior is in society's interest. Then you define such behavior as good. Then you argue that good behavior, while perhaps disagreeable in the short run, is in the long-run interest of those who engage in it. Every parent will recognize this ploy: my son should take out the garbage because it is in his long-run interest to learn good work habits, not because I don't want to take it out or don't want to live with a shirker. The conflict between individual interests and the common interest, between selfishness and unselfishness, is thus transformed into a conflict between short-run and long-run self-interest. Unfortunately, the argument is often false.

Early in *Losing Ground*, Murray calculates what he calls the "latent" poverty rate, that is, the percentage of people who fall below the poverty line when we ignore transfer payments from the government such as social security, AFDC, unemployment compensation, and military pensions. The latent poverty rate rose from 18 percent in 1968 to 22 percent in 1980. Murray calls this "the most damning" measure of policy failure, because "economic independence—standing on one's own abilities and accomplishments—is of paramount importance in determining the quality of a family's life." This is a classic instance of wishful thinking. Murray wants people to work (or clip coupons) because such behavior keeps taxes low and maintains a public moral order of which he (and I) approve, so he asserts that failure to work will undermine family life. He doesn't try to prove this empirically; he says it is self-evident. ("Hardly anyone, from whatever part of the political spectrum, will disagree.") But the claim is not only not self-evident; it is almost certainly wrong.

One major reason latent poverty increased after 1968 was that social security, SSI, food stamps, and private pensions allowed more old people to stop working. These programs also made it easier for old people to live on their own instead of moving in with younger relatives. Having come to depend on the government, old people suffer from latent poverty. But is there a shred of evidence that these changes undermined the quality of their family life? If so, why were the elderly so eager to trade their jobs for social security and so reluctant to move in with their daughters-in-law?

Another reason latent poverty increased after 1968 was that more women and children came to depend on AFDC instead of on a man. According to Murray, a woman who depends on the government suffers from latent poverty, while a woman who depends on a man does not. But unless a woman can support herself and her children from her own earnings, she is always dependent on someone ("one man away from welfare"). Murray assumes that AFDC has a worse effect on family life than Harold. But that depends on Harold. Phyllis may not be very smart, but if she chooses AFDC over Harold, surely that is because she expects the choice to improve the quality of her family life, not undermine it. Even if, as Murray imagines, most AFDC recipients are really living in sin with men who help support them, what makes Murray think that the extra money these families get from AFDC makes their family life worse?

Murray's conviction that getting checks from the government is always bad for people is complemented by his conviction that working is always good for them, at least in the long run. Since many people do not recognize that working is in their long-run interest, Murray assumes such people must be forced to do what is good for them. Harold, for example, would rather loaf than take an exhausting, poorly paid job in a laundry. To prevent Harold from indulging his self-destructive preference for loafing, we must make loafing financially impossible. America did this quite effectively until the 1960s. Then we allegedly made it easier for him to qualify for unemployment compensation if he lost his job, making him less eager to find another. We also made it easier for him to live off Phyllis's AFDC check. Once Harold had tasted the pleasures of indolence, he found them addictive, like smoking, so he never acquired either the skills or the self-discipline he would have needed to hold a decent job and support a family. By trying to help we therefore did him irreparable harm.

Although I share Murray's enthusiasm for work, I cannot see much evidence that changes in government programs during the 1960s significantly affected men's willingness to work. When we look at the unemployed, we find that about half of all unemployed workers were getting unemployment benefits in 1960. The figure was virtually identical in both 1970 and 1980.[22] Thus while the rules governing unemployment compensation did change, the changes did not make joblessness more attractive economically. Murray is quite right that dropping the man-in-the-house rule made it easier for Harold to live off Phyllis' AFDC check. But there is no evidence that this contributed to rising unemployment. Since black women receive nearly half of all AFDC money, Murray's argument implies that as AFDC rules became more liberal and benefits rose in the late 1960s, unemployment should have risen among young black men. Yet Murray's own data show that black men's unemployment rates fell during the late 1960s. Murray's argument also implies that young black men's unemployment rates should have fallen in the 1970s, when the purchasing power of AFDC benefits was falling. In fact, their unemployment rates rose.[23]

Where We Went Wrong

While Murray's claim that helping the poor has really hurt them seems to me indefensible, his criticism of the ways in which government tried to help the poor from 1965 to 1980 still raises a number of issues that defenders of these programs need to face. Any successful social policy must strike a balance between collective compassion and individual responsibility. The social policies of the late 1960s and 1970s did not strike this balance very well. They vacillated unpredictably between the two ideals in ways that neither Americans nor any other people could live with over the long run. This vacillation played a major role in the backlash against government efforts to "do good." Murray's rhetoric of individual responsibility and self-sufficiency is not the basis for a social policy that would be politically acceptable over the long run either, but it provides a useful starting point for rethinking where we went wrong.

One chapter of *Losing Ground* is titled "The Destruction of Status Rewards"— not a euphonious phrase, but a useful one. The message is simple. If we want to promote virtue, we have to reward it. The social policies that prevailed from 1964 to 1980 often seemed to reward vice instead. They did not, of course, reward vice for its own sake. But if you set out to help people who are in trouble, you almost always find that most of them are to some extent responsible for their present troubles. Few victims are completely innocent. Helping those who are not doing their best to help themselves poses extraordinarily difficult moral and political problems.

Phyllis, for example, turns to AFDC after she has left Harold. Her cousin Sharon, whose husband has left her, works forty hours a week in the same laundry where Harold worked before he took to drink. If we help Phyllis much, she will end up better off than Sharon. This will not do. Almost all of us believe it is better for people to work than not to work. This means we also believe those who work should end up better off economically than those who do not work. Standing the established moral order on its head by rewarding Phyllis more than Sharon will undermine the legitimacy of the entire AFDC system. Nor is it enough to ensure that Phyllis is just a little worse off than Sharon. If Phyllis does not work, many—including Sharon—will feel that Phyllis should be substantially worse off, so that there will be no ambiguity about Sharon's virtue being rewarded.

The AFDC revolution of the 1960s sometimes left Sharon worse off than Phyllis. In 1970 Sharon's minimum-wage job paid $275 a month if she worked forty hours every week and was never laid off. Once her employer deducted social security and taxes, she was unlikely to take home more than $250 a month. Meanwhile, the median state (Oregon) paid Phyllis and her three children $225 a month, and nine states paid her more than $300 a month. This comparison is somewhat misleading in one respect, however. By 1970 Sharon could also get AFDC benefits to supplement her earnings in the laundry. Under the "thirty and a third" rule, adopted in 1967, local welfare agencies had to ignore the first $30 of Sharon's monthly earnings plus a third of what she earned beyond $30 when they computed her need for AFDC. If Sharon lived in Oregon, had three children, and took home $250 a month from her job, she could get an additional $78 a month from AFDC, bringing her total monthly income to $328, compared to Phyllis's $225. But Sharon could only collect her extra $78 a month by becoming a "welfare mother," with all the humiliations and hassles that implies. So she seldom applied. Instead, she nursed a grievance against the government for treating Phyllis better than it treated her.[24]

Upsetting the moral order in this way may not have had much effect on people's behavior. Sharon might well continue to work even if she could get almost as much on welfare. But this is irrelevant. Even if *nobody* quit work to go on welfare, a system that provided indolent Phyllis with as much money as diligent Sharon would be universally viewed as unjust. To say that such a system does not increase indolence—or doesn't increase it much—is beside the point. A criminal justice system that frequently convicts the innocent and acquits the guilty may deter crime as effectively as a system that yields just results, but that does not make it morally or politically acceptable. We care about justice independent of its effects on behavior.

Yet while Murray claims to be concerned about rewarding virtue, he seems interested in doing this only if it doesn't cost the taxpayer anything. Instead of endorsing the thirty-and-a-third rule, for example, on the grounds that it rewarded work, he lumps it with all the other undesirable changes that contributed to the growth of the AFDC rolls during the late 1960s. His rationale for this judgment seems to be that getting money from the government undermines Sharon's self-respect *even if she also holds a full-time job*. This may often be true but, when it is, Sharon presumably does not apply for AFDC.

On balance, I prefer the Reagan administration's argument against the thirty-and-a-third rule. The administration persuaded Congress to drop the rule in 1981, substituting a dollar-for-dollar reduction in AFDC benefits whenever a recipient worked regularly. As a result, a mother of three is now better off in seven states if she goes on AFDC than if she works at a minimum-wage job. The administration made no pretense that this change was good for AFDC recipients or that it made the system more just. It simply argued that supplementing the wages of the working poor was a luxury the American taxpayer could not afford, or at least did not want to afford. While this appeal to selfishness is not morally persuasive, it offends me less than Murray's claim that such changes are really in the victims' best interests.

The difficulty of helping the needy without rewarding indolence or folly recurs when we try to provide "second chances." America was a second chance for many of our ancestors, and it remains more committed to the idea that people can change their ways than any other society I know. But we cannot give too many second chances without undermining people's motivation to do well the first time around. In most countries, for example, students work hard in secondary school because they must do well on the exams given at the end of school in order to get a desirable job or go on to a university. In America, many colleges accept students who have learned nothing whatever in high school, including those who score near the bottom on the SATs. Is it any wonder that Americans learn less in high school than their counterparts in other industrial countries?

Analogous problems arise in our efforts to deal with criminals. We claim that crime will be punished, but this turns out to be mostly talk. Building prisons is too expensive, and putting people in prisons makes them more likely to commit crimes in the future. So we don't jail many criminals. Instead we tell ourselves that probation, suspended sentences, and the like are "really" better. Needless to say, such a policy convinces both the prospective criminal and the public that punishment is a sham and that the criminal justice system has no moral principles.

Still it is important not to overgeneralize this argument. Many people apply it to premarital sex, for example, arguing that fear of economic hardship in an important deterent to illegitimacy and that offering unwed mothers an economic second chance makes unmarried women more casual about sex and contraception. In this case, however, the problem turns out to be illusory. Unmarried women do not seem to make much effort to avoid pregnancy even in states like Mississippi, where AFDC pays a pittance. This means that liberal legislators can indulge their impulse to support illegitimate children in a modicum of decency without fearing that generosity will increase the number of children born into this unenviable situation.

The problem of second chances is intimately related to the larger problem of maintaining respect for the rules governing rewards and punishments in American society. As Murray rightly emphasizes, no society can survive if it allows people to violate its rules with impunity on the grounds that "the system is at fault." Murray also argues that the liberal impulse to blame "the system" for blacks' problems played an important part in the social, cultural, and moral deterioration of black urban communities after 1965. That such deterioration occurred in many cities is beyond doubt. Blacks were far more likely to murder, rape, and rob one another in 1980 than in 1965. Black males were also more likely to father children they did not intend to care for or support. Black teenagers were less likely to be working.

All this being conceded, the question remains: were these ills attributable to people's willingness to blame the system, as Murray claims? During the late 1960s crime, drug use, child abandonment, and academic lassitude were increasing in the prosperous white suburbs of New York and Los Angeles—and, indeed, in London, Prague, and Peking—as well as in Harlem and Watts. Murray is right to emphasize that the problem was worst in black American communities. But recall his explanation: "we—meaning the not-poor and the undisadvantaged—had changed the rules of their world. Not our world, just theirs." If that is the explanation, why do we see the same trends among the rich?

Losing Ground does not answer such questions. Indeed, it does not ask them. But it does at least cast the debate over social policy in what I believe are the correct terms. First, it does not ask how much our social policies cost, or appear to cost, but whether they work. Second, it makes clear that a successful program must not only help those it seeks to help but must do so in such a way as not to reward folly or vice. Third, it reminds us that social policy is about punishment as well as rewards, and that a policy which is never willing to countenance suffering, however deserved, will not long endure. The liberal coalition that dominated Washington from 1964 to 1980 did quite well by the first of these criteria: its major programs, contrary to Murray's argument, did help the poor. But it did not do as well by the other two criteria: it often rewarded folly and vice, and it never had enough confidence in its own norms of behavior to assert that those who violated these norms deserved whatever sorrows followed.

= 3 =

Crime

Like rain on election day, crime is good for the Republicans.[1] Whenever crime seems to be increasing, significant numbers of Americans tend to blame liberal permissiveness and turn to conservative political candidates, partly because they endorse a sterner approach to raising children, policing the streets, and punishing criminals, and partly because they oppose government "giveaways" to the poor, blacks, and other groups that commit a lot of crimes. While orthodox liberals answer that "getting tough" won't really help and that the way to reduce crime is to make society more just and opportunity more equal, this response to crime has seldom moved the electorate. When crime rates rise, liberals almost always find themselves on the defensive.

The political effect of crime on the public may be the result of an intellectual mistake, but if so it is an understandable one. Modern liberalism is a product of the eighteenth century, and as its name suggests, its most consistent and powerful impulse has been to expand personal liberty or, as we often say today, "opportunity." In recent decades American liberalism has been primarily concerned with making sure that minorities, women, the poor, and other disadvantaged groups have the same opportunities as affluent white males, so it has acquired an increasingly egalitarian cast—but its strongest impulse is still to eliminate constraints and provide people with more choices.

Liberals have traditionally hoped that more freedom would lead to more of almost everything else they valued. Many Americans viewed the 1960s and early 1970s as a test of this hypothesis. Restrictions on personal behavior diminished dramatically during this period, altering everything from sexual habits and hair styles to relations with the po-

92

lice and employers. Deference to authority in all its guises also declined, making people feel they had more choices.

Among blacks, the end of de jure segregation and the advent of affirmative action opened even more opportunities. Black college-entrance rates almost doubled between 1960 and 1975, and large numbers of young black adults moved into professional and managerial jobs for the first time. Yet for blacks as for whites, the most important change was probably subjective rather than objective. The influence of both black and white authority figures declined precipitously during this period, leaving young blacks with the feeling that there were no clearly defined limits on the choices open to them. They could become anything—or nothing.

In the early 1960s most liberals had hoped that this kind of liberalization would make us all feel a stronger sense of solidarity (or "fraternity") with one another. Once our own rights were more fully recognized, we were supposed to become more attentive to the rights of others. Increasing affluence and opportunity were also supposed to give those at the bottom of the social pyramid a stronger feeling that they had something to lose if they broke the law. The liberal innovations of the 1960s and early 1970s were therefore supposed to reduce the frequency of murder, rape, assault, robbery, and burglary. Instead, all these crimes became far more common. Rightly or wrongly, many Americans concluded that increased liberty, especially for the poor, had actually caused the decline in "fraternity."

Public concern about crime is obviously selective. The mere fact that some behavior is illegal does not worry most Americans much. Every year millions of Americans defraud the Internal Revenue Service by underreporting their income or overstating their deductions. The amounts stolen in this way almost certainly exceed the amounts stolen by muggers on the streets. Yet very few Americans view tax fraud as a serious threat to themselves or to the republic. The reason seems obvious. Unlike robbery, tax evasion has no individual victims. It forces the rest of us to pay higher taxes than we otherwise would, but it does not create the same kind of fear or the same sense of personal violation as being raped or even having your house burgled. We react to most other white-collar crimes with equal indifference. Given a choice, almost everyone would rather be robbed by computer than at gunpoint. This does not make white-collar crime morally preferable to blue-collar crime, but it does explain why white-collar crime is not a major political issue.

The politics of criminology mirror the politics of crime. Any complete account of why people commit crimes must include two elements: a description of how criminals differ from noncriminals and an explanation of how they got that way. In most cases, however, conservative criminologists emphasize the psychological differences between criminals and noncriminals, while liberals emphasize the social circumstances that produce these psychological differences. Indeed, extreme liberals sometimes argue that there are no stable psychological differences between criminals and the rest of us, and that criminals are just ordinary people who find themselves in especially trying or especially tempting circumstances. The extreme conservative position, in contrast, seems to be that social circumstances have nothing to do with crime; some people are just born rotten.

The political motives behind these differing approaches to crime are obvious. Traditional moral reasoning holds us responsible for our psychological states but not, in most cases, for the circumstances in which we find ourselves. Attributing crime to psychological deficiencies is thus compatible with holding criminals morally accountable for their acts, while attributing crime to the circumstances in which criminals find themselves is to some degree morally exculpatory.

Portraying crime as a product of psychological deficiencies also encourages us to place the ultimate blame on parents rather than on society. If we hear a social scientist say that black teenage muggers are unusually aggressive, egocentric, or impulsive, for example, we instinctively impute these defects of character to poor upbringing. Since Americans see upbringing as the responsibility of the family rather than society, the ultimate villains turn out to be the mugger's parents (who are also black), not the federal government, capitalism, white racism, or other targets of liberal reform.

The Politics of Heredity

James Q. Wilson has played a major role in discrediting liberal ideas about crime among both scholars and public officials over the years. Today he is probably the most influential single writer on crime in America. In 1977 he began teaching a course on crime at Harvard with

Richard J. Herrnstein, an experimental psychologist whom the left had bitterly attacked in the early 1970s for his views on the role of heredity in determining IQ scores and economic success. In 1985 Wilson and Herrnstein turned their lecture notes into a book, *Crime and Human Nature*,[2] which tries to summarize what we know about criminal behavior. Unlike Wilson's earlier books on crime, this one is both discursive and inconclusive; indeed, it reads more like a textbook than a trade book. Nonetheless, it has become controversial, largely because it argues that genetic variation helps to explain why some people commit serious crimes while others do not.

Most liberals and radicals are instinctively suspicious of any claim that genes influence human behavior. In part, no doubt, this reflects the fact that we know almost nothing about *how* genes influence behavior. Indeed, we know very little about how they influence physical development. Confronted with the DNA of a dinosaur, for example, geneticists could not even tell you whether it would grow up to be large or small, much less how it would behave. But liberal resistance to genetic explanations is more than just a matter of scholarly caution. Genetic explanations of human behavior arouse opposition because we think they imply that undesirable behavior is a product of forces society cannot control. If we are told that genetic variation explains much of the variation in children's performance on cognitive tests, we take this to mean that schools can do very little to improve slow learners' performance on such tests. In the same way, if we are told that criminal behavior is traceable to genetic differences between criminals and the rest of us, we treat this as an assertion that some people are born criminals and that there is nothing either their parents or society can do to make them better citizens.

This response to genetic explanations of human behavior, while nearly universal, is fundamentally wrong. Wilson and Herrnstein recognize that it is wrong, but they nonetheless say very little about the ways in which social institutions can alter genes' effects on behavior. As a result, their book has helped to perpetuate liberal opposition to genetic explanations. In what follows I will argue that such opposition is misguided. Since I will use Wilson and Herrnstein's genetic explanations of crime as examples, I may leave the reader with the impression that *Crime and Human Nature* is devoted exclusively to such matters. In fact, two thirds of the book has nothing to do with genes, and even the remaining third concerns traits that have nongenetic as well as genetic determinants. Still it is the genetic argument that has made the book controversial.

Heredity or Environment: A False Dichotomy

In order to illustrate both the basic logic of genetic explanations and their potential pitfalls, it is helpful to begin with an example in which the causal links are relatively clear, such as hair length. In our society variation in hair length is largely attributable to the fact that some people have their hair cut shorter than others. In most cases, moreover, men cut their hair shorter than women. This means that if you are born with two X chromosomes, your hair usually ends up longer than if you are born with an X and a Y chromosome. In a statistical sense, therefore, the presence or absence of a Y chromosome predicts much of the variation in hair length—let us say 60 percent. But the fact that genes currently predict hair length fairly accurately tells us nothing about society's ability to alter hair length. If men and women became convinced that equal hair length was important, achieving this result would be no harder than making hair length equal among males alone. Likewise, if some zealot decided that shorter (or longer) hair would contribute to human happiness, he would be a fool to abandon his campaign simply because someone pointed out that people's genes currently "explained" 60 percent of the variation in hair length. And if some social scientist read a study showing that genes explained 60 percent of the variation in hair length, he would be an even greater fool to conclude, as many now do, that environmental influences explained only 40 percent. Environmental variation (in the way people have their hair cut) would explain virtually all the variation in hair length, despite the fact that genetic variation explained 60 percent.

Similar problems arise when we try to analyze the effects of genes on crime. As the authors of one of the most important empirical studies of heredity and crime point out:

> There are no genes for criminality, but only genes coding for structural proteins and enzymes that influence metabolic, hormonal, and other physiological processes, which may indirectly modify the risk of "criminal" behavior in particular environments.[3]

Two seemingly innocuous points in this formulation require special emphasis: the notion that genes exert their effects "indirectly" and the notion that their effects depend on the "particular environments" in which individuals find themselves. The effects of gender on crime illustrate both how genes' effects can be indirect and how they can vary considerably from one particular environment to another.

As Wilson and Herrnstein point out, men are five to ten times more likely than women to commit almost every crime on which American society keeps records. Men also commit more crimes than women in all other societies that keep records, though the magnitude of the difference varies somewhat. This statistical association obviously means that an individual's genes affect his or her chances of committing a crime. But the important question is why this happens. Does a Y chromosome exert physical effects that somehow make men less law-abiding than women no matter how society treats them? Or does having a Y chromosome make us commit more crimes simply because it alters the way society expects us to behave? Wilson and Herrnstein are reticent on this question.

Most feminists argue that sex differences in crime, like all sex differences in social behavior, are a product of culture rather than of physiology. This is a false distinction. It is certainly true that human societies have traditionally tolerated or even encouraged more aggression among males than among females, but this cultural pattern itself demands an explanation. It is not enough to say that male aggression is part of a systematic pattern of male domination. We must ask why male domination has been universal and female domination essentially unknown.

One possible explanation is that men are usually bigger and stronger than women. This difference appears to arise largely because having a Y chromosome influences physical growth, though in many societies social norms accentuate the difference by encouraging men to exercise more than women. Because of these physical differences, men have been able to beat or overpower their wives without much risk of retribution. To survive in such a world, women have had to accommodate rather than confront, seduce rather than overwhelm. That is what daughters have been taught to do the world over. Parents seem especially likely to emphasize these virtues in cultures where domestic violence is commonplace. Liberated women who treat their spouses as equals can survive only in cultures where men do not exploit their physical advantages.

Differences in size may not be the only reason we tolerate more aggression among boys than among girls. There has been a lively debate in recent years about whether hormonal differences between men and women contribute to male aggressiveness, independent of their effects on size and strength. My point is not to defend any particular physical explanation of cultural norms, but merely to argue that cultural support for the prevalence of male rather than female aggressiveness is so nearly universal that it can hardly have arisen simply by chance. If male aggression and violence are not just historical accidents, they must be directly or indirectly attributable to genetic differences between the sexes.

Certainly culture also has a life of its own, which is only partially constrained by physiology. Cultures usually encourage men and women to act in ways that accentuate the effects of physical differences, but this is not universal law. Suppressing physical aggression among young males is often construed as an attempt to "sissify" them in America, for example, but many European and Asian societies do this routinely. Most European and Asian societies also have fewer violent crimes than we do, though the pattern is neither uniform nor consistent over time.

Wilson and Herrnstein recognize that a Y chromosome can have social as well as physical consequences, but they largely ignore the possibility that other genes have equally complex and ambiguous effects. Their discussion of race is a striking example, both because it is a sensitive topic about which I would expect them to be especially cautious and because race is widely regarded as similar to gender.

As Wilson and Herrnstein note, blacks currently account for about half of all arrests for rape and murder and two thirds of all arrests for robbery in the United States, even though they constitute less than one eighth of the population. Since about two thirds of all robbery victims also say that their assailant was black, we cannot blame these arrest statistics on police prejudices. The conclusion that blacks are five to ten times more likely than whites to commit most violent crimes is almost inescapable. This means that the genes determining skin color are as closely correlated with criminal violence in the United States as the genes determining gender. Once again the question is why. The traditional liberal view has been that your skin color affects your behavior by affecting the way others treat you, which then affects the way you treat others. Conservatives often suspect that skin color is a proxy for other unidentified physiological differences that somehow make blacks less law-abiding than whites, though they seldom say this in print.

Crime and Human Nature devotes an entire chapter to assessing various explanations of black crime. The authors begin with a discussion of what they call "constitutional" differences between blacks and whites. A constitutional difference between two individuals or groups, they tell us, is "present at or soon after birth" and its "behavioral consequences appear gradually during the child's development." They give three examples of differences between blacks and whites that they think might be constitutional in this sense: differences in body type, differences in personality, and differences in IQ scores. They conclude that while such differences exist, there is no way of knowing whether racial differences in personality traits or IQ scores are "heritable." By this they mean that there is no way of knowing whether such differences would persist in a color-blind world.

Unfortunately, Wilson and Herrnstein ignore the most obvious—and most obviously heritable—constitutional difference between blacks and whites, namely physical appearance. We don't know for sure that appearance affects criminality, but the possibility surely deserves serious consideration. Sandra Scarr is currently studying the social adjustment of black children adopted into white families, for example. Almost all these children grew up in white neighborhoods and attended predominantly white schools. If constitutional factors don't matter, these children should commit the same number of crimes as whites adopted into similar families. If black adoptees commit more crimes than white adoptees, constitutional factors must matter in some way.

Suppose Scarr finds high crime rates among black adoptees. This could have at least three explanations. One possibility is that parents, teachers, and friends treat black adoptees differently from white adoptees and that black adoptees turn to crime as a result. A second possibility is that people treat black and white adoptees the same way, but that blacks nonetheless see themselves as "different," seek out black friends, emulate these friends' behavior, and end up in trouble as a result. A third possibility is that people treat blacks and whites similarly but that blacks react differently for some physiological reason.

The first of these explanations is compatible with traditional liberalism. The last is compatible with scientific racism. Yet in all three cases the difference between black and white adoptees' behavior would be constitutional in Wilson and Herrnstein's sense of the term, since it would be a direct or indirect consequence of physical differences that are "present at birth" and whose "behavioral consequences appear gradually during the child's development." Unfortunately, nothing in *Crime and Human Nature* warns the reader that a constitutional explanation of black crime could also be a social explanation. Wilson and Herrnstein treat the two kinds of explanation as if they were mutually exclusive.

The examples of gender and race suggest that heredity and environment are not mutually exclusive explanations of human diversity, since genes can influence behavior by influencing the environment. Most of us recognize this ambiguity in the cases of gender and skin color, but we tend to assume that if other genes affect human behavior they must exert their effects directly, rather than influencing the environment individuals encounter. If a study shows that genetic differences among white males are associated with differences in crime rates, IQ scores, or alcoholism, we assume that this is because genetic variation causes variation in the way white males respond to the same environment, not because white males with different genes are treated differently. As we shall see, this assumption is unwarranted. The ambiguities that plague efforts to disentangle the contributions of heredity and environment to differences between males and females or between blacks and whites recur in virtually every other example of genetic influence.

The Evidence for Genetic Effects

If we set aside race and sex, how much of the variation in criminal behavior do genes appear to explain? The best data come from a study of Danish boys adopted by nonrelatives between 1927 and 1947. Almost all these boys were adopted into families where neither parent had ever been convicted of a crime. Of the 3718 boys adopted by apparently law-abiding families, one third had a biological parent—usually the father—who had been convicted of one or more crimes, and one ninth had biological parents with three or more convictions. Table 3.1 shows what had happened to these boys at the time of the followup. The more often the biological parents had been convicted, the more often their sons were convicted.[4]

There have been three other studies of adopted children, including a fairly large study in Sweden. All suggest that sons resemble their natu-

Table 3.1   Criminal Convictions among Danish Males Adopted by Nonrelatives
Who Had Never Been Convicted of a Crime

Category	Convictions per 100 adoptees	Actual numbers of adoptees
Natural parents had		
no convictions	33	2,492
one conviction	42	574
two convictions	54	233
three or more convictions	80	419
All adoptees	41	3,718

Source: Estimated from data in Sarnoff A. Mednick, William F. Gabrielli, and Barry
Hutchings, "Genetic Influences in Criminal Convictions: Evidence from an Adoption
Cohort," *Science,* May 25, 1984, pp. 891–894.

ral fathers more than we would expect if genes had no connection with
criminality. Such studies are not entirely conclusive. To begin with,
adopted children have usually had some contact with their natural parents, or at least with their natural mother, prior to adoption. The authors of the Danish study report, however, that the age at which
children were adopted did not affect the degree of resemblance between them and their biological parents. This suggests that early childhood contact with the natural parents was not critical, perhaps because
such contact was usually with the natural mother, and it was usually
the natural father who had a criminal record.

A second potential problem with adoption studies is that adoption
agencies often place children from advantaged backgrounds in advantaged homes, creating artificial resemblance between biological and
natural parents. The authors of the Danish study report that statistical
adjustment for this kind of socioeconomic matching did not appreciably change their results. The psychologist Leon Kamin has argued that
subtler forms of selective placement might conceivably explain the
Danish findings, but the constraints under which the Danish adoption
officials worked make this seem unlikely.[5]

The most plausible explanation of the adoption data is therefore the
one that Wilson and Herrnstein accept, namely that adopted sons resemble their natural fathers because adopted sons and natural fathers
have half their genes in common and genes exert some influence on the
likelihood that both fathers and sons will be convicted of crimes.[6]

While the adoption studies certainly suggest that genes matter, they do not suggest that genes matter very much. To begin with, genes seem mainly to influence men's chances of committing minor offenses. There is currently no solid evidence that, if we set aside skin color, men's genes affect their chances of committing violent crimes, although such evidence may well emerge. Even for less serious offenses, genetic influences are comparatively unimportant. One way to assess genes' importance is to ask how closely the behavior of adopted sons resembles that of their natural parents. If we do this we find that natural parents' criminal records account for only about 2 percent of the variation in their sons' criminal records.[7]

Another way to assess the importance of genes is to compare the effects of having a criminal parent to the effects of various social determinants of criminal behavior. Table 3.1 shows that children of repeat offenders committed 2.4 times as many crimes as children of non-offenders. Wilson and Herrnstein report that adolescents enrolled in poorly run London comprehensive schools have crime rates three times those of students from similar backgrounds who enrolled in well-run schools. The crime rate in American cities and suburbs is also about three times that in rural areas, and the murder rate for America as a whole in 1980 was at least double that in 1960.[8] These comparisons suggest that genetic effects are neither trivial nor crucial. When we compare the effects of heredity to the effects of growing up in one country rather than another, however, genes look relatively unimportant. The murder rate in New York City in the late 1960s was at least twenty times that in Madrid, Dublin, Paris, or Brussels. And the murder rate in the United States as a whole was about five times that in Australia, despite the fact that a significant fraction of the Australian population was descended from English convicts.

While adoption studies certainly suggest that a man's genes have some influence on the number of crimes he will commit, they do not tell us why this is the case. In this respect they are logically analogous to studies showing that gender or skin color influences criminal behavior. The existence of such a statistical association is intriguing, but it does not have any practical meaning unless we know why it arises. At present, we don't.

The association between body type and crime, with which Wilson and Herrnstein begin their discussion of the constitutional determinants of crime, illustrates the importance of identifying causal mechanisms. Wilson and Herrnstein report a series of studies showing that "heavy-boned and muscular" mesomorphs are overrepresented in American prisons, while stringy ectomorphs and flabby endomorphs are underrepresented. They do not discuss the extent to which body type depends on heredity, but everyday experience suggests that the influence cannot be negligible. It seems to follow that genes influence criminal behavior partly by influencing body type.

How can this be? Wilson and Herrnstein assume that body type cannot influence criminal behavior directly, so they look for other factors that could be correlated with both. Their candidate is personality. Mesomorphs, they suggest, are likely to be dominated by "the spirit of unrestrained, impulsive self-gratification." This may conceivably be true, but the studies they cite certainly do not convince me of the fact. In any event, the association between body type and crime may have a much simpler explanation that they do not consider.

American society makes relatively little collective effort to discourage physical aggression among young males. Preadolescent boys who are larger and stronger than average may therefore find that they can literally "throw their weight around" without much fear of collective retribution. Some of these boys—perhaps especially those with low IQ scores—are likely to find that violence, or a threat of violence, is the best way of getting what they want from others. A stringy ectomorph or a flabby endomorph is less likely to find that violence pays, so he is more likely to develop other strategies for getting what he wants. Given these differing incentives, Wilson and Herrnstein's own model of the determinants of crime predicts that mesomorphs should be especially tempted to become playground bullies, then to be drawn into teenage street gangs, and eventually to end up in prison.

While such a linkage between body type and crime seems natural, it is obviously not inevitable. Only a small percentage of mesomorphs, even from poor families, become criminals. If body type affects criminality by affecting the costs and benefits of aggressive behavior, moreover, it should have less effect in societies where adults consistently punish physical aggression among schoolboys. (Japan and France come to mind as possible examples.) The same should also be true in any American school that consistently punishes physical aggression. Body type should also make less difference for girls, among whom physical aggression is far less acceptable than it is among boys. I know of no effort to test theories of this kind. Scholarly research remains divided between those who believe that biology is destiny and those who prefer to ignore it. Even Wilson and Herrnstein, who are interested in both the biological and the social determinants of behavior, have relatively little to say about how the two interact.

The Role of IQ

The association between heredity, IQ and crime provides a more important and more fully documented example of the way genes might influence criminal behavior. Wilson and Herrnstein believe that criminal behavior depends partly on IQ and that IQ scores depend partly on heredity. It obviously follows that criminal behavior must depend partly on heredity. Yet while the premises and logic of this syllogism seem impeccable, the conclusion need not imply what most readers are likely to think it does.

Before discussing the links between heredity, IQ, and crime, I must say something about the vexed question of what IQ tests measure. Despite the claims of some early twentieth-century psychologists, "intelligence" is not a fixed one-dimensional trait. Nor does it mean the same thing in all cultures. All modern societies label people intelligent if they are good at solving problems that require thought. But since different kinds of thought require different skills, people who are good at solving one kind of mental puzzle may not be good at others. This means we can define and measure intelligence only if we can agree on which sorts of thinking we value most. In a society dominated by engineers, intelligence would be largely associated with quantitative skills. In a society dominated by lawyers or theologians, it would mean verbal skills. In a society dominated by politicians and diplomats, it might mean skill at figuring out what other people think and want. In our society it means all this and more. Measuring intelligence is thus no different from measuring how much people know about medieval history or molecular biology: it depends on social convention. A useful test is one that accurately mimics the demands that some particular set of social conventions makes on us.

Alfred Binet designed the first IQ tests to estimate the ability of French children to do schoolwork, so he included many problems that demanded the kinds of skills that schools teach and reward. Many IQ tests now contain other kinds of problems as well, but an IQ test's power to predict performance still depends on its resemblance to schoolwork. The Wechsler Intelligence Scale for Children (WISC) has a "verbal" and a "performance" section. Despite its name, the verbal section includes not only a vocabulary test and a test of verbal analogies but tests of arithmetic reasoning, general information, and ability to solve hypothetical problems. Children's scores on this section of the WISC tend to predict a multitude of things, including how long they will stay in school and whether they will end up in prison. The performance section, which bears less resemblance to schoolwork, adds almost nothing to the predictive power of the verbal section. For practical purposes, therefore, the WISC is just a measure of academic skills. Whether we should call it an intelligence test is a political question. My own preference would be to abandon the term, since IQ tests seem to me to define intelligence far more narrowly than adult society does. But whatever we call the test, we need to recognize that it has no magical significance. IQ scores provide essentially the same information as a battery of conventional achievement tests covering vocabulary, reading comprehension, arithmetic reasoning, and general information.

Interpreting Heritability Estimates

The claim that genetic differences account for much of the variation in IQ scores is even more controversial than the claim that such scores measure intelligence. By the late 1930s studies of adopted children had provided strong evidence that genes influenced IQ scores. But these studies threw no light on how genes exerted their influence. Both hereditarians and their critics almost always assumed that if genes affected IQ scores they must do so by affecting the physical capacity to learn, independent of environmental influences. But there were—and are—a multitude of other possibilities. Since no one could identify most of the genes that affected IQ scores, much less specify how they exerted their influence, the adoption studies proved less than either hereditarians or their critics assumed. Such studies suggested that the causal chain leading from genes to cognitive skills was a fairly strong one, but they told us nothing about how it worked.

The Nazis' abuse of genetic theories put an end to public discussion of hereditary differences in human beings for a generation. Throughout the 1950s and 1960s American liberals talked and wrote as if IQ and achievement scores varied for purely environmental reasons. Arthur Jensen revived public debate about the question in 1969 when he published a controversial article in the *Harvard Educational Review* summarizing the statistical evidence that genes affect IQ scores.[9] Jensen's presentation guaranteed liberal opposition, since he argued that genes could explain not only IQ differences among members of the same racial group but also differences between racial groups. In a statistical sense, the latter claim was a tautology. Even if IQ differences between blacks and whites were wholly attributable to white racism and disappeared in societies dominated by blacks, black-white differences in societies such as our own would still be indirectly attributable to genetically determined differences in appearance.

But that was not what Jensen or his readers meant when they talked about genetic differences between blacks and whites. Jensen meant that even if blacks and whites encountered identical environments, blacks would end up with lower IQ scores than whites, presumably because blacks' genes made it harder for them to learn the skills and information that IQ tests measured. This theory could only be tested in a color-blind society. No such society has ever existed, and it is difficult to imagine how one could exist. Jensen's critics therefore argued, quite correctly, that his racial case was based on speculation, not evidence. This allowed most liberals and radicals to dismiss his entire hereditarian argument, on the grounds that anyone who thought whites genetically superior to blacks was bound to be wrong about almost everything.

Hereditarian theories suffered another political setback in the 1970s, when Leon Kamin demonstrated that Sir Cyril Burt, the leading English advocate of the genetic hypothesis, had fabricated most of his data. As a result, many liberals still believe that heredity has no effect on IQ scores. But the hereditarian case does not rest on Burt's data alone. American studies of resemblance among relatives also indicate that genes have a major influence on IQ scores. Wilson and Herrnstein suggest that 60 percent of the variation in IQ scores is in some way attributable to genetic variation. This is less than the 80 percent that Herrnstein cited in the early 1970s,[10] before Burt's data had been exposed as fraudulent, but it still strikes me as a bit high. The exact number is far less important than its interpretation, however. The crucial point is that all such figures include not only genes' effects on what children learn from a given environment, but also their effects on the way parents, teachers, schools, and peers treat a child, as well as on the environments children select for themselves. Wilson and Herrnstein fail to mention this.

There is, then, a critical difference between the way we estimate the heritability of a trait and the way we usually interpret such estimates. Since there is no practical method for separating the physical and social effects of genes, heritability estimates include both. This means that heritability estimates set a lower bound on the explanatory power of the environment, not an upper bound. If genetic variation explains 60 percent of the variation in IQ scores, environmental variation *must* explain the remaining 40 percent, but it *may* explain as much as 100 percent. If, for example, genes affected IQ scores solely by affecting children's appearance or behavior, and if their appearance or behavior then affected the way they were treated at home and at school, everything genes explained would also be explicable by environmental factors. In such a world, environmental differences would explain 100 percent of the variation in IQ scores. But if genetic variation explained 60 percent of the variation in children's environments, there would be no contradiction between the claim that genes explained 60 percent of the variation in IQ scores and the claim that the environment explained 100 percent. My earlier example of hair length illustrates the same idea. In that case individual preferences explained 100 percent of the variation in hair length, but having an X rather than a Y chromosome explained 60 percent of the variation in individual preferences.[11]

Unfortunately, most social scientists and laymen interpret heritability statistics as if they set an upper bound on environmental influences rather than a lower bound. In everyday language, the statement that something is hereditary means that it is "not environmental." In the same way, if someone says that 60 percent of the variation in IQ scores is genetic, we take this to mean that even if we treated all children exactly alike, their IQ scores would still vary greatly. This is simply wrong. The proposition that genes explain 60 percent of the variation in IQ scores is entirely compatible with the proposition that treating all children alike would result in their all having identical IQ scores. I do not mean to suggest, of course, that treating all children alike really would make their IQ scores identical. No sensible person believes this. My point is merely that hereditarians cannot refute such claims simply by showing that genes influence IQ. Hereditarians can only discredit the extreme environmental position by showing that, when we treat children exactly alike, their IQ scores still differ. Since we never treat children exactly alike, the claims of extreme environmentalists are in practice irrefutable even though implausible.

IQ and Crime

The link between IQ scores and crime is almost as controversial as that between genes and IQ scores. Surveys of teenagers find that those with low IQs report having committed a greater number of serious crimes than those with high IQs. Teenagers with low IQs also get arrested more often than those with high IQs. And adults with low IQs are overrepresented in prisons. Until quite recently, however, most criminologists dismissed the association between IQ and crime as meaningless. They did not deny that criminals who had been arrested or convicted mostly had below-average IQ scores. Nor did they usually suggest that this was solely the result of police or judicial prejudice against low-IQ suspects and defendants. Instead, they argued that IQ tests were culturally biased against the poor and that convicts had low scores on such tests because they mostly came from disadvantaged backgrounds.

There is some truth to the argument that IQ tests are biased against the poor, but not much. To begin with, class background explains only 10 to 20 percent of the variation in adolescents' IQ scores, so the idea that IQ scores are simply disguised measures of social advantage is exaggerated.[12] Furthermore, the association between IQ scores and criminal behavior persists, at least among teenagers, even when we look at people from the same class background.[13]

Once again, the question that ought to be explored is not whether IQ scores predict the statistical likelihood that individuals will engage in murder, rape, robbery, and the like, but why they do so. The prevailing view among sociologists is that children with low IQs learn less in school, earn low grades, and react negatively to this experience. In order to protect their self-respect, many reject the standards of the adult world that defines them as incompetent. Unable to win at being smart in school, some of them turn to being cool and tough. As they get older they also find that the adult world offers them no clear, legitimate route to material success. They know they are not "college material." Unless they have family connections, the more demanding blue-collar crafts are also closed to them. They can see that they would have to work extremely hard to support a family on the wages available in the unskilled or semiskilled jobs they can expect to get. Confronted with this bleak prospect many look for an alternative. At least in the short run, crime is the best-paid job open to an unskilled teenager, even though most of those who make their living this way can expect to spend time in prison, and many die violently.

Wilson and Herrnstein give qualified support to this explanation of the connection between IQ scores and crime, but they do not seem interested in its social or political implications. If the conventional sociological view is correct, adolescents with low IQs commit crimes not because they are inherently more hostile, amoral, or impulsive than their high-IQ classmates, but because both schools and labor markets treat them in ways that make them hostile, amoral, and impulsive. If this is true, the connection between IQ and crime probably varies considerably from one society to another. In societies like our own, youngsters with low IQs cannot do much that others value. This almost inevitably means that they will be treated like dirt and will react accordingly. In societies where youngsters with low IQs can make a more valuable contribution to the common good—through conscientious or courageous performance of simple duties, for example—they might be more likely to become self-respecting, law-abiding citizens. We do not have any data on IQ and crime in such societies, so this hypothesis is hard to test. But Wilson and Herrnstein do not even raise the question of whether low-IQ youngsters might be more law-abiding in a less "academic" (or a less competitive) society. *Crime and Human Nature* is a book about the way individual differences affect criminality in one particular kind of society, namely our own, not about the way societies can alter—or eliminate—the effects of individual differences.

Are Genetic Theories Inherently Reactionary?

The notion that having one set of genes rather than another can lead, however indirectly, to variations in criminal behavior of the same magnitude as the variations attributable to attending one school rather than another, living in one community rather than another, or growing up in one decade rather than another, does not strike me as either startling or alarming—but it certainly alarms most people who think of themselves as liberals or radicals. So far as I can tell, this reaction has two sources.

First, as I have already noted, many people assume that if your genes affect your behavior, then your behavior is immune to environmental modification. As we have seen, and as Wilson and Herrnstein also emphasize, this is nonsense. To say that men commit more crimes than women, blacks more than whites, or slow learners more than fast learners is not to say that we cannot reduce crime among blacks, males, or slow learners. Such persons did not, after all, commit anything like as many crimes a generation ago as they do today.

Genetic explanations of crime also alarm us because we fear they will lead to more brutal treatment of criminals. The notion that criminals are "different" has been used to rationalize horrifying abuses in the past, and the same thing could happen again. The danger here, however, is not that a realistic understanding of genetic influences will lead us to think of criminals as subhuman, but that the mythology surrounding genetic explanations will do so. The most serious risk is that we will come to think of criminals as incorrigible. If people commit crimes not because of the situations in which they find themselves but because of what they personally bring to the situation, then the fact that they have committed crimes in the past can create a strong prima facie expectation that they will commit more crimes in the future. Such reasoning leads many people to favor locking up even first offenders more or less indefinitely.

But the same misguided logic can also come into play if you think that criminals differ from the rest of us for purely environmental reasons. If a child has been neglected or abused for many years, this experience is as irreversible as having inherited the wrong genes. The consequences of having been abused in childhood may be reversible, of course, but this is equally true for the consequences of having inherited the wrong genes. A medical analogy is helpful here. Suppose you have a deaf child. The disorder may be inherited, or it may be the result of childhood disease or accident. But the prospects of curing the disorder do not depend in any direct sense on whether it is a product of nature or nurture. Rather, they depend on what is actually wrong and how much your doctors know. Furthermore, if the disorder cannot be cured, the question of how you should educate such a child does not depend, at least in any simple way, on what caused the problem. The same principle holds for behavioral problems.

In the right setting, moreover, genetic explanations can be helpful rather than damaging. Research on adopted children in Sweden shows, for example, that if a Swede's natural father was an alcoholic, his own chances of becoming an alcholic are significantly greater than if his father was not an alcoholic.[14] This does not mean that there is an "alcoholism gene," any more than there is a "crime gene." But it does suggest that your genetic makeup can influence your susceptibility to alcohol addiction. Far from resisting this notion, many alcoholics seem to find it quite helpful, and Alcoholics Anonymous has endorsed it. Genetic explanations of alcoholism dramatize the idea that alcoholics cannot engage in social drinking just because others do. Telling alcoholics that they are genetically different is also a way of transforming their problem from a character defect into an illness. This not only makes society less punitive but makes the alcoholic feel less guilty. In many cases, of course, guilt is both an appropriate and a productive response to past behavior. But it does not seem to be a good thing for alcoholics, who often drink to escape it.

It does not follow that genetic explanations of crime would have a salutary effect on chronic offenders' behavior. Much would depend on the mechanisms that actually link genes to crime, about which we still know very little. I can imagine some chronic offenders using simplistic genetic theories to excuse their behavior. ("It's not my fault I keep breaking the rules. I'm just one of those people who can't follow the rules no matter how hard I try. Some people are just born to be criminals.") But social explanations of crime can be abused in much the same way. If we say that crime is a product of poverty, racism, or parental abuse, this too may provide those who are poor, black, or abused with an excuse for committing more crimes. It can also encourage others to believe that poor, black, or abused criminals are incorrigible.

Inequality and Crime

If liberals have trouble with the idea that people's genes influence their chances of committing crimes, conservatives have trouble with the idea that poverty causes crime. Conservatives do not deny that the poor commit more crimes than the rich. But instead of assuming that poverty causes crime, conservatives usually assume that poverty and crime have a common cause, namely the deficient character or misguided values of the poor.

Wilson and Herrnstein have surprisingly little to say about the effects of either poverty or social class on crime. They devote a chapter to labor markets but none to the effects of either social class or poverty. Their introduction justifies this omission with the rather lame observations that "class is an ambiguous concept" and that crime and class could have common causes. Fortunately, other writers are less reticent.

Elliott Currie's *Confronting Crime* is both short and readable, and unlike *Crime and Human Nature* it concentrates on what we can do to reduce crime.[15] Nonetheless, Currie's book got far less attention than Wilson and Herrnstein's, partly because Currie was not as well known and partly because Currie's approach to crime is currently out of fashion. Prepublication excerpts from Wilson and Herrnstein's book appeared in the *New York Times;* excerpts from Currie's book appeared in *Dissent.*

Currie argues that crime is a product of economic inequality, broadly construed. This claim will appeal to anyone who, like myself, favors more equal economic rewards. Egalitarians are as addicted to universal panaceas as everyone else. We want to believe that equality is the answer to every problem for the same reason libertarians want to believe that free markets are the answer to every problem. It is easier to remember and promote a single universal formula than many ad hoc ones.

The notion that equality can reduce crime also has obvious political appeal. Egalitarianism is usually rooted in some combination of sympathy for the disadvantaged and guilt about privilege. But egalitarians know that appeals to compassion and moral principle are seldom enough to move the polity toward more egalitarian policies. We would therefore like to argue that reducing inequality also has practical benefits for the privileged. Even those who benefit from today's competitive system and have no instinctive sympathy for losers might, we imagine, endorse egalitarian reform if they thought it was the only alternative to having their house burgled. But precisely because liberals and radicals derive such obvious political and emotional benefits from believing that economic equality can reduce crime, we must look at the evidence for this belief with special care.

Currie adduces a variety of evidence for his claim that economic inequality causes crime, but three facts are central to his argument. First, the economically disadvantaged commit a disproportionate share of all crimes, especially serious crimes. Second, American cities with relatively equal distributions of household income or relatively equal job opportunities for blacks and whites have lower rates of violent crime than cities where job opportunities and incomes are less equal. Third, countries with a high level of economic inequality usually have more homicides than equally affluent countries with less inequality. In each case, however, the facts are subject to more than one explanation.

In the absence of reliable data on individuals, Currie's argument about class background and crime begins by contrasting rich and poor communities. In Illinois, for example, he contrasts East St. Louis, where nearly 40 percent of all families are poor, with Oak Lawn, where only 3 percent are poor. In East St. Louis one person in every thousand was murdered in 1983—almost twelve times the national average. In Oak Lawn no one was murdered in 1983. While East St. Louis is an extreme case, Oak Lawn is not. The same pattern recurs all across America.

To some extent the difference between Oak Lawn and East St. Louis reflects the fact that Oak Lawn is white while East St. Louis is black. But when we separate blacks from whites we still find large class differences in criminal behavior, even in the same city. Marvin Wolfgang and his colleagues followed a large sample of boys born in Philadelphia in 1946. Boys living in low-income neighborhoods had been charged with almost twice as many criminal offenses by the time they turned eighteen as boys of the same race living in high-income neighborhoods.[16] The difference would presumably have been even greater if the "high-income" neighborhoods had been truly well-to-do, like Oak Lawn. In fact, they were merely neighborhoods in which the typical family had an income above the Philadelphia average.

While there is a lot more crime in poor neighborhoods than in affluent ones, the relationship between parental income and crime *within* any given neighborhood is relatively weak. This presumably reflects the way people choose the neighborhoods in which they live. If a poor family is anxious to keep its children out of trouble and help them join the middle class, it will often make substantial sacrifices to live in a better neighborhood and enroll its children in a better school. Poor families living in middle-income neighbporhoods are thus likely to be more ambitious and more law-abiding than those living in poor neighborhoods. Conversely, middle-income parents are unlikely to remain in poor neighborhoods if they find delinquent behavior alarming in children. As a result, children from such families get in trouble with the law almost as often as children from poor families in the same neighborhood.[17]

While the poor commit more crimes than the rich, they do not commit these crimes solely because they have low incomes. If low incomes alone drove people to crime, graduate students and clergymen would also commit a lot of crimes. These examples suggest that we should not exaggerate the effects of income per se. Economic inequality involves much more than just money. Sociologists often find that a father's occupation has more effect on his children's behavior than his income does, and this may well be true for teenage crime. This does not invalidate Currie's basic argument, but it does suggest that reducing economic inequality would require us to reorganize work as well as redistribute income. While Currie would doubtless agree, conceding this point makes egalitarian reform look considerably harder.

But to what extent do economic disadvantages cause crime? As Wilson and Herrnstein point out, the same defects of character could cause both poverty and crime. Many people who are poor may just be more ignorant, more aggressive, or—as Wilson and Herrnstein claim—more impulsive and "present-oriented" than their affluent brethren. If that were the case, closing the economic gap between the rich and poor would not be likely to reduce crime among the poor, since it would not remove the defects of character that caused crime in the first place.

Comparing Cities and Nations

One way to assess this argument is to look at communities rather than individuals. Poor communities should have more crime than rich communities, regardless of whether poverty causes crime or character defects cause both poverty and crime. But if we look at communities with the same percentage of poor people, and if those with a large economic gap between rich and poor have more crime than those with a small gap, we cannot easily argue that this is just because unequal communities attract ne'er-do-wells. A more plausible explanation would be that what sociologists call "relative deprivation" leads to crime.

A study by Judith and Peter Blau, cited in both Currie's book and Wilson and Herrnstein's, supports this conclusion.[18] Blau and Blau asked what characteristics of America's 125 largest metropolitan areas were associated with high levels of violent crime in 1970. Because of local differences in whether citizens report crimes to the police and in the way the police record crimes, much of the apparent variation in cities' crime rates is spurious, but this does not appear to be a serious problem for murder. Blau and Blau found high murder rates both in cities where whites worked in much more skilled and better-paid occupations than blacks and in cities where the difference in incomes between rich and poor was unusually high. In cities where differences in both income and jobs were less marked, such as Utica, New York, or

Johnstown, Pennsylvania, the murder rates were lower. The absolute amount of poverty made no difference, except insofar as it was associated with inequality.

But Blau and Blau also found that ethnic and cultural differences had large effects on murder rates. Even when people in cities had similar economic characteristics, cities with more blacks had more murders. Cities with many divorced and separated adults also had more than the average number of murders, even after taking account of their economic and racial mix. This was not just a matter of bad blood between ex-spouses; cities with many divorced adults also had more than their share of robberies, presumably because divorce rates are high where other social ties are also weak.

Differences between countries also appear to derive from a mixture of economic and cultural influences. The size of the income gap between the rich and the poor accounts for about a sixth of the variation in countries' murder rates.[19] This is far from trivial, but it suggests that other factors are even more important than economic inequality in explaining variations in murder rates. Table 3.2 underlines this point. In the late 1960s your chances of being murdered in Mexico were twice those in the United States, while your chances in the United States were twice those in India, five times those in Australia, and ten times those in France or Spain. The gap between rich and poor was surely greater in Mexico than in the United States in the late 1960s. But it seems safe to assume that the gap between rich and poor was also greater in India than in the United States, and yet India was much safer.[20] This was not just because India was more rural than America.

Table 3.2   Murders per 100,000 Inhabitants in Selected Places, 1966–1970

Country	Rate	Principal city	Rate
Trinidad and Tobago	14.0	Port of Spain	15.3
Mexico	13.2	Mexico City	13.3
United States	6.6	New York City	11.5
India	2.7	Bombay	2.9
Japan	2.2	Tokyo	1.8
Australia	1.3	Sydney	1.6
France	0.6	Paris	0.6
Spain	0.5	Madrid	0.6

Source: Dane Archer and Rosemary Gartner, *Violence and Crime in Cross-National Perspective* (New Haven: Yale University Press, 1984), table 5.2.

Your chances of being murdered in New York City were four times those in Bombay. And while most European countries were both more law-abiding and more egalitarian than America, France had about as much income inequality as America but had far less violent crime.[21]

Comparisons between nations or cities, like comparisons between individuals, are always subject to the objection that the observed patterns of association may not be truly causal. Look at Table 3.2. Many readers may suspect that the differences between Mexico, the United States, India, Australia, France, and Spain are really attributable to cultural differences between the Mexicans, Americans, Indians, Australians, French, and Spanish who inhabit these nations, not to differences in economic opportunities or outcomes. But we cannot test such intuitions unless we can say precisely what it is about different ethnic groups that leads us to expect their homicide rates to vary. That turns out to be very difficult. "Cultural" explanations of crime tend to be tautological: "the Japanese commit fewer crimes than the Mexicans because the Japanese have more respect for the law," for example.

The Historical Record

Because of these difficulties, changes over time are probably our best guide to causal connections. The historical experience that still shapes most Americans' views about crime began in the early 1960s and ended in the early 1970s. It was marked by many egalitarian reforms and by a dramatic increase in crime. Those on the right tend to assume a causal link between the two phenomena. Those on the left deny it. Before looking for causal links, however, we need to ask what really happened.

The increase in crime during the late 1960s is beyond question. The figures on murder are the most reliable indicator of the trend because they are not subject to much reporting error.[22] The economic significance of the egalitarian reforms initiated during the late 1960s is harder to assess. The incomes of the poorest fifth of all families rose from 25 percent of the national average in 1963 to 28 percent in 1973—only a modest improvement but nonetheless a step toward equality rather than away from it. The absolute improvement in living standards was greater. Only 11 percent of all Americans were officially poor in 1973, compared to about 20 percent in 1963.

Currie recognizes that increased income inequality cannot explain the rise in crime between 1963 and 1973. Instead, he emphasizes unemployment among black teenagers. But economic statistics for teenagers do not predict trends in crime very well either. Between 1962–63 and 1968–69, for example, the black teenage male unemployment rate fell from 24.7 to 21.8 percent, and the white teenage male rate fell from 14.8 to 10.1 percent. Nonetheless, the murder rate rose by half. This pattern was reversed in the early 1980s. Between 1979 and 1983 teenage unemployment rose by almost half among both blacks and whites, but the murder rate fell by a sixth. The great depression of the 1930s was also associated with a dramatic decline in murder. During the late 1920s and early 1930s murder had become about as common as it is today. Then between 1933 and 1940 the murder rate fell by a third. This decline occurred despite levels of unemployment far higher than any recorded in the 1970s or 1980s.[23]

More recent history also seems to me to contradict Currie's claim that economic inequality leads to more crime. During the 1980s the real incomes of the poorest American families fell while the real incomes of the more affluent rose. From 1979 to 1987 the share of total income going to the poorest fifth of all families fell from 26 to 23 percent of the national average. Currie's analysis implies that this increase in economic inequality should have led to rising crime rates. In fact, crime declined somewhat.

Looking further back in history, we find a dramatic long-term, worldwide decline in crime during the second half of the nineteenth century. Yet this too appears to have been a period of increasing economic inequality. The decline appears to have been a byproduct of industrialization, which brought millions of men into relatively large hierarchical organizations for the first time. These organizations demanded a lot of self-control and regimentation. Their existence also led to the creation of a public school system that regimented the lives of the young in new ways and tried to make them internalize "Victorian" habits and values. Declining crime rates appear to have been one byproduct of this cultural transformation.

Among America's urban blacks, in contrast, crime rates increased steadily during the second half of the nineteenth century. Roger Lane argues that black and white crime rates diverged because urban blacks were excluded from the industrial and white-collar jobs that were transforming white immigrants into law-abiding citizens. Black culture was linked to a different sort of labor market and evolved in a fundamentally different way.[24] This argument is hard to test rigorously. Nonetheless, it links economic institutions to cultural values in a way that appeals to both my economic liberalism and my cultural conservatism. Both economic conservatives and cultural liberals will presumably find it less appealing.

I do not mean to suggest on the basis of either nineteenth-century experience or the experiences of the 1960s, 1970s, and 1980s that economic inequality helps to reduce crime. Crime rates depend on how people respond to economic inequality rather than on the actual level of inequality, and these responses appear to vary with the historical circumstances—a polite way of saying that we have no clear idea what determines people's responses.

Yet even if Currie's claim that egalitarian reforms can reduce crime is overstated, his book still has the enormous virtue of concentrating our attention on societal rather than individual determinants of crime rates. This is, of course, the very "error" that Wilson and Herrnstein seek to correct. Yet the reader who compares Tables 3.1 and 3.2 can easily see that differences between societies have far more effect on crime rates than the genetic differences between individuals to which Wilson and Herrnstein give a central place in their book.

Liberals and radicals will, no doubt, take this conclusion as a vindication of what they knew all along. But for those who hope to reduce crime, it may not be such good news. Figuring out how genes affect human behavior is a formidable task, but the prospects for significant progress over the next couple of generations seem to me somewhat encouraging. Our methods for identifying specific genes and for tracing their physical effects have improved steadily. While this does not necessarily mean that we will be able to sort out genes' behavioral consequences, it seems likely to make the task easier.

When we turn from physiology to culture and ask why the United States, Mexico, and the Caribbean have more crime than most of Europe and Asia, the obstacles to intellectual progress look even more formidable than when we try to understand the effects of genes. The record of the past generation is also less encouraging. We are not, I think, any closer to understanding why cultures differ from one another, or why they change over time, than we were thirty years ago. Worse yet, young social scientists are seldom interested in such questions. Without a clearer understanding of why Europeans and Japanese respect one another's person and property more than Americans do, it is hard to see what practical benefits we can reap from simply knowing that culture and history are important. Yet our failure to understand the deeper causes of variation in crime rates does not mean that crime must remain as high as it is. What went up twenty-five years ago, for whatever unknown reason, can come down, even though criminologists cannot currently offer any reliable advice about how to make this happen.

= 4 =

The Ghetto

The poor are climbing back onto the American political agenda.[1] Books about their plight are receiving more attention, foundations are planning new programs to help them, and middle-of-the-road legislators are worrying about the rising poverty rate among children. Indeed, today's political mood is in some ways reminiscent of the mood in the early 1960s, just before we launched our ill-fated War on Poverty.

Times have changed in at least one crucial respect, however. Instead of talking about the poor, we now talk about the underclass, which by common consensus includes only the undeserving poor: men who have no regular job, women who depend largely on welfare to survive, street criminals, winos, and addicts. The deserving poor, notably the elderly and two-parent families in which the man works steadily but cannot earn enough to feed all his children, are definitely not part of the underclass. The popularity of the term thus signals a political shift: instead of blaming poverty on society, as we did in the late 1960s, we are now more inclined to blame poverty on the poor.

Recent writing on the underclass usually suggests that it is a new phenomenon. But ethnographic descriptions of the "lower class" in the early 1960s, such as Elliot Liebow's classic *Tally's Corner* or Oscar Lewis' *La Vida,* describe people who seem much like those who populate recent descriptions of the underclass.[2] The fact that many believe the underclass is growing also gives it a symbolic significance that it did not have a generation ago, when most Americans thought the rising tide of prosperity would soon wash it away.

The undeserving poor have always posed a problem for compassionate liberals. When the poor are doing all they can to better themselves, it is easy to argue that they deserve a helping hand. When people are too old, too sick, too deranged, or too retarded to help themselves, it is also easy to argue that compassion requires others to help. But when sane, healthy adults refuse to follow norms of behavior that most of society endorses, the claim that we should help them arouses intense controversy.

Those who favor compassion usually deny that the poor are undeserving. The poor are not poor, they maintain, because they have the wrong values or because they suffer from what philosophers call "weakness of the will." The poor behave as they do, according to the compassionate, only because they confront different choices from the rest of us—or because they have no choices at all. If they had our choices, they would act as we act. Compassionate liberals have therefore been hostile to those who write about the underclass, and especially those who see the underclass as having a "deviant" culture that approves (or at least fails to disapprove) of idleness, single parenthood, theft, and violence. This way of characterizing the poor is, they feel, a device for "blaming the victim."

William Julius Wilson, a distinguished sociologist from the University of Chicago, has been struggling since the late 1970s to find a way out of this rhetorical corner. As he argues in the opening pages of *The Truly Disadvantaged:*

> The liberal perspective on the ghetto underclass has become less persuasive and convincing in public discourse principally because many of those who represent traditional liberal views on social issues have been reluctant to discuss openly, or, in some instances, even to acknowledge, the sharp rise in social pathologies in ghetto communities.[3]

An economic radical, a cultural conservative, and a political pragmatist, Wilson wants liberals to acknowledge that "there is a heterogeneous grouping of inner-city families and individuals whose behavior contrasts sharply with that of mainstream America." He also wants to explain why this is more true today than in the past and to show how we might reverse the trend.

Wilson's major aim is to explain the increases in joblessness and single-parent families in black urban communities over the past generation. He recognizes that many factors are at work, but his basic argument has three strands:

1. Joblessness has increased among young black men partly because there are fewer unskilled and semiskilled blue-collar jobs in the big cities where blacks now live. I will call this his "structural unemployment" hypothesis.
2. The two-parent black family is disappearing because male joblessness has made marriage less attractive. I will call this his "no marriageable men" hypothesis.
3. Both single parenthood and male joblessness have also increased among poor blacks because the black middle class has been moving out of the ghetto. As a result, black inner-city schools have deteriorated, ghetto businesses have closed, the police have fewer allies in their struggle to control crime, jobseekers have fewer employed neighbors to help them find jobs, and the young have fewer good role models. I will call this his "physical isolation" hypothesis.

Each of these hypotheses contains a kernel of truth, but none seems to me altogether convincing unless it is embedded in a larger story about cultural change.

Black Male Joblessness

Joblessness among young black men has increased dramatically since 1970. Official unemployment statistics do not tell this story very well, since they exclude "discouraged workers" who have not looked for work during the previous month. Many writers, including Wilson, therefore prefer to look at the proportion of young men who have no job, regardless of whether they are looking for one. This figure can be equally misleading, however, because it rises whenever school enrollment rises.

What we ought to measure is the number of men who are neither working nor in school nor in the armed forces. Most of these men are idle in the traditional sense of that term. Using this definition, 8 percent of all nonwhite men in their early twenties were idle during a typical week between 1965 and 1969, 20 percent were idle in 1975–1979, 26 percent in 1980–1983, and 21 percent in 1984–85. Rates for eighteen- and nineteen-year-olds were roughly similar to those for twenty- to twenty-four-year-olds.[4] Rates for older men were lower, but not much lower. Rates for men of all ages show the same increase since 1970. None shows any consistent trend before 1970.

Wilson blames rising black joblessness on the fact that most blacks now live in the central cities of major metropolitan areas, where "information processing" has been replacing manufacturing as the dominant economic activity. As a result, central-city jobs require more schooling than they used to. Wilson argues that this has made it harder for members of the black underclass to find work.

This argument is not new. Manufacturing jobs began moving out of central cities early in the twentieth century. In 1968 John Kain published a seminal paper arguing that this trend, combined with housing policies that excluded blacks from most suburbs, contributed significantly to black joblessness.[5] The most persuasive strands of what has come to be called the spatial-mismatch hypothesis emphasize the difficulty inner-city residents have finding a job many miles from home and the difficulty they have reaching such a job once they find it.

Living in the wrong place does seem to increase joblessness among ghetto teenagers. Firms that hire teenagers for minimum-wage work rely mainly on help-wanted signs and walk-in applicants. A job in a suburban McDonald's is therefore likely to be filled before an inner-city teenager hears about it unless the local teenagers can all find better jobs and the manager has to seek out inner-city residents. Even then, a minimum-wage job in the suburbs will not pay for a car with which to get to work. Nor does it pay enough to justify spending two or three hours a day commuting by bus.

The spatial-mismatch hypothesis is far less compelling when applied to mature men than when applied to teenagers. Black men do have trouble learning about suburban job vacancies, but that is not because they live in the inner city. Distance is a problem only when employers let it become one. Distance does not prevent suburban whites from finding good jobs in the downtown business district, because downtown employers publicize openings in such a way as to ensure that qualified suburbanites get the news. Suburban manufacturers do not advertise their vacancies in places where inner-city blacks would learn about them (major metropolitan dailies or the state employment service, for example), because they do not want those applicants. Suburban firms see inner-city blacks as less skilled, less reliable, and less diligent than the white workers they can hire for the same wages.[6] Such prejudices are often exaggerated, but they are not exaggerated by distance. They are created and sustained by images in the mass media and firms' own experience with black workers.

Nor do transportation problems provide a plausible explanation for high rates of joblessness among mature inner-city men. Large suburban manufacturing firms almost never recruit mature workers from within walking distance. A few suburban blue-collar men commute on public transportation, but most drive. If blacks could get good jobs with suburban firms, they too could afford to buy cars and drive to work. The average black would probably spend longer than the average white commuting, but not much longer.

Empirical research supports these a priori judgments. A growing body of evidence suggests that location has a moderate effect on teenagers' chances of working, but there is not much evidence that it matters for older men. Recent work has found a widening employment gap between black men in central cities and those in the suburbs. But that trend only tells us that black men with steady jobs have been fleeing the central city. This could mean that black men who remain in the central city face growing difficulty finding or reaching work, as Wilson suggests. But it could just mean that black men with jobs no longer want to raise their children in ghetto neighborhoods.[7]

The moral of this story is that at least for mature men most metropolitan areas constitute a single labor market, not separate urban and suburban labor markets as Kain, Wilson, and many others have assumed. But this does not necessarily mean that Wilson is incorrect when he blames rising black joblessness on structural changes in the economy. It just means that we have to look at changes in the economy as a whole rather than in central-city economies.

When we look at the economy as a whole, we find that young blacks were not the only group that had more trouble finding work after 1970. Idleness is only about half as common among young whites as among young blacks. But whenever the black rate rises or falls, the white rate for the same age group rises or falls by about the same percentage. This suggests that both rates depend largely on the balance between supply and demand in the labor market as a whole. To see why this balance has changed, a little history is helpful.

Between 1958 and 1960 the overall unemployment rate averaged 6 percent. Most liberals regarded this as evidence of Republican economic incompetence, and during the 1960s the Democrats used monetary and fiscal policy to push down unemployment. By 1968–1970 the unemployment rate averaged only 4 percent. This change was especially beneficial to those who have always borne the brunt of unemployment, namely unskilled blacks. Unemployment among black high-school dropouts fell from 16 percent to 9 percent.[8]

Inflation began to acceleate in the late 1960s, and by 1973 most economists were convinced that the only way to control it was to let unemployment rise. By 1978–1980 we had let unemployment climb back to its 1958–1960 level of 6 percent. The big losers were the same people who had benefited from tight labor markets in the 1960s. Unemployment rose from 9 percent to 21 percent among black high-school dropouts and from 5 percent to 11 percent among white dropouts. Among college graduates, in contrast, unemployment only rose from 1.4 to 4.2 percent for blacks and from 1.1 percent to 2.1 percent for whites.

Nonetheless, inflation persisted. In order to curb it, the Federal Reserve Board pushed the economy into the worst recession since the 1930s. Unemployment rose above 10 percent in the early 1980s, and inflation receded. By 1989 unemployment was below 6 percent, and inflation was also fairly low. Most economists felt that pushing unemployment much lower would mean more inflation, so there was little political pressure to do this.

This history suggests to me that the rise in idleness among young black men is largely attributable to the fact that we have stopped running the economy at full throttle. Slack labor markets have always had catastrophic effects on urban blacks (though the effect was less obvious during the 1950s because many more blacks still worked in the rural south, where they were underemployed rather than unemployed).[9] If we could get the overall unemployment rate back down to 3 or 4 percent, joblessness among blacks would also drop precipitously.

Consider Massachusetts: by the mid-1980s the Reagan administration's military spending binge had cut unemployment in the Boston area below 3 percent. This boom was led by high-tech industries, and much of it took place in the suburban ring around Boston, where few blacks live. Nonetheless, black unemployment in the Boston area was down to 5.6 percent by 1985. Tight labor markets lower unemployment among young black men even more.[10] The trouble is that no one knows how to sustain these conditions nationwide without encouraging another round of inflation.

While our inability to maintain a tight labor market deserves most of the blame for increased idleness among young blacks, it is not the only culprit. Demand for unskilled workers has been especially soft. So far as I know, nobody has tried to measure recent changes in the educational requirements of American jobs. But occupations with above-average *wages* grew about 20 percent faster than those with average or below-average wages between 1973 and 1982.[11] High-wage occupations almost always require more education than low-wage occupations. It seems likely, therefore, that occupations with above-average educational requirements are growing faster than occupations that require little or no formal education.

But while educational requirements seem to be rising, real wages are not. All those new accountants, computer programmers, lawyers, and college professors are supposed to make the economy work more efficiently, but they haven't delivered. Output per worker has hardly changed since 1970. As a result, real annual earnings have stagnated (though hours have fallen slightly and fringe benefits have risen).[12]

The economic situation has been especially bad for the young. Most firms want to maintain a certain balance between experienced and inexperienced workers. Because of the baby boom, immigration, and the fact that more young mothers work part time, the number of inexperienced workers has grown much faster than the number of experienced workers since 1970. As a result, employers have bid up experienced workers' pay while letting inexperienced workers' pay lag behind inflation.

Young high-school dropouts have suffered the most. Even after correcting for the fact that the Consumer Price Index exaggerated inflation during the 1970s, the purchasing power of twenty-five- to thirty-four-year-old male high-school dropouts fell 18 percent between 1967 and 1987. High-school graduates of the same age lost 3 percent. Meanwhile, college graduates gained 9 percent.[13] Unemployment statistics tell much the same story. Recall that overall unemployment averaged 6 percent both in the late 1950s and the late 1970s. Yet unemployment among high-school dropouts was much higher in the late 1970s than in the late 1950s (11 pecent versus 7 percent for whites, and 21 percent versus 16 percent for blacks).[14]

The increase in educational requirements for jobs after 1970 was nothing new. The same trend had been apparent throughout the twentieth century. But from 1920 to 1965, the supply of poorly educated workers also shrank rapidly. Native-born Americans stayed in school longer, and Congress excluded almost all poorly educated foreigners from the American labor market.

All this changed in the mid-1960s. The proportion of young whites completing high school leveled off (see Chapter 5). Latin Americans with very little formal schooling began entering the country in larger numbers. And more high-school students began seeking after-school jobs (perhaps partly because of declining academic requirements). As a result, the supply of young, unskilled workers began to outstrip demand. Their wages lagged, and their chances of being idle rose. As always, young black dropouts were especially vulnerable.

In trying to understand the effects of these changes, it is important to distinguish three groups who are all jobless: those who would take any job they could get, those who only want a good job, and those who do not want a job at all. Official statistics do not draw such distinctions, but we can get some help from other sources.

In 1979–1980, when the National Longitudinal Survey of Youth asked unemployed sixteen- to twenty-one-year-olds to name the lowest wage they would accept, roughly half named amounts that exceeded the legal minimum by more than 50 percent.[15] This pattern did not vary by race. When the National Bureau of Economic Research asked unemployed sixteen- to twenty-four-year-old blacks in the poorest areas of Boston, Chicago, and Philadelphia how hard they thought it would be to find a minimum-wage job, 46 percent thought it would be "very easy" and 25 percent thought it would be "somewhat easy."[16] Surveys of this kind suggest that a lot of idleness is voluntary. This does not mean that the men in question don't want to work. Most do. But many do not want to work so badly that they will take (or keep) a minimum-wage job with no fringe benefits, no job security, and no prospects of promotion.

Minimum-wage jobs are acceptable to many teenagers, who have no family to support and just want pocket money. But no native-born American male can imagine supporting a family on $3.35 an hour. If that is the only "respectable" alternative, he will usually conclude that respectability is beyond his reach and slip into crime, alcohol, heroin, or psychotic delusions.

Not *all* idleness is voluntary. Some young men, especially inexperienced, semiliterate teenagers, cannot find even a minimum-wage job. When the Carter administration created large numbers of minimum-wage summer jobs for teenagers, there were always more applicants than places. Making minimum-wage public jobs available to everyone on a year-round basis would surely reduce idleness substantially, even though it would not eliminate the problem. Equally important, it would alter the moral climate of the country, making it impossible for anyone to argue that they could not find work.

Still the big problem is to create more jobs that pay a living wage. Historically, this has meant a wage at least two thirds of the national average—which would put it at $6 an hour today.[17] With wage inequality growing, jobs of this kind have become harder and harder for the young to find. That means not just more joblessness but more trouble of every sort.

America's economic history since 1945 suggests that we need what Marx called a "reserve army of the unemployed." Without it, workers will push up their wages faster than their productivity, inflation will accelerate, and the Federal Reserve Board will throw the economy into a recession in order to restore price stability. Still we must ask why the pool of idle workers should be so disproportionately black. Such a pattern was easy to understand in 1960, when employers refused to hire blacks for many jobs as a matter of principle and blacks had far less schooling than whites. But since 1960 we have outlawed formal discrimination, instituted affirmative action, and drastically reduced racial differences in educational attainment among those entering the labor force. These changes should have altered the old rule that unemployment and idleness are twice as common among blacks as among whites. It hasn't.

In 1970, 44 percent of blacks in their early twenties had not completed high school, compared with 22 percent of whites. By 1985 the figures were 19 percent for blacks and 13 percent for whites.[18] Yet this change had almost no effect on the ratio of black idleness to white idleness. The reason is simple: the "two-to-one rule" holds even when blacks and whites have the same amount of education.

One partial explanation is that blacks have learned less in school than whites. But as I pointed out in Chapter 1, differences in test performance account for no more than a quarter of the earnings gap between black and white men. Why should employers be willing to pay white men more than they pay blacks with the same amount of schooling and the same test scores? Wilson is surely right that racial discrimination based solely on skin color has declined since 1960. Most employers now pay blacks who can talk, think, and act like whites almost as much as they pay "real" whites. But employers' distaste for ghetto culture does not seem to me to have declined. Indeed, it may have increased. A generation ago, most employers expected young ghetto blacks to "know their place." Today employers anticipate that ghetto blacks will be far more assertive. Few employers want unskilled workers who are assertive, regardless of their race. Even fewer want assertive workers from an alien culture they don't understand.

Even when young ghetto blacks manage to get a job, they are not likely to keep it long. Many quit because they take offense at the way their supervisors treat them or get fired because their employers take offense at the way they behave. If we want to understand racism in the 1980s, we must look at conflicts of this kind.

When blacks assert that racism is endemic in American society, they usually mean that whites assume white culture is superior to black culture. The charge is correct. Despite a certain amount of rhetoric about cultural pluralism, the American melting pot has worked because most immigrants (or their descendants) were eager to adopt established American ways of thinking, acting, and feeling, not because we found ways of enabling separate-but-equal cultures to live together.

For Europeans who came to America because they were dissatisfied with their homeland, assimilation has often been difficult, but it has not for the most part been intrinsically humiliating. European immigrants came with no animus against America, and they had reason to believe that if they learned to act like Americans they would be accepted as such. For blacks, however, the situation was altogether different. Blacks did not volunteer to become Americans, and they had good reason to doubt that they would be accepted as Americans even if they did learn to mimic them. In order to become fully assimilated into white America, moreover, blacks must to some extent identify with people who have humiliated and oppressed them for three hundred years. Under these circumstances, "assimilation" is likely to be extraordinarily difficult.

The persistence of a distinctive black culture in America means that we must ask ourselves whether true pluralism can be made to work here. I doubt that it can. I cannot imagine employers making the kind of effort they would have to make to become truly bicultural. Nor can I imagine many whites concluding that black and white cultures should enjoy true parity. In the end, I think most whites will conclude that their culture is simply better than black culture and that appeals for pluralism are just liberal eyewash.

Unfortunately, Wilson has very little to say about cultural conflict of this kind. Neither does anyone else. But unless we consider cultural conflicts and macroeconomic changes together, I don't think we can fully explain the appalling level of joblessness among blacks today.

Single-Parent Families

Wilson's second major aim in *The Truly Disadvantaged* is to explain why two-parent black families are disappearing. Again the facts are clear. In 1960, 20 percent of all black children were living in fatherless families. By 1985 the figure was 51 percent.[19] A 1978 census survey found that only one of seven absent black fathers had made child support payments during the previous year.[20]

The proximate causes of this change are clear. Single motherhood increased partly because fewer black women were marrying and partly because those who married split up more often. In 1960 about 75 percent of all black children were born to mothers who had a husband living with them. By 1985 the figure was less than 40 percent, and in some big cities it was less than 25 percent.[21] Some of these unwed mothers eventually marry, but since most black marriages end in divorce, a black child's chances of growing up in an intact family are only about one in seven.[22]

Despite two decades of heated ideological controversy, we don't know much about how a father's absence (or a stepfather's presence) affects a child's social or emotional development.[23] We do know, however, that not having a man in the house has serious economic consequences. Two thirds of all black children in fatherless families are poor, and this figure has not changed since 1970.[24]

Many conservatives blame the decline of the two-parent black family on welfare. This theory seemed quite plausible in the early 1970s. Welfare benefits had risen dramatically from 1960 to 1973, recipients had become eligible for both food stamps and free medical care, the rules governing recipients' lives had become much more permissive, and the proportion of single mothers receiving benefits had grown dramatically as a result. It was natural to assume that making welfare more attractive had made single parenthood more attractive too.

Once this suspicion became widespread among legislators, however, they began to restrict eligibility again, allowed benefits to lag behind inflation, imposed new work requirements on many recipients, and began pressuring local welfare departments to kick clients off the rolls if they had not conformed to all the agency's reporting requirements.

These changes made welfare less attractive, and the proportion of single mothers on the rolls began to fall.[25]

Despite the declining attractions of welfare, single parenthood continued to spread. Since making welfare less attractive did not discourage single parenthood after 1973, it no longer seems likely that raising benefits encouraged it before 1973. Nor do state-to-state comparisons suggest that welfare benefit levels have much impact on family structure. Even after taking into account differences in income, racial mix, and the like, states with high benefits have no more out-of-wedlock births than states with low benefits. Generous benefits do seem to encourage divorce and discourage remarriage, but the effect is quite small.[26]

Since welfare played such a small role in the decline of the two-parent black family, we need another villain. Wilson argues that single parenthood spread among blacks because fewer black men were able to support their families. As a result, fewer black women had an economic incentive to marry. To estimate a woman's chances of finding a marriageable man, Wilson calculates the ratio of men with civilian jobs to all women of the same age and race. This ratio has always been much lower among blacks than among whites, partly because black men are more likely to die young, partly because the survivors are more likely to be in prison or asylums, and partly because those on the streets are less likely to have jobs. The dearth of promising husbands surely helps explain why black women have traditionally married less than their white counterparts. The fact that black men are more likely to die, go to prison, go mad, or be jobless also helps explain why black women's marriages are less stable than white women's.

But Wilson is not trying to explain black-white differences. He is trying to explain changes over time within the black community. Here his story is less convincing. Wilson's calculations seem to show, for example, that black teenage girls have far less chance of finding a suitable husband today than thirty years ago. But this is because Wilson compares the number of teenage girls with the number of employed teenage boys. That is not the right comparison. Teenage boys have never earned enough to support a family, even when they had jobs, and they seldom married even in the 1950s. Table 4.1 shows that even in 1960 less than 4 percent of all black men who worked throughout the year were married. The fact that fewer black teenage boys have jobs today cannot, therefore, explain why fewer black teenage mothers are mar-

Table 4.1   Weeks Worked and Marital Status of 16- to 44-Year-Old Black Males, 1960 and 1980

| Age | Weeks worked last year | | | | Sample size |
	50–52	1–49	None	Total	
16–19					
1960	10.4	42.8	46.9	100.0	559
1980	9.0	37.2	53.8	100.0	1132
20–24					
1960	38.7	52.8	8.5	100.0	551
1980	36.6	42.1	21.3	100.0	1231
25–29					
1960	50.3	43.8	5.9	100.0	537
1980	52.1	33.9	14.1	100.0	1031
30–44					
1960	56.4	38.5	5.1	100.0	1597
1980	59.7	28.4	11.9	100.0	2030
	Percent married				
16–19					
1960	3.5	6.3	1.1	3.6	
1980	3.9	1.2	.7	1.1	
20–24					
1960	54.0	35.1	23.4	41.4	
1980	30.6	15.3	6.1	18.9	
25–29					
1960	75.9	68.1	31.2	69.8	
1980	55.7	40.7	23.5	46.1	
30–44					
1960	81.0	74.1	42.7	76.5	
1980	70.0	60.7	38.1	63.5	

Source: Calculated from 1/1000 public use samples of 1960 and 1980 census records; tabulations by Gary McClelland. Totals may not add to 100.0 due to rounding.

ried. Black teenage girls have hardly ever married unless their boyfriend was older than they were. An economic explanation of declining marriage rates must therefore look at changes in the economic situation of older men.

Wilson's data on nonwhite men between the ages of twenty-five and forty-four show two things. First, the ratio of marriageable men to women hardly changed during the 1950s and 1960s. There were about 70 employed nonwhite men for every 100 women throughout this period. It follows that Wilson's argument cannot explain the spread of single parenthood during the 1960s. Second, the ratio of marriageable men to women fell after 1970, but it did not fall much. In 1982 there were still 63 employed nonwhite men for every 100 women between the ages of twenty-five and forty-four. The growing shortage of marriageable black men almost certainly contributed to the declining rate of marriage. But the shortage did not increase nearly enough to account for the huge increase in single parenthood after 1970.

Table 4.1 also shows changes between 1960 and 1980 in the percentage of black men who had not worked during the previous year. The fraction of black men who did not work rose both among the young and among the middle-aged, but it was still only 12 percent among men aged thirty to forty-four in 1980. The table also shows that a man's employment history is strongly correlated with his marital status. Among black men between twenty-five and forty-four, working throughout the year roughly doubled the chances of being married.

Nonetheless, the increase in black male joblessness between 1960 and 1980 made only a modest contribution to the decline in black men's chances of being married. In 1960, 77 percent of all black men between thirty and forty-four were living with a wife. By 1980 the figure had fallen to 64 percent—a thirteen-point drop. To see what would have happened if black men had all worked regularly, we can look at trends among those who did. Such men's chances of being married fell from 81 to 70 percent—an eleven-point drop. The decline in marriage rates among black men who worked regularly was thus almost as large as the decline among all black men. The same pattern holds if we control earnings as well as weeks worked. Marriage must, therefore, have been losing its charms for noneconomic reasons as well.[27]

The stable two-parent family is losing ground throughout American society. The trend is the same in Beverly Hills as in Watts. Single parenthood has always been much more common among poor blacks than in any other group, so doubling its frequency for everyone hurts poor black children more than any other group. But the trend is up everywhere, not just in the underclass. This increase has not followed trends in the economy in any obvious way. Single parenthood began to spread during the 1960s, when the economy was booming. It spread during the 1970s, when the economy stagnated. It spread in the early 1980s, during the worst economic downturn in a half century.

These observations suggest that we will never be able to understand the spread of single parenthood if we focus on economic and demographic factors alone. We need to think about broader cultural changes as well.

Single parenthood began its rapid spread during the 1960s, when elite attitudes toward sex, marriage, divorce, and parenthood were undergoing a dramatic change. This change was obvious in the mass media, in the law, and in the widely publicized activities of celebrities. In the space of a decade we moved from thinking that society ought to discourage extramarital sex, and especially out-of-wedlock births, to thinking that such efforts were an unwarranted infringement on personal liberty. Instead of feeling morally superior to anyone who had a baby without marrying, the young began to feel morally superior to anyone who disapproved of unwed mothers. Even quite conservative institutions such as the public schools changed their line on illegitimacy. Instead of expelling unwed mothers lest they set a bad example for their classmates, school boards began trying to keep unwed mothers in school in order to minimize the cost of the mother's "mistake."

As having babies out of wedlock and getting divorced became more socially acceptable, couples' self-interest began to assert itself. Instead of assuming that they had to get married if they were expecting a baby, prospective parents began to ask themselves whether they wanted to get married. And instead of assuming that they had to stay married, unhappy spouses began to wonder if it was worthwhile to stay married. For a growing minority, the answer was no. The men often wanted freedom. The women often thought they could do without, or do better than, the lout who made them pregnant. Improved job opportunities for women also encouraged them to look at their potential mates more critically.

These changes in attitude almost certainly improved the lives of the educated elite. Comparatively few educated women became pregnant accidentally, and a large fraction of those who did had abortions, so few well-educated women became unwed mothers unless they wanted to. Such women's chances of becoming single mothers because of divorce did climb, but most of these women found another husband if they wanted one. Even those who did not remarry were usually able to make a reasonable life for themselves and their children. If their ex-husband had a good job, he could afford sizable child-support payments, even if he was maintaining another household. If he stopped making his payments, the mother could still get a job that paid enough to make ends meet.

For less privileged couples, however, the demise of traditional norms about marriage and divorce posed more serious problems. Many of these women reject abortion, and few are obsessive about contraception. Now that their boyfriends feel freer to walk out after they conceive a child, these women are more likely to end up as single mothers even when they do not want to. Moreover, couples with neither money nor education have always had more trouble keeping their marriages together than more privileged couples. Once poor couples' relatives began to accept marital breakups as normal, their divorce rate soared. Divorce is far costlier for women with limited schooling and job skills than for college-educated women. Poorly educated ex-husbands can seldom afford to support two households, and they seldom make adequate child-support payments. Nor are these women in a strong competitive position if they want to remarry.

Poor children have suffered the most from our newly permissive approach to reproduction. Shotgun weddings and lifetime marriages caused adults a lot of misery, but they ensured that almost every child had a claim on some adult male's earnings unless his father died. That is no longer the case.

This change is, I think, a byproduct of growing individualism and commitment to personal freedom. Americans have always believed that every couple had a God-given right to conceive children, but until recently we assumed that this right carried with it an obligation to marry, to live together, and to support these children. To enforce this obligation we exerted very strong social pressure on couples to marry if they conceived children, and to stay married thereafter. Today we are rich enough that affluent couples can afford the luxury of supporting two households. As a result, elite support for the two-parent norm has eroded.

Even when almost every "respectable" adult thought unwed parenthood, desertion, and divorce immoral, it was hard to keep families together in poor communities. Now that the mass media, the schools, and even the churches have begun to treat single parenthood as a regrettable but inescapable part of modern life, we can hardly expect the respectable poor to carry on the struggle against illegitimacy and desertion with their old fervor. They still deplore such behavior, but they cannot make it morally taboo. Once the two-parent norm loses its moral sanctity, the selfish considerations that always pulled poor parents apart often become overwhelming.

In making this cultural argument, I do not mean to deny the importance of the economic factors that concern Wilson. I only want to suggest that economic factors alone cannot explain the changes that began in the 1960s. It is the conjunction of economic vulnerability and cultural change that has proved disastrous.

Neighborhood Effects

Wilson's most important contribution to the underclass debate is probably his emphasis on the role of neighborhoods in shaping the lives of the poor. Neighborhoods have been largely neglected since the mid-1960s, when economists replaced sociologists as the nation's most influential experts on the downtrodden. Now neighborhoods are enjoying something of an intellectual revival largely because of Wilson's work.

His success at reviving interest in neighborhoods derives mainly from a single fact: in 1985 the Census Bureau released data showing that poor urban families were more likely to have poor neighbors in 1979 than in 1969.[28] This change was especially marked among poor urban blacks. No one knows for sure whether the 1990 Census will show a similar trend during the 1980s, but the available evidence points in that direction. Using official poverty thresholds (which slightly overstate the increase in poverty during the 1970s), the poverty rate among blacks living in central cities fell from 41 percent in 1959 to 24 percent in 1969. It then climbed to 31 percent in 1979. By 1989 it had reached 33 percent.[29] Such evidence as we have suggests that the level of residential segregation by race and income in large metropolitan areas has been quite stable over the past generation.[30] Any increase in the overall poverty rate among central-city blacks is therefore likely to bring an increase in the proportion of poor blacks who have poor neighbors.

Wilson argues that poverty rates also increased in poor black neighborhoods during the 1970s because middle-income blacks were moving to better housing elsewhere. Middle-income blacks did move out of poor black neighborhoods, but recent research suggests that poorer blacks moved out too.[31] As a result the overall demand for housing fell in these neighborhoods, many buildings were burned or abandoned, and the total population declined dramatically. But because everyone was moving out, the same economic mix was being recreated elsewhere. When we look at major metropolitan areas as a whole, therefore, economic segregation did not increase much.

Nonetheless, poor inner-city blacks were less likely to have middle-income neighbors in 1979 than in 1969, just as Wilson claims, and this was probably even more true by 1989. The causes of this change are controversial but not really critical to Wilson's story. His story is about the consequences of the change. In order to understand these consequences one must remember that Wilson is not concerned with poverty per se. If he were, he would portray the 1960s as a decade of extraordinary progress, simply because black poverty in central cities fell from 41 to 24 percent. He would also note that, common as poverty was in the late 1980s, it was not as common as it had been in the 1950s. He does not stress these facts because the changes that really concern him involve behavior rather than income. In particular, he is worried by the declining rate of employment among black men and the rising proportion of black children growing up in fatherless families. These phenomena are clearly more common in poor central-city neighborhoods today than ever before.

Wilson's story focusses on poor neighborhoods because he believes that as the proportion of middle-income residents declines, deviant behavior becomes more common among the poor. Black women who live in very poor neighborhoods are more likely to become unwed mothers at an early age than those from similar families who live in more affluent neighborhoods.[32] Black men who grow up in poor areas also work somewhat fewer hours per year and earn lower wages as young adults than blacks from similar families who grow up in richer areas.[33]

In some cases, however, affluent neighbors may not have such benign effects on poor youngsters. In a study of Chicago teenagers' criminal behavior, John Johnstone found that poor teenagers with affluent neighbors reported having committed more serious crimes than poor teenagers who lived in poor neighborhoods.[34] This suggests that poor teenagers may feel worse off when they have rich neighbors and that resentment may lead to crime. Unfortunately, no one has replicated Johnstone's study elsewhere, so we don't know how seriously to take it.

Setting aside crime, it seems fair to assume that when middle-income blacks flee from the ghetto, the poor blacks who remain behind are worse off. But the middle-income blacks who leave are also better off.

The net effect on blacks as a group depends, therefore, on whether the cost to the poor outweighs the benefits to the more affluent. Wilson does not discuss this issue.

We don't know whether living in a poor neighborhood has more effect on a poor girl's chances of becoming a single mother than on a middle-income girl's chances. Nor do we know whether the academic costs of poor classmates are greater for poor blacks than for middle-income blacks. Nor do we know how economic (or racial) segregation affects whites at different economic levels. Indeed, the list of what we don't know goes on and on.[35]

The main reason we don't know the answers to such questions is that research of this kind requires many false starts, gradual improvements in measurement and data analysis, and lots of replications. Getting reliable answers takes several decades. Unfortunately, those who pay for such research want quick results. When the first results turn out to be inconclusive, they either shift their attention to another problem or conclude that all social science is a waste of money. (Given the way we organize and fund social science, that is largely true.) Because we know so little about the relative cost of living in the ghetto for different groups, Wilson's argument that increasing economic segregation has hurt blacks as a group remains intriguing, but unproven.

The Legacy of Discrimination

Wilson believes that "historic discrimination is more important than contemporary discrimination in understanding the plight of the black underclass." For this argument to be convincing, we need a detailed account of how past discrimination affects blacks' present competitive position. For reasons I have already discussed, I think such an account must deal not just with blacks' economic resources but with their culture as well.

Why is it that black first-graders in racially mixed schools have more trouble with reading and math than their white classmates? The standard answer is that blacks come from "disadvantaged" backgrounds. But that answer is not sufficiently precise to be useful. We need to know what specific disadvantages make it harder for blacks to master reading and arithmetic, and how these disadvantages exert their effect. We know, of course, that black parents typically have less education and less money than white parents. But, as Table 4.2 indicates, when

Table 4.2 Mean Tenth-Grade Vocabulary Scores by Socioeconomic Status,
Family Structure, and Race, 1980

Socioeconomic status and family structure	Non-Hispanic White	Non-Hispanic Black	Hispanic	White standard deviation
Lowest quartile SES				
Intact family	9.76 (1831)	7.24 (729)	7.74 (1178)	3.80
Other family	9.92 (980)	7.19 (433)	7.61 (614)	3.83
Second quartile SES				
Intact family	11.27 (3161)	8.15 (332)	8.96 (667)	3.75
Other family	11.28 (974)	7.94 (348)	8.30 (264)	3.96
Third quartile SES				
Intact family	12.27 (3414)	9.12 (303)	9.95 (571)	3.81
Other family	11.70 (931)	8.45 (237)	9.14 (174)	3.99
Top quartile SES				
Intact family	13.97 (4299)	10.38 (213)	11.71 (374)	3.84
Other family	13.56 (831)	9.71 (145)	10.29 (104)	3.85

Numbers in parentheses are sample sizes. Vocabulary is measured by a 19-item test with a sample mean of 11.02 and a standard deviation of 4.38. The within-cell standard deviations for blacks average about 4 points. The sampling errors of cell means are thus roughly $(16/N)^{.5}$ and the sampling errors of differences between cells are roughly $[16/N_1 + 16/N_2]^{.5}$.

SES is the equally weighted sum of the respondent's standardized scores for father's education, mother's education, father's occupation, family income, and items in the house, with missing items deleted from the index.

The tabulations were done by Tony Maier using the High School and Beyond 10th Grade Sample.

we match black and white parents on years of education, occupation, income, and family structure, white children still outperform black children on standardized tests. This holds not just for the vocabulary test shown in the table but for tests of reading comprehension, arithmetic reasoning, computational skills, and almost all kinds of information. How are we to explain this?

Table 4.3   IQ Scores of Four-Year-Olds by Race and Socioeconomic Status

Socioeconomic Status	Mean		Standard deviation		Number of cases	
	White	Black	White	Black	White	Black
Lowest 25 percent	95.6	88.0	14.9	13.3	1267	4620
Middle 50 percent	101.2	92.0	15.3	13.7	5579	8106
Highest 25 percent	110.9	98.1	16.5	14.6	4870	1476

Source: Sarah Broman, Paul Nichols, and Wallace Kennedy, *Preschool IQ: Prenatal and Early Developmental Correlates* (New York: Wiley, 1975), p. 43. The SES measure is based on the household head's education and occupation and on family income. The sample was drawn from women giving birth in 12 large urban hospitals in the early 1960s. High-SES blacks and whites and very low-SES blacks are undersampled. The cell mean for low-SES blacks is likely to be biased upward.

Theories abound. Some emphasize differences between black English and white English. Some claim that black parents pay less attention to their children's cognitive development than white parents do. Some say that centuries of racist propaganda have undermined blacks' intellectual self-confidence and that blacks therefore give up sooner than whites when they don't understand something.

In the absence of strong evidence, many well-intentioned blacks and whites have chosen to ignore such differences. They assume that blacks don't learn as much as whites because they attend worse schools or because teachers don't expect them to learn. There is certainly a lot of truth in both claims. But, as Table 4.3 shows, blacks and whites from the same socioeconomic background know different amounts when they *enter* school. Unless we are prepared to blame this on genes, we have to look at the way in which historic discrimination has shaped black families and black culture.

Social scientists have never been very good at describing cultural differences. We cannot explain why Jews learn more in school than gentiles, or why most Asian Americans learn more than European Americans, any better than we can explain why whites learn more than blacks. Those who are best at answering such questions write like novelists, not like social scientists, which means that they have trouble persuading anyone who does not agree with them to begin with.

Wilson has relatively little to say about cultural differences between the black underclass and the rest of America. He rejects the idea of a distinctive "culture of poverty" because the phrase has come to imply that the moral values and social norms of the undeserving poor are immutable. Wilson prefers to talk about "ghetto culture," a term he hopes will convey his conviction that the moral values and the social norms of the ghetto are a product of its physical isolation and economic distress.

Such arguments about nomenclature are at bottom political arguments about whether changing the opportunities available to ghetto residents would change their behavior. But that is not quite the right question. Wilson concedes that cultures do not adapt to changing circumstances instantaneously. And most advocates of cultural determinism concede that cultures are not completely immutable. Wilson's quarrel with conservatives who write about the culture of poverty, then, is a quarrel about *how long* it would take for ghetto culture to adapt to new circumstances. Neither side has much evidence on this point.

For many liberals, of course, even Wilson's structural approach to ghetto culture will smack of blaming the victim. This criticism has obvious rhetorical force. The term "victim" implies innocence, and blaming the innocent is obviously wrong. But the oppressed are not just innocent victims. They make choices that help shape their lives, just as everyone else does. If people make these choices on narrowly self-interested grounds, their communities begin to unravel. In poor communities as in rich ones, clergymen, teachers, mothers, and other moral leaders must continually struggle both to limit and to redefine self-interest. Censoriousness and blame are their principal weapons in this struggle: blame for teenage boys who steal from their neighbors, blame for drunken men who beat up their wives, blame for young women who have babies they cannot offer a "decent home," blame for young men who say a four-dollar-an-hour job is not worth the bother, blame for everyone who acts as if society owes them more than they owe society.

The unwritten moral contract between the poor and the rest of society is fragile at best. We usually treat the poor badly, they often treat us badly, and perhaps worst of all, they often treat each other badly. But the solution cannot be to tear up the moral contract or to deny that the poor are responsible for their behavior. That approach must eventually lead to a Hobbesian war of all against all. The only viable solution is to ask more of both the poor and the larger society.

Wilson's concluding chapter outlines what American society's obligations might be under such a revised social contract. He wants tighter labor markets, more job training, children's allowances, subsidized childcare for working mothers, and other programs that would bring the underclass into mainstream society. All this would surely help. But if moral ideas and norms of behavior have a life of their own, as I have argued, Wilson's package of institutional reforms must be complemented by a self-conscious effort at cultural change, of the kind that Jesse Jackson and others have promoted. There is not much that white liberals can do to reinforce poor urban blacks' sense of obligation to one another, to their unborn children, or to the society from which they must derive their livelihood. But we can at least stop disparaging the moral rhetoric that black leaders must use if they are to make a dent in such problems. In the last analysis, Wilson's greatest contribution may be his discussion of how liberals' reluctance to blame blacks for anything happening in their communities has clouded both black and white thinking about how we can improve those communities.

= 5 =

The Underclass

Late in 1981 Ken Auletta published three articles in the *New Yorker* on what he called the American underclass.[1] Auletta was not the first to use the term "underclass,"[2] but he was largely responsible for making it part of middle-class America's working vocabulary.[3] Six years later William Julius Wilson published *The Truly Disadvantaged,* the first book to present systematic evidence that the underclass was growing and also the first to propose plausible hypotheses about why this was happening.

In order to determine whether the underclass is growing, we need to define it. There is widespread agreement that "underclass" is an antonym for "middle class," or perhaps more broadly for "mainstream" (a term that has come to subsume both the middle class and working class). But this kind of consensus does not take us very far, since Americans have never agreed on what it meant to be middle class or working class. Thus it is just as hard to answer the question "Is the middle class shrinking?" as to answer the question "Is the underclass growing?"

The ambiguity of phrases like "middle class" and "underclass" derives from the fact that Americans use a multitude of different criteria to rank one another, including how much income they have, where they get it, whether they have mastered the cultural skills most Americans value, and whether people conform to American ideals about social behavior. Because we all use different criteria to rank one another, we end up assigning different people to the social elite, to the middle class, and to the underclass. If you rank people primarily according to how much income they have, while I rank people according to where they get their money, we will put different people in the underclass.

143

Likewise, if you think the underclass is composed of men who mug their neighbors or women who have babies out of wedlock, while I think of the underclass as composed of people who lack the social and cultural skills required to deal with mainstream American institutions, we will often disagree about whether specific individuals belong to the underclass or not. In this chapter I consider four ranking schemes, each of which implies a different definition of the underclass.

Income level. Some social scientists equate membership in the underclass with persistent poverty. In everyday usage, however, the underclass does not include the elderly poor, the working poor, or others who are poor through no fault of their own. The underclass includes only those families whose poverty is attributable to a violation of one or more widely shared social norms, such as the family head's failure to work regularly or to marry before having children. I will call this group the "impoverished underclass."

Income sources. Sociologists have traditionally assigned people to classes primarily on the basis of where they get their money rather than how much money they have. They assume that the upper class gets its income from capital, the middle and working classes get their money from regular jobs (or job-related pensions), and the lower class gets its money from irregular work, crime, public assistance, and handouts. I will call this last group the "jobless underclass."

Cultural skills. Many Americans assign people to classes primarily on the basis of how they talk, how much they know, and how they deal with other people. From this perspective the middle class is composed of people who think, talk, and act like those who manage America's major institutions. The underclass is composed of people who lack the basic skills required to deal with these institutions. For lack of a better term I will call this group "the educational underclass."

Moral norms. Americans also talk a lot about middle-class "values," and some social critics use the term "underclass" to describe people who seem indifferent to these values. Three middle-class values (or as I would prefer to say, ideals) are especially salient in discussions of this kind:

- Working-age men should have a steady job. Those who violate this norm constitute the jobless underclass.

- Women should postpone childbearing until they are married. Those who violate this norm constitute what I will call the reproductive underclass.

- Everyone should refrain from violence. Those who violate this norm constitute what I will call the violent underclass.

Whether you conclude that the underclass is growing depends on which of these ranking schemes you adopt.

Many Americans also think of the underclass as almost exclusively nonwhite. This perception may be partly due to racism, but it derives primarily from our habit of equating people's class position with their address. Using most of the ranking schemes described above, the underclass includes considerably more whites than nonwhites. But the underclass constitutes only a small fraction of the white population, and American neighborhoods are only moderately segregated along economic lines. As a result, underclass whites are seldom a majority in any neighborhood. This means that if you equate membership in the underclass with living in an underclass neighborhood, not many whites will qualify.[4]

Nonwhites are far more likely than whites to have underclass characteristics, and they almost always live in racially segregated neighborhoods. Because the underclass constitutes a relatively large fraction of the nonwhite population, it is a majority or near majority in some nonwhite neighborhoods. Those who equate membership in the underclass with living in an underclass neighborhood therefore see the underclass as nonwhite.[5]

I have not incorporated either race or geographic isolation into my definitions of the underclass, but I will ask whether each of my definitions implies that the underclass has become blacker or more geographically isolated over time. The data available for answering these questions are far from ideal. With regard to geographic isolation, the only trend data are for the 1970s, and even those data are not all one might wish. With regard to race, we have a lot of data on blacks but very little on racially distinctive Latinos.[6]

The Impoverished Underclass

Many early discussions of the underclass treated the term as a synonym for the persistently poor.[7] By the late 1980s, however, a fairly broad consensus had developed that the underclass was a subset of the poor and that it included only those families and individuals whose poverty was somehow attributable to their behavior. The underclass had, in

Table 5.1 Poverty Rates, Characteristics of the Poor, and Economic Growth, 1959–1988

Rates and characteristics	1959	1967	1974	1981	1988
Poverty rate					
1. Thresholds adjusted using CPI-U	22.4	14.2	11.2	14.0	13.1
2. Thresholds adjusted using CPI-U-X1	23.2	14.2	10.5	12.2	11.6
3. Thresholds adjusted using CPI-U-X1 and income adjusted for recipient value of noncash benefits	23.1	14.0	9.7	10.8	10.5
Composition of the poverty population					
4. Percent black	25.1	30.5	30.7	30.0	30.6
5. Percent of poor families with children that were headed by women	28.0	39.5	57.2	54.8	63.7
Economic growth					
6. Per capita income (1988 dollars)	NA	7,939	10,029	11,016	13,123
7. Unemployment rate	5.3	3.7	5.5	7.5	5.4

Sources by row:

1. U.S. Bureau of the Census, "Money Income and Poverty Status in the United States, 1988," *Current Population Reports,* Series P-60, no. 166 (Government Printing Office, 1989), table 18.

2. Ibid., table F-2, for 1974, 1981, and 1988, and Table 18 for 1967. The CPI-U-X1 is not available for 1959, but since it rose at almost the same rate between 1967 and 1988 as the fixed-weight price index for Personal Consumption Expenditures in the National Income and Product Accounts, I assumed that the same was true from 1959 to 1967. On this assumption the old CPI overstates inflation between 1959 and 1967 by 2.7 percent. I therefore assumed that substituting the CPI-U-X1 for the CPI should raise the 1959 poverty thresholds by about $1 - 1/1.027 = 2.63$ percent. The CPI overstated inflation between 1967 and 1988 by 10.0 percent. This error raised the estimated 1988 poverty rate from 11.6 to 13.1 percent. I therefore assumed that each 1 percent increase in the poverty threshold increased the poverty population by $(.131/.116 - 1)/.10 = 1.29$ percent. It follows that raising the 1959 poverty thresholds by 2.63 percent should raise the poverty population by $(1.29)(2.63) = 3.4$ percent. Since the 1959 poverty rate using the CPI was 22.4 percent, I assumed that using the CPI-U-X1 would have raised it to $(22.4)(1.034) = 23.2$ percent.

3. Bureau of the Census, "Estimates of Poverty Including the Value of Noncash Benefits, 1987," Technical Paper 58 (Government Printing Office, 1988), table 1, shows the effect of adding the "recipient value" of food and housing benefits to respondents' incomes in 1979 through 1987. This adjustment lowered the official poverty rate by 1.7 points in 1979, 1.6 points in 1980, 1.4 points in 1981, 1.3 points in 1982, and 1.2 or 1.1 points from 1983 through 1987. The size of the reduction was not proportional to the base rate. I therefore assumed that taking account of noncash benefits would lower poverty rates based on the CPI-U-X1 by 1.4 points in 1981 and 1.1 points in 1988. Bureau of the Census, *Statistical Abstract of the United States* (Government Printing Office, 1979), table 522, and 1988, table 553, shows that governmental expenditure on food and housing programs roughly doubled in real value between 1974 and 1980, so I assumed that their effect on the size of the poverty population also doubled. This implied that they reduced the poverty rate by .8 points in 1974. Analogous reasoning suggested a reduction of about .2 points in 1967.

4–5. "Money Income" (1989), tables 18 and F-2. The estimates for 1967–88 are for those who fall below thresholds based on the CPI-U-X1. The estimates for 1959 are for those who fall below thresholds based on the CPI-U.

6. Ibid., table F-15. These estimates are adjusted for inflation using the CPI-U-X1.

7. *Economic Report of the President* (Government Printing Office, 1989).

other words, become a synonym for those whom an earlier generation called the undeserving poor. To see if this impoverished underclass is growing, I proceed in three steps. First, I look at changes in the prevalence of short-term poverty. Second, I look at changes in the proportion of the short-term poor who are likely to be poor for a long period. Third, I look at changes in the proportion of the poor who behave in ways that most Americans consider blameworthy.

Changes in the overall poverty rate. The federal government classifies individuals as poor if their reported (or in some cases imputed) family income for the previous calendar year was less than the official poverty line. This line, which varies with family size and the age of family members, was created in 1965 and was supposedly tied to the cost of a nutritionally adequate diet.[8] In practice, however, it is best understood as a line that happened to divide the poorest fifth of Americans from the richest four fifths in 1963.[9] The line has been adjusted every year to take account of changes in the Consumer Price Index. It has not been adjusted to take account of changes in what more affluent families can afford to buy, so it is supposed to represent an absolute rather than a relative standard.[10]

Table 5.1 shows changes between 1959 and 1988 in three different measures of the prevalence of poverty. Row 1 shows the official poverty rate, published every year by the Census Bureau. This rate has two well-known flaws: it uses a faulty price index to adjust the poverty line for inflation, and it ignores noncash benefits. Because of these flaws, it understates the decline in poverty over the past generation. Row 2 shows how the official rate changes when we use a better measure of inflation.[11] Although using a better inflation index makes poverty decline somewhat more over time, the basic story is the same as when we use the official rate.[12]

Row 3 adjusts the estimates in row 2 for the growth of noncash government benefits. The adjustment tries to assign food stamps and government housing subsidies the monetary value that recipients would assign them. It does not assign a cash value to Medicaid or Medicare because these programs have not allowed poor families to reduce their medical expenditures. Unlike food stamps and housing subsidies, therefore, Medicare and Medicaid have not allowed the poor to spend more on other goods and services.[13] But Medicare and Medicaid have greatly increased poor people's access to medical services. Readers should keep this in mind when assessing the poverty counts in row 3.

While the official poverty series shows no overall progress between 1967 and 1981, the revised series in row 3 shows that poverty dropped by nearly a quarter during this period. All three series agree, however, in showing minimal progress since 1981. All three also show somewhat more poverty in 1988 than in 1974. Real per capita income rose 31 percent between 1974 and 1988 (see row 6), so we cannot blame the increase in poverty after 1974 on economic stagnation. Unemployment was also slightly lower in 1988 than in 1974, so we cannot blame slack labor markets. Poverty persisted because both earnings and per capita family income became more unequal.[14] The reasons why inequality increased are controversial and poorly understood. Indeed, the hypothesis that America has a growing underclass appeals to many people precisely because it purports to explain this puzzle.[15]

Is poverty more persistent? The next question is whether the proportion of the poor who remain poor over a prolonged period has risen or not. One simple way to address this question is to ask whether annual turnover in the poverty population has increased or decreased. Terry Adams, Greg Duncan, and Willard Rogers have calculated the proportion of urban families who were poor one year but not the next from 1969 through 1983.[16] They found no clear trend during the 1970s: about a third of the urban families that were poor in one year escaped poverty the following year, although many undoubtedly fell back into poverty in some subsequent year. Poverty became more persistent between 1979 and 1983, but that may have been because the overall poverty rate rose by a third during these years. The increasing persistence of urban poverty in the early 1980s was also partially offset by a decline in the persistence of rural poverty.

Duncan and Rogers also examined changes in the proportion of children living in families whose mean income over a six-year interval (including food stamps) fell below the poverty line.[17] They found no statistically reliable changes between 1967–1972 and 1981–1986. The use of a long time frame did, however, magnify racial differences. The estimated incidence of long-term poverty in 1967–1972 was 30 percent for black children compared to only 4.4 for white children. In 1981–1986 the figures were 38 percent for blacks and 5 percent for whites.

The available evidence suggests, in short, that poverty was somewhat more persistent in the early 1980s than in the 1970s. Whether this trend continued in the late 1980s remains uncertain.

Inheritance of poverty. When social critics talk about "persistent poverty" they often mean poverty that persists from one generation to the next rather than just from one year to the next. I have not been able to locate any data on changes in the inheritance of either poverty or chronic joblessness, but as we shall see, the influence of white parents' educational attainment on their children's attainment has not changed significantly in recent times, while the influence of black parents' attainment on their children's attainment has declined.

Many people believe that poverty is becoming more hereditary because they think it is increasingly confined to blacks. Table 5.1 does not support this view. Blacks constituted 31 percent of the poor in 1967, and they still constituted 31 percent of the poor in 1988.[18] Black poverty has become more urban, which makes it more visible to opinion leaders. But moving the black poor from rural to urban areas is not likely to have made their poverty more hereditary.

The undeserving poor. Poverty may be a necessary condition for counting someone as a member of the underclass, but few observers think it sufficient. The term caught on because it focused attention on those poor people who violated mainstream rules of behavior. There are at least four socially acceptable reasons for being poor: old age, physical disability, school enrollment, and low hourly wages (so long as you work steadily). Table 5.2 shows how the proportion of people who were poor for each of these reasons changed between 1968 and 1987.[19]

The elderly accounted for a much smaller fraction of all poverty in 1987 than in 1968. So did family heads who worked throughout the year. As a result, only 54 percent of poor households had socially acceptable reasons for being poor in 1987, compared to 74 percent in 1968. This change inevitably reduced public sympathy for the poor.

Once we exclude all poor household heads who are elderly, disabled, enrolled in school, or working steadily, we are left with a group whom most Americans regard as undeserving: men and women who "should" work regularly but don't, and who are poor as a result. Table 5.2 shows that, if we define the impoverished underclass in this way, it grew from 3.9 percent of all households in 1968 to 6.7 percent in 1987—an increase of more than two-thirds. This definition is problematic in at least two respects, however. First, it is not clear that we should exclude everyone who is disabled from the underclass. Second, it is not clear that we should include every able-bodied household whose head worked less than forty-eight weeks during a given year.

Table 5.2   Alternative Estimates of Percent of Households in the Impoverished Underclass, 1968 and 1987

Characteristics/Estimates	1968	1987
Percent of poor household heads with selected characteristics		
Over 65	39.0	21.5
Under 65 but disabled	11.8	13.9
Under 65, not disabled, but in school	6.7	7.8
Under 65, not disabled, not in school, and		
Worked all year	16.7	10.7
Worked part year	13.6	24.3
Did not work	12.3	21.8
Total[a]	100.0	100.0
Alternative estimates of percent of households in impoverished underclass		
All poor households[b]	15.2	14.5
All poor households headed by nonstudents under 65 who[c]		
Worked less than 48 weeks	5.7	8.7
Worked less than 48 weeks and were not disabled	3.9	6.7
Did not work at all and were not disabled	1.9	3.2

Source: Tabulations by Sheldon Danziger using the March 1969 and 1988 Current Population Survey tapes. Danziger found 310,000 more poor families and unrelated individuals on the 1988 data tape than the Census Bureau found, but this has almost no effect on the results. As used in this table, the term "household" does not coincide with Census Bureau usage. Here a household head is either the head of a family or an individual who does not live with any relatives.

a. Totals may not add to 100 because of rounding error.

b. This is the estimated poverty rate for family heads and unrelated individuals and was calculated from "Money Income and Poverty Status in the United States, 1988," *Current Population Reports,* Series P-60, no. 166, tables 18 and 20. The estimates are not comparable to those in Table 5.1 because they weight large and small families equally. The poverty thresholds are adjusted for inflation using the CPI-U. The income estimates do not include the value of noncash benefits.

c. Calculated by multiplying the overall poverty rate for family heads and unrelated individuals by the estimated proportion of such individuals with the relevant characteristics (shown in the top panel of the table).

Household heads who once held steady jobs but were then disabled by an illness or accident over which they had no control are not part of the underclass as most people conceive it. But household heads who cannot work because of disabilities caused by alcohol or drug abuse certainly do fit the popular image of the underclass. People who cannot work because they are mentally ill also fit the popular stereotype, presumably because many people equate membership in the underclass with deviant behavior rather than moral turpitude. I do not know what fraction of all disabilities were related to alcohol, drugs, or mental illness in either 1968 or 1987. But if we include *all* disabled household heads in the underclass in both years, Table 5.2 shows that it grew from 5.7 to 8.7 percent of all households. If alcohol, drugs, and mental illness accounted for a larger fraction of all disabilities in 1987 than in 1968, as many assume, the growth rate would be even higher.

Counting all poor household heads who worked less than forty-eight weeks during a year as members of the underclass is also problematic. No doubt some of the poor heads who worked less than forty-eight weeks in 1987 or 1968 had been irregularly employed for many years and remained irregularly employed in subsequent years. They clearly belong to the impoverished underclass. But some poor heads who worked less than forty-eight weeks held steady jobs in the recent past, experienced a long spell of unemployment that pushed their income below the poverty line in 1987 or 1968, but then found another steady job in a subsequent year. These households should not be classified as underclass. To see how much misclassification of such households might distort conclusions about the size of the impoverished underclass, the last row of Table 5.2 restricts the underclass to households in which the head did no paid work whatever. This change cuts the impoverished underclass in half. Nonetheless, it still appears to have grown by about two-thirds between 1968 and 1987.

One reason fewer poor household heads worked in 1987 than in 1968 is that more heads were women. Although there is now a fairly broad consensus that single mothers ought to work, this norm is relatively new, at least when applied to whites. But even when most Americans thought that a single mother should stay home with her children, they still tended to think that she had brought her poverty on herself if she had her children out of wedlock or had been divorced. Poor widows were the only female heads who qualified as deserving, and most of them were over sixty-five.

Table 5.2 leaves little doubt that a declining fraction of poor household heads looks deserving by current American standards. If the impoverished underclass includes households that are poor because the head does not conform to our current ideas about how people ought to behave, this class is clearly bigger today than it was in the late 1960s.

The Jobless Male Underclass

Men without regular jobs populate every journalistic and scholarly description of lower-class life. Indeed, American sociologists have traditionally seen chronic joblessness as a defining characteristic of the lower class, and many people now equate membership in the underclass with joblessness. Auletta's book on the underclass, for example, focuses on twenty-two men and women who were enrolled in a job-training program for the "hard-core" unemployed. Wilson also describes the underclass as a group "outside the mainstream of the American occupational system."[20]

Yet while many writers see chronic joblessness as a necessary condition for membership in the underclass, few see it as sufficient. A computer engineer who makes a fortune, sells his company, and never works again is not a member of the underclass, even if he spends most of his time in an alcoholic stupor. Nor is a disabled construction worker part of the underclass if he has good disability benefits and a working wife. It is the combination of chronic joblessness and inadequate income that makes a man part of the underclass.

The best way to measure chronic joblessness would be to ask working-age adults how many months they had worked over, say, the past five years, but the data that are actually available cover only one year. These data come from the March Current Population Survey (CPS), which asks how many weeks adults worked during the previous calendar year. In analyzing these data I will focus on trends among men between the ages of twenty-five and fifty-four. These prime-age men have almost all completed school and military service, and they are too young to have retired. Americans expect men of this age to work unless they have a physical or mental illness that makes working impossible.

Trends in long-term joblessness. Using men's reports of how many weeks they worked last year, we can calculate the percentage of men who were jobless in an average week. We can then divide those who were not working in a given week into two groups: the long-term jobless who did not work at all during the year, and the short-term jobless who worked between one and fifty-one weeks.[21] Men who hold steady jobs can lose them. When the economy is in a recession, such men may spend a long time looking for a new position. When the economy is reasonably healthy, however, such men seldom remain jobless for long. Even if they cannot find another steady job immediately,

Figure 5.1

Rates of Long-term, Short-term, and Total Joblessness among White Men Aged 25 to 54, 1963–1987

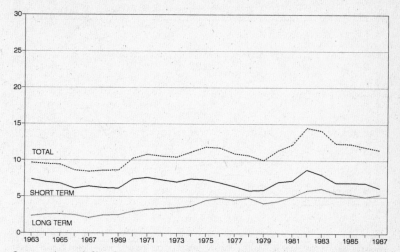

Source: Annual files from the March Current Population Survey, assembled by Robert Mare and Christopher Winship. Tabulations by Christine Kidd, Rich Mrizek, and David Rhodes.

they can usually find temporary work while they look for something better. Except during serious recessions, therefore, a man who does not work for an entire calendar year is either not looking for work, is very choosy about the jobs he will take, or is a very undesirable employee. Such men are clearly candidates for membership in the underclass.

Figure 5.1 shows trends in both long-term and short-term jobless-ness among prime-age white men. The rate of short-term joblessness shows no clear trend from 1963 through 1987, hovering around 7 per-cent except during recessions, but long-term joblessness has clearly risen (from about 2 percent in 1963 to 5 percent in 1987). Note that the business cycle has very little influence on long-term joblessness among prime-age white men. Even the deep recession of 1982–83 only pushed long-term white joblessness about one point above the trend line. This fact implies that most prime-age white men who look for work find at least a few weeks of employment every year. It seems to follow that the increase in long-term joblessness among whites is probably not a byproduct of slacker labor markets.

Figure 5.2
Rates of Long-term, Short-term, and Total Joblessness among Black Men Aged 25 to 54, 1963–1987

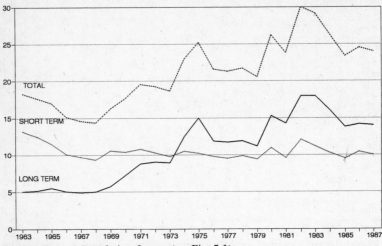

Source: Current Population Survey (see Fig. 5.1).

Figure 5.2 shows analogous trends for prime-age black men. Short-term joblessness is more common among blacks than whites (averaging 10 rather than 7 percent), but again there is no clear upward trend over time. Long-term joblessness, in contrast, shows a dramatic upward trend after 1969 among black men. This increase is much steeper among blacks than whites. The business cycle also has far more effect on long-term joblessness among blacks than whites. A lot of prime-age black men who want to work are apparently unable to find any sort of job for at least a year when the economy is in trouble. Most of these men return to work when the economy revives, but some apparently do not, so the rate at the peak of each business cycle is higher than it was at the previous peak.

Long-term joblessness and poverty. Much writing about the underclass treats long-term joblessness as almost synonymous with poverty. This is a mistake. More than half the prime-age men who do no paid work in a given year now live in families with incomes above the poverty line. Many live in families with incomes more than twice the poverty line. Figure 5.3 shows trends in the proportions of prime-age black and white men who were not only jobless for the entire year but also

Figure 5.3

Percentage of Men Aged 25 to 54 Who Were Both Long-Term Jobless and Poor, by Race, 1963–1987

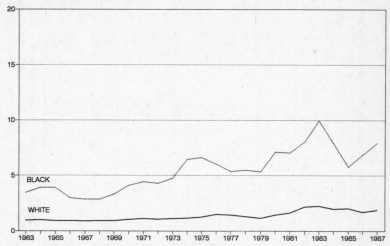

Source: Current Population Survey (see Fig. 5.1).

poor.[22] Most of these men presumably fit the popular image of the underclass. Defined in this way, the underclass included about 1 percent of prime-age white men and just under 4 percent of prime-age black men in the early 1960s. By 1985–1987 it included almost 2 percent of prime-age white men and 6 to 8 percent of prime-age black men.

Errors in the estimates. The CPS does not survey inmates of institutions. Most prime-age inmates are in prisons or mental hospitals. Such men are quite likely to be jobless when they are not locked up, so the CPS almost certainly underestimates the fraction of the total population that belongs to the jobless underclass.

Trend estimates based on the CPS may also be biased, because American society has changed its policies with regard to locking up the mentally ill and criminals. During the 1970s, for example, most states moved a lot of mental patients out of hospitals onto the streets. This change almost certainly increased the estimated rate of long-term joblessness. At roughly the same time, however, most states also began locking up felons for longer periods. This change almost certainly reduced the estimated rate of long-term joblessness.

Changes in the duration of incarceration and hospitalization roughly

Table 5.3 Percent of Men Aged 25 to 54 Who Did Not Work at Any Time during Calendar Year, by Race and Education, 1963–1987

Schooling and race	1963–65	1966–68	1972–74	1978–80	1985–87	Change between 1963–65 and 1985–87	
						Diff.	Ratio
No high school							
White	5.2	5.6	9.7	13.5	18.7	13.5	3.48
Black	6.8	7.7	14.5	23.2	32.7	25.9	4.81
Some high school							
White	2.5	2.5	4.5	7.3	10.7	8.2	4.28
Black	4.9	4.6	11.5	15.7	21.6	16.7	4.41
High school graduate							
White	1.6	1.5	2.5	3.3	4.9	3.3	3.06
Black	4.8	3.1	8.0	9.9	12.7	7.9	2.65
Some college							
White	1.8	1.5	2.6	3.3	3.9	2.1	2.17
Black	2.4	1.4	7.0	10.1	9.2	6.8	3.83
College graduate							
White	1.7	1.4	1.9	2.0	2.2	.5	1.29
Black	1.0	2.9	6.3	8.8	7.2	6.2	7.20
Total							
White	2.5	2.3	3.5	4.1	5.2	2.7	2.08
Black	5.3	5.0	10.2	12.4	14.0	8.7	2.64

Source: Annual files from the March Current Population Survey compiled by Robert Mare and Christopher Winship. Tabulations by Rich Mrizck, Christine Kidd, and David Rhodes. Three-year averages are shown to minimize sampling error. Recession years are omitted in order to dramatize the secular trend.

offset one another during the 1970s. The decennial census found that 0.6 percent of all prime-age white men and about 2.4 percent of all prime-age black men were inmates in both 1970 and 1980.[23] Including inmates in the jobless underclass would therefore raise its estimated size by about a third but would not alter its estimated rate of growth during the 1970s. During the 1980s, however, the prison population continued to grow while the number of men in mental hospitals stopped falling. Figure 5.3 may therefore understate growth in the jobless underclass since 1980.

The CPS also misses a significant number of jobless men who do not head a household of their own. Some of these men are homeless. Others live with a relative or a girlfriend. The head of the household in which such a man is staying often considers him to be a temporary guest rather than a permanent household member and does not list him when the CPS asks who lives in the household. A full count of such men would almost certainly increase the estimated size of the underclass and might conceivably increase its estimated growth rate.

Skills and joblessness. Both liberals and conservatives often claim that long-term joblessness increased after 1970 because demand for unskilled workers declined. Table 5.3 shows that the absolute increase in long-term joblessness has indeed been largest among men without high-school diplomas. With one minor exception, the percentage increase in long-term joblessness has also been largest among men without high-school diplomas.[24]

Men's earnings when they work also constitute an indirect measure of their skills. Chinhui Juhn has shown that the mean number of weeks worked by men whose expected weekly earnings exceeded the national average hardly changed between 1967 and 1987. Among men whose expected weekly earnings were between the fortieth and twentieth percentiles, there was a modest decline in weeks worked. Among men whose expected weekly earnings fell below the twentieth percentile, there was a large decline.[25]

The reasons for the link between skills and joblessness are controversial. Liberals often claim that there are not enough jobs to go around, or at least not enough unskilled jobs. Many conservatives claim that low-wage jobs are widely available and that jobless men just won't take them. Some conservatives conclude that jobless men do not want to work. Others argue, more plausibly, that while jobless men may want to work, they only want good jobs, for which they are not qualified.

Some liberals accept the second argument, asserting that no grown man should be expected to take a job at McDonald's. No one has yet undertaken the kind of research that would be necessary to determine what sorts of jobs the long-term jobless are really willing to take.

We do know, however, that wages have become more unequal since 1970. (The weekly earnings of men in the top half of the wage distribution rose about 6 percent between 1970 and 1987, while the weekly earnings of men in the bottom tenth of the wage distribution fell 25 percent.[26]) If an unskilled man's reservation wage depends on what the average man earns, any increase in inequality will create a situation in which fewer men can find jobs that pay enough to make work seem worthwhile. Juhn's calculations suggest that changes of this kind could explain much of the decline in male employment since 1970.[27]

The changing cost of joblessness. Many conservatives have suggested that joblessness increased after 1970 because the welfare state reduced its cost. We know, for example, that disability benefits became more readily available after 1970. This change presumably encouraged some low-wage workers with health problems to stop working, although the magnitude of the effect is uncertain.[28] But we also have reason to believe that general assistance benefits, which are the main income-maintenance program available to men who do not get disability benefits, have probably declined in real terms since 1970. In addition, prime-age men probably have fewer close kin to whom they can turn for help if they cannot find a job they want. Declining fertility means that men have fewer brothers and sisters whom they can ask for help. And declining marriage rates mean that fewer men have wives to support them if they do not work.

One way to assess the cumulative impact of all these changes is to compare the family incomes of men who did and did not work in various periods. Figure 5.4 shows that long-term joblessness increased a black man's chances of being poor by about 40 percentage points in the early 1960s. The poverty rate among jobless black men declined during the late 1960s, which is consistent with the conservative story. But poverty also declined at about the same rate among men who worked. The net benefit of working therefore remained unchanged. This situation persisted throughout the 1970s and 1980s. Long-term joblessness increased the percentage of black men who were poor by about 40 points in 1985–1987, just as it had in 1963–1965. Among

Figure 5.4

Poverty Rates among Men Aged 25 to 54 by Race and Employment Status, 1963–1987

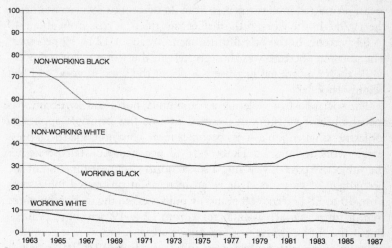

Source: Current Population Survey. "Non-working" means having worked zero weeks during the relevant year.

whites, long-term joblessness raised a man's chances of being poor by only 30 points. At least using this crude measure, however, the economic cost of long-term joblessness has not changed.

The geographic distribution of joblessness. Most people who talk about the underclass assume that long-term joblessness has increased primarily in poor inner-city neighborhoods. Many infer that the work ethic must have collapsed in these neighborhoods. In order to test such claims we need data on changes in the geographic distribution of joblessness within metropolitan areas. Unfortunately, the Census Bureau only collects such data every ten years, and the 1990 census results were not available when I completed this essay. We do, however, have data from the 1970 and 1980 censuses.

The Census Bureau divides metropolitan areas into tracts with 2000 to 8000 residents. For each tract the bureau estimates what I will call the rate of "protracted" joblessness: the percentage of men over the age the rate of sixteen who worked twenty-six or fewer weeks during the year prior to the census. Mark Hughes has studied changes during the

1970s in the geographic distribution of protracted joblessness within eight metropolitan areas (Atlanta, Chicago, Cincinnati, Cleveland, Detroit, Louisville, Newark, and Paterson).[29] Averaging across all eight areas, protracted joblessness rose from 26 percent to 39 percent during the 1970s. In the worst fifth of all census tracts, it rose from about 40 to 58 percent. In the best fifth it rose from about 12 to 19 percent.[30] The absolute increase was thus greatest in the worst neighborhoods, while the proportional increase was about the same in good and bad neighborhoods.[31]

The social cost of violating a community norm usually declines as the number of violators increases. I assume this principle applies to joblessness: when joblessness becomes more common, the social pressure to work declines. But I know no evidence that would tell us whether the subjective cost of violating a social norm is a linear function of the percentage of violators. If it is, an increase in protracted joblessness from 40 to 58 percent (18 points) would weaken the work ethic three to four times as much as an increase from 12 to 19 percent (5 points). But if the subjective cost of violating a social norm were a nonlinear function of the rate of joblessness, an increase from 12 to 19 percent (a factor of 1.6) might have as much effect as an increase from 40 to 58 percent (a factor of 1.5).[32]

The Census Bureau does not report on the geographic distribution of *poor* jobless men, but we can make educated guesses. Figure 5.3 shows that the proportion of prime-age men who were both long-term jobless and poor roughly doubled between 1963 and 1987. Since a wide range of evidence suggests that major metropolitan areas are about as segregated along economic lines today as in the past, it seems likely that the proportion of men who were both jobless and poor roughly doubled in both good and bad census tracts. This would imply a much larger absolute increase in bad tracts.

Racial composition of the jobless underclass. Table 5.4 shows that 29 percent of the jobless male underclass was black in 1963–1965, 28 percent was black in 1972–1974, and 29 percent was black in 1985–1987. The only big change in the racial composition of the underclass was the increase in "other races"—Native Americans, Asians, and Hispanics who described their race as "other." They constituted 7.7 percent of the jobless underclass in 1985–1987, compared to only 1.6 percent in 1963–1965.

The fact that blacks constitute the same fraction of the jobless under-

Table 5.4 Racial Mix of Men Aged 25 to 54 in the Total Population and in the Jobless Underclass, Selected Years

Race	1963–65	1972–74	1985–87
All men aged 25 to 54			
Percent white	89.9	89.2	86.4
Percent black	9.2	9.3	10.3
Percent other races	.9	1.6	3.3
Total	100.0	100.0	100.0
Men aged 25 to 54 who were poor and did not work at any time in calendar year			
Percent white	69.3	68.8	63.1
Percent black	29.1	28.2	29.2
Percent other races	1.6	3.0	7.7
Total	100.0	100.0	100.0

Source: Annual files from the March Current Population Survey compiled by Robert Mare and Christopher Winship. Tabulations by Rich Mrizek, Christine Kidd, and David Rhodes. Three-year averages are shown to minimize sampling error.

class today as in the early 1960s may come as a surprise, since blacks constitute a rising fraction of the long-term jobless. The explanation is that poverty rates have declined more among jobless black men than among jobless white men.

Many people assume that long-term joblessness rose faster among blacks than whites simply because demand for unskilled workers declined. But Table 5.3 shows that when we compare men with the same amount of schooling, long-term joblessness increased more among blacks than whites.[33] Furthermore, as we shall see, racial disparities in both reading skills and high-school graduation rates have fallen dramatically since 1970. All else equal, therefore, we would expect black-white differences in employment to have narrowed as well.

Nor can wage changes explain why joblessness rose faster among blacks than whites. When Chinhui Juhn estimated the effect of changes in real wages, she found that the expected decline in employment was the same for blacks and whites. At any given real wage level, white men were just as likely to work in 1987 as in 1970. Among black men, in contrast, joblessness rose even with real wages held constant.[34]

One possible explanation for the growing racial disparity in long-term joblessness is that while civil-rights laws have forced employers to pay their black workers as much as they pay whites in similar jobs, employers still do not believe that black men are worth as much as whites (see Chapter 1). Employers may therefore have become more reluctant to hire blacks. Another possible explanation is that the civil-rights movement made black men less willing to accept poorly paid menial jobs, even though these were still the only jobs open to many unskilled blacks (see Chapter 4).

The proportion of prime-age men who live with a wife and children has also declined faster among blacks than whites. Not having a family to support almost certainly reduces a man's willingness to take a job he does not want. Changes in family structure may therefore have pushed up reservation wages faster among black than white men.

Another popular explanation for the rise in black male joblessness is the alleged growth of the illegal economy, especially the drug trade. Illegal income obviously reduces a man's incentive to take a poorly paid job. In the long run, moreover, illegal work makes it harder to find a legal job, because most men who work in the illegal economy accumulate a criminal record. But blacks have no monopoly on illegal activity, and there is no direct evidence that their share of illegal income has grown over the past generation. If blacks' share of illegal income *had* grown, I would expect them to account for a rising fraction of all arrests. No such trend is apparent. Blacks' share of total arrests fell slightly during the 1970s and rose slightly during the 1980s, but the overall change was quite small.[35]

Another reason long-term joblessness could have risen more among blacks than whites is that American blacks still live in the central cities of their metropolitan areas, while jobs—especially blue-collar jobs—have been moving to the suburbs. For reasons discussed in the previous chapter, this argument seems quite plausible for black teenagers but is not very convincing when applied to prime-age men.[36]

Culture and joblessness. Because long-term joblessness began rising around 1970, some conservatives have blamed the increase on the baby boomers' alleged allergy to work. But Figure 5.5 shows that long-term joblessness increased for all age groups after 1970, not just for those born after 1945. Long-term joblessness also kept rising during the 1980s, despite widespread repudiation of the antiwork values that attracted young adults in the late 1960s and early 1970s.

Nor has the increase in long-term joblessness been confined to disadvantaged blacks. The same trend was apparent among black college graduates and among all but the best-educated whites. White college

Figure 5.5

Percentage of Men Who Did Not Work at Any Time during the Year, by Age, 1959–1987

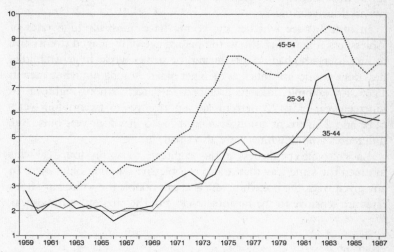

Source: *Handbook of Labor Statistics, 1989,* table 48.

graduates are the one group that has remained almost immune (see Table 5.3). Nobody has proposed a very convincing theory of cultural change that applies to everyone but college-educated whites.

Joblessness among younger men. Many descriptions of the underclass emphasize joblessness among teenagers and young adults rather than among older men. In part, this is because the official teenage unemployment rate is much higher than the adult rate. In 1989, for example, the official rate among sixteen- to nineteen-year-old blacks averaged 32 percent for males and 33 percent for females—more than three times the rate for blacks over the age of twenty. Among white teenagers, unemployment averaged 14 percent for males and 12 percent for females.[37] Official unemployment statistics for young people can be quite misleading, however, because they include students looking for part-time jobs and exclude men in the armed forces.

What we need to know is how many young men are doing nothing the larger society regards as useful. For males, our best approximation is probably the percentage who are not in school, not in the armed forces, and not working in a civilian job. Robert Mare and Christopher

Winship have estimated the proportions of young men who were idle in this sense during a typical week between 1964 and 1985.[38] Figure 5.6 shows their estimates for eighteen- to nineteen-year-olds and twenty- to twenty-four-year-olds.

In order to see whether the young have unusually high rates of joblessness, Figure 5.7 shows the percentage of men aged twenty-five to fifty-four who had no job during the survey week. In general, idleness does not decline much as men get older. Among nonwhite men in 1985, for example, idleness averaged 25 percent among eighteen- to nineteen-year-olds, 22 percent among twenty- to twenty-four-year-olds, and 22 percent among twenty-five- to fifty-four-year-olds. Age differences among whites were also small.[39]

Race also affects idleness among eighteen- to twenty-four-year-olds in much the same way that it affects joblessness among older men. In any given week the nonwhite rate is about double the white rate. Both rates are sensitive to the business cycle, but the rates at both the peak

Figure 5.6
Percentage of Men Aged 18 to 24 Who Were Not Employed, in the Military, or Enrolled in School in an Average Week, by Race, 1964–1985

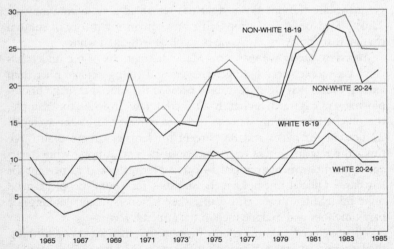

Source: Current Population Survey and Department of Defense estimates. Data provided by Robert Mare and Christopher Winship.

Figure 5.7
Percentage of Men Aged 25 to 54 Who Were Not Employed in an Average Week, by Race, 1954–1988

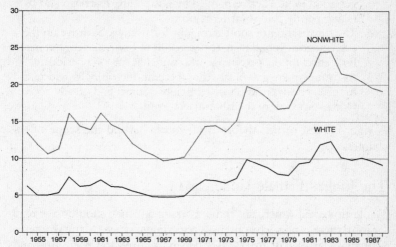

Source: *Handbook of Labor Statistics, 1989,* tables 3 and 15. Estimates shown un-weighted means for men aged 25–34, 35–44, and 45–54.

and trough of the business cycle have risen fairly steadily since the late 1960s.

Figure 5.6 shows the proportions of young men who were idle in the week they were surveyed. It does not show how long such men remained idle. Contrary to folklore, the proportion of young men who reported that they did not work at any time during a calendar year has not risen over the past generation. Ten percent of all twenty- to twenty-four-year-old men reported that they did not work during 1987. The figure was 8 percent in 1979, 10 percent in 1969, and 8 percent in 1959.[40]

So far as I know, nobody has tried to explain why both short-term and long-term joblessness rose between 1959 and 1987 among mature men, while only short-term joblessness rose among younger men. My tentative hypothesis has five parts:

1. Good jobs (steady jobs that paid enough to support a family) became scarcer after 1970.

2. Firms increasingly reserved these jobs for the college-educated and for men with good work histories.
3. Young men without higher education therefore found it harder to get good jobs. They responded by postponing marriage and by taking poorly paid short-term jobs.
4. The substitution of short-term jobs for steady jobs drove up the percentage of young men who were idle in a typical week but had little effect on the percentage who were idle for long periods.
5. As young men get older, they become increasingly reluctant to take poorly paid short-term jobs. Some find steady jobs. Others drop out of the labor market entirely.

A vigorous test of this theory is obviously beyond the scope of this chapter.

The Jobless Female Underclass

While almost all Americans think working-age men should have regular jobs, there is no such consensus regarding women. Many women of all social classes still marry and depend entirely on their husbands for support. Some Americans now regard such dependency as old-fashioned, but few regard it as evidence of shiftlessness. If a woman cannot persuade a man to support her, however, most Americans now think she should work, even if she has children.

Until the 1960s, most legislators thought single white mothers should stay home and care for their children, even if that meant the government had to pay their bills. Congress made its first major effort to encourage work among single mothers in 1967, when it allowed welfare recipients to retain part of their earnings. Since then, both federal and state legislators have devised dozens of different schemes for moving single mothers "off the welfare rolls and onto payrolls." Yet the proportion of single mothers with paid jobs only rose from 52 percent in 1960 to 57 percent in 1988 (see Table 5.5).[41] Since the proportion of married mothers with jobs rose from 26 to 62 percent during this period, it seems reasonable to infer that the rewards of work rose far less for single mothers than for married mothers.

Confronted with statistics of this kind, most people have an easy explanation: Single mothers don't work because they can get welfare instead. Some see this decision as a simple matter of economics: those who can get a good job do so, but those who can only get low-wage work choose welfare because it pays better. Others deny that single mothers are income maximizers, arguing that many are now enmeshed in a culture that makes them unlikely to work even if work pays significantly better than welfare. Advocates of this view conjure up images of women who grew up on welfare, had a baby out of wedlock while they were still teenagers, went on welfare themselves, and have never lived with anyone who held a regular job.

Surprisingly little research has been done on the relationship between welfare and work. Popular concern has focused largely on the number of single mothers collecting welfare rather than on the number who work, so scholars have done the same. Most people assume that when more single mothers collect welfare, fewer work—and that when fewer collect welfare, more work. But the truth is that few Americans care whether single mothers work, so long as they do not collect welfare. The federal government did not even calculate the proportion of single mothers who worked until 1981, and even today such statistics get almost no attention.

Table 5.5 shows that the proportion of single mothers collecting welfare has fluctuated dramatically since 1960, rising from 29 percent in 1964 to 63 percent in 1972, and then gradually declining to about 45 percent in 1988. These fluctuations had almost no effect on the proportion of single mothers who worked, which remained roughly constant.

One reason more single mothers began collecting welfare in the late 1960s was that Congress allowed them to supplement their meager welfare checks with low-wage work. Under the thirty-and-a-third rule, welfare recipients who worked could keep the first $30 of their monthly earnings, plus a third of all additional earnings. In practice, the way welfare agencies calculated work-related expenses often allowed single mothers to keep more. These rules remained in effect from 1967 to 1981, and during these years roughly a sixth of all welfare recipients told the welfare department that they worked. In 1981, the Reagan administration persuaded Congress to abandon this policy, once again reducing a welfare mother's check by the full amount of her earnings (except for work-related expenses). As a result, far fewer recipients told the welfare department that they worked. Some left the welfare rolls entirely. Others continued to work but took off-the-books employment or worked under false social security numbers (see Chapter 6).

Unfortunately, the weak relationship between trends in employment

Table 5.5 Income Sources of Female-Headed Families with Children, 1960–1988

	1960	1964	1968	1972	1976	1980	1984	1988
Percent of families with children headed by women	9.4	10.0	11.0	13.3	16.3	18.6	20.2	21.2
Percent of families with children headed by welfare mothers	2.5	2.9	4.1	8.4	9.9	10.2	9.9	9.5
Percent of women with children who work								
Spouse present	26	30	35	38	42	51	55	62
No spouse present	52	na	52	49	49	56	53	57
Percent of women heading families with children who								
Collect AFDC	27	29	37	63	61	55	49	45
Collect AFDC and work	na	na	6	10	10	8	2	3
Mean monthly value of AFDC and food stamps in 1988 dollars	560	554	609	774	782	715	670	660

Sources by row:

1. "Money Income and Poverty Status in the United States, 1988," *Current Population Reports*, Series P-60, no. 166, p. 62. Data are designated as applying to the previous year in the source but are based on the March CPS for the years shown here.

2. Rows 1 and 5: This estimate does not include families with male heads who received AFDC, either because they were unemployed or because they were disabled.

3. *Handbook of Labor Statistics, 1989*, p. 242.

4. Robert Moffitt, "Work and the US Welfare System," Institute for Research on Poverty, University of Wisconsin, Special Report 46 (Madison, 1988), table 4. I estimated the values for 1972, 1976, and 1980 by interpolation from Moffitt's data on the immediately preceding and immediately following years. The value for 1988 is taken from "Money Income, 1988," p. 73. The value for 1960 is from a 1/1000 Public Use Sample of 1960 census records.

5. The rate shown here is the number of AFDC families headed by single women divided by the total number of families with children under 18 headed by single women. The number of female-headed families with children comes from "Money Income, 1988," p. 62. The total number of families receiving AFDC comes from *Social Security Bulletin, Annual Statistical Supplement, 1988* (Government Printing Office), p. 334. I estimated the proportion of AFDC families headed by women by interpolation and extrapolation from data on the number of AFDC families that included a disabled or unemployed husband, taken from U.S. House of Representatives, Committee on Ways and Means, *Background Material and Data on Programs within the Jurisdiction of the Committee on Ways and Means* (Government Printing Office, 1989), p. 563. I assumed that Puerto Rico, Guam, and the Virgin Islands accounted for 1.5 percent of the caseload in all years. I estimated the AFDC count for 1988 from data supplied by Emmett Dye of the Social Security Administration for *fiscal* years 1986–1988, by assuming that the count for calendar 1988 = .75(fiscal 1988) + .25(fiscal 1989).

6. Estimated from column 5 and data on the employment status of AFDC recipients in Committee on Ways and Means (1989), and Moffitt.

7. *Background Material and Data on Programs within the Jurisdiction of the Committee on Ways and Means* (1987), p. 662. I readjusted the published estimates for inflation using the fixed-weight price index for Personal Consumption Expenditures from the National Income and Product Accounts, taken from *Economic Report of the President* (Government Printing Office, 1989), table B-4. All estimates are for a family of four. The estimates for 1960 through 1988 assume that a family did receive food stamps. In reality, food stamps expanded gradually. In May, 1969, 53 percent of all AFDC households got either food stamps or surplus food. This figure had reached 68 percent by 1973 and 83 percent by 1983. It was still 83 percent in 1987 (see Committee on Ways and Means, 1989, p. 564). The estimate for 1988 assumes that AFDC benefits for a family of four rose at the same rate between 1986 and 1988 as the average monthly benefit per family, that food stamps constituted 30.5 percent of total benefits (see Committee on Ways and Means, 1986, p. 662), and that the value of food stamps rose at the same rate as the Consumer Price Index between 1986 and 1988.

and trends in welfare receipt also raises questions about the quality of the data in Table 5.5. From 1960 through 1968, about a fifth of all single mothers appeared to be getting by without either working or collecting welfare. By 1972 such mothers had disappeared. The magnitude and speed of this change seem implausibly large, suggesting that the basic data may contain errors.[42] Because the data are problematic, it is hard to be sure that changes in welfare benefits do not affect the proportion of single mothers who work.

Who collects welfare? If the underclass were growing, and if welfare had played a significant role in its growth, as many believe, we would expect a rising fraction of recipients to be black, concentrated in poor central-city neighborhoods, and raised in underclass families.

In reality, blacks constitute a declining fraction of all welfare recipients (40 percent in 1987, compared to 45 percent in 1969).[43] Roughly a third of all single mothers were black in both years, so the effect of race on a single mother's chance of collecting welfare must also have declined slightly between 1969 and 1987.[44]

Mark Hughes has investigated neighborhood differences in the proportion of households receiving public assistance.[45] The proportion of households collecting public assistance in the eight metropolitan areas discussed earlier rose from 6 percent in 1969 to 10 percent in 1979. The absolute difference between the best and the worst census tracts grew substantially in all eight cities. The proportional difference between the best and worst tracts declined, however, so the fraction of public-assistance recipients living in the worst census tracts fell. Whether this means that the social stigma attached to welfare fell more in good or bad neighborhoods is unclear.

I have not been able to locate data on changes over time in the family background of welfare recipients.

The Educational Underclass

Americans constantly use cultural cues to estimate one another's social standing. These cues include the way people talk, what they know, their taste in consumer goods and services, and how they spend their time. Sometimes we use these cues because we do not know how much money an individual has or where it comes from. But most Americans also think these cultural attributes are important in their own right.

America does not collect much data on the distribution of social and cultural skills. We do not know, for example, how many Americans can speak middle-class English or how many could do so in the past.[46] Nor do we know how well different sorts of workers can meet a middle-class supervisor's expectations regarding punctuality, courtesy, friendliness, meticulousness, or bringing problems to the supervisor's attention. Still less do we know how well random samples of workers would have been able to meet such expectations in the past.

This section therefore focuses on only two crude measures of cultural competence: the proportion of individuals who finish high school and the proportions who can read and calculate at various levels of competence. I will describe young people who do not complete high school or do not learn the basic cognitive skills that schools try to teach as the "educational underclass."

High-school graduation rates. High-school graduation can mean two different things in America: graduating from a regular high school or earning a certificate of General Educational Development (GED) by passing a test. The Census Bureau treats high-school diplomas and GED certificates as equivalent.

Broadly speaking, three quarters of all American teenagers graduate from high school, and another 10 percent earn GED certificates. Table 5.6 shows that the proportion of teenagers earning high-school diplomas peaked around 1970, declined slightly over the next ten years, and recovered somewhat in the 1980s.[47] But while the regular graduation rate declined slightly in the 1970s, more young adults earned GED certificates. As a result, the proportion of twenty-five- to twenty-nine-year-olds with either a high-school diploma or a GED certificate has remained roughly constant (about 85 percent) since the mid-1960s. Table 5.6 also suggests that this figure is unlikely to change much over the next decade.[48]

Racial and ethnic differences in dropping out. Because high schools do not report the race of those who earn diplomas, we must rely on census surveys to see how graduation rates vary by race. The Census Bureau publishes two statistical series that throw light on dropout rates: the proportion of twenty-five- to twenty-nine-year-olds who had neither a high-school diploma nor a GED in a given year, and the proportion of sixteen- to twenty-four-year-olds who were no longer in school and had neither a diploma nor a GED

Most people who eventually earn a GED have done so by the time they are in their late twenties, so the proportion of twenty-five- to

Table 5.6 High School Graduation Rates by Year of Expected Graduation, 1950–1987

Age	1948–52	1958–62	1963–7	1968–72	1973–7	1978–82	1983–7	1988–9
High school graduates as a percent of 17-year-olds	56.3	67.5	74.5	76.3	74.1	72.2	73.2	73.9
GED certificates 5 years after graduation year as a percent of 17-year-olds	na	na	na	8.5	10.8	10.3	na	na
Percent of 25–29-year-olds reporting high school diploma or GED	60.7	75.4	83.1	85.4	86.1	na	na	na

Sources by row:

1. National Center for Education Statistics, *Digest of Education Statistics, 1989* (Government Printing Office, 1989), p. 103. The estimates shown are averages for the 5-year interval, based on states' reports of the number of high-school graduates and Current Population Survey estimates of the number of 17-year-olds.

2. National Center for Education Statistics, p. 104. The proportion of the cohort receiving a GED certificate is estimated from the mean number of GED certificates awarded in the 5-year interval when the cohort was 22 years old. This approximation is based on age distributions given in the source.

3. National Center for Education Statistics, *Youth Indicators, 1988* p. 52. The estimates cover 25–29-year-olds surveyed 10 years after the midpoint of the graduation interval shown at the top of the table.

twenty-nine-year-olds with neither a high-school diploma nor a GED is a good proxy for the proportion of the birth cohort that will never earn either credential. The main drawback of this measure is that it cannot tell us much about recent trends in dropping out. The percentage of twenty-five- to twenty-nine-year-olds without a diploma in 1985, for example, reflects the holding power of high schools in the mid-1970s.

The proportion of sixteen- to twenty-four-year-olds who are not in school and have neither a diploma nor a GED provides a better picture of recent trends. Some of the those currently enrolled in high school will drop out before earning a diploma, and some older dropouts will eventually earn a GED. Experience suggests, however, that these two sources of bias roughly offset one another. As a result, the proportion of sixteen- to twenty-four-year-old dropouts is about the same as the proportion of twenty-five- to twenty-nine-year-old dropouts seven years later. Thus while Table 5.7 presents both measures, I will concentrate on the results for sixteen- to twenty-four-year-olds.

The proportion of sixteen- to twenty-four-year-old whites who had left school and had neither a regular diploma nor a GED hardly changed between 1975 and 1988. This apparent stability is somewhat misleading, however, because a rapidly growing fraction of all whites is Hispanic, and they have a much higher dropout rate than either blacks or non-Hispanic whites.[49] The obvious solution to this problem would be to look at trends among non-Hispanic whites, but the Census Bureau does not report data for this group. Table 5.7 therefore uses a second-best approximation, namely the dropout rate for all non-Hispanic whites, Asians, and Native Americans. After excluding Hispanics, the dropout rate for whites, Asians, and Native Americans was two points lower in 1988 than it had been in 1975 (9.5 versus 11.5 percent).

For blacks, the story is even more encouraging. Their dropout rate fell from 28 percent in 1970 to 15 percent in 1988. Most of this decline occurred in the 1970s, but the rate continued to fall in the 1980s. As a result, the disparity between blacks and non-Hispanic whites, Asians, and Native Americans declined from eleven points in 1975 to five points in 1988.

If not finishing high school is a good measure of coming from an underclass family, as many believe, Table 5.7 shows that the underclass is not only getting smaller but also getting whiter. Likewise, if not finishing high school indicates that an individual will grow up to be part of the underclass, the underclass will be smaller and whiter tomorrow than it is today.

Table 5.7 High School Dropout Rates and College Graduation Rates, by Race and Year, 1960–1985

Race	1960	1970	1975	1980	1985	1988
High school dropout rate						
Percent of 25–29-year-olds reporting neither a high-school diploma nor a GED						
White	36.3	22.2	15.6	13.1	13.2	13.4
Nonwhite	61.4	41.6	26.2	23.0	17.6	18.0
Black	–	43.9	29.0	23.4	19.4	19.2
Hispanic	–	–	48.3	42.1	39.0	37.8
Non-Hispanic whites, Asians, Native Americans	–	–	13.4	11.2	10.4	10.3
Percent of 16–24-year-olds who were neither in school nor high school graduates						
Total		15.0	13.9	14.1	12.6	12.9
White		13.2	12.6	13.3	12.2	12.7
Black		27.9	22.8	18.3	15.7	14.9
Hispanic		—	29.2	35.2	27.6	35.8
Non-Hispanic whites, Asians, Native Americans		—	11.5	11.4	10.4	9.5
Percent of 16–24-year-old dropouts who were						
Black		22.6	20.6	17.9	16.8	16.5
Hispanic		—	11.9	17.4	18.4	27.6
College graduation rate						
Percent of 25–29-year-olds reporting 4 or more years of college						
White	11.8	17.3	22.8	23.7	23.2	23.5
Nonwhite	5.4	10.0	15.4	15.2	16.7	18.1
Black	—	7.3	10.7	11.7	11.5	12.3

Sources: Rows 1–5 and 13–15 are from National Center for Education Statistics, *Youth Indicators, 1988,* p. 52, and *Digest of Education Statistics 1990,* pp. 18–19. Rows 6–12 are from Mary J. Frase, "Dropout Rates in the United States, 1988" (Washington: National Center for Education Statistics, NCES 89-609, 1989), tables A4 and A5. I made the estimates for non-Hispanic whites, Asians, and Native Americans by subtracting blacks and Hispanics from the total population. In 1980, 2.7 percent of all Hispanics classified themselves as black (*1980 Census of Population: General Social and Economic Characteristics, United States Summary,* PC80-1-C1 (1983), table 75). My estimates exclude these individuals twice.

Parental education of dropouts. Advocates of the underclass hypothesis often argue that while the overall black dropout rate may have declined, that is because the black middle class has grown. Poor blacks, they say, are even worse off than they used to be.

Table 5.8 tests this hypothesis using data collected by the General Social Survey (GSS) between 1972 and 1989. The top half of the table shows dropout rates for blacks and whites whose parents had different amounts of schooling.

- The dropout rate declined more among children whose parents had not completed high school than among children with better-educated parents.

- The dropout rate declined more among blacks than among whites whose parents had the same amount of schooling.

- The dropout rate among blacks whose parents had not completed high school declined less after 1970 than in earlier decades. Indeed, their apparent gains after 1970 could be due to sampling error ($p = .06$). But there is no evidence that disadvantaged black children did *worse* after 1970 than in earlier decades. Nor did the gap between disadvantaged and advantaged black children widen after 1970.

- The dropout rate for white children whose parents had not completed high school may have risen slightly after 1970, although this too could be sampling error ($p = .06$).

Trends in high-school graduation rates could be misleading if family background were exerting more influence on high-school graduates' chances of attending college. To see if this is a problem, the bottom half of Table 5.8 uses parental education to predict the total number of years of school or college that GSS respondents completed. Among whites, each extra year of parental schooling yielded an extra 0.33 years of schooling for their children. This relationship hardly changed between 1940 and 1982.[50] In the 1940s, an extra year of parental education had about the same impact on black and white children. After 1950, however, disadvantaged black children made bigger gains than either advantaged black children or white children. As a result, the effect of parental education on black children's attainment declined steadily. Among teenagers who finished high school during the 1970s or early 1980s, an extra year of parental education had only two thirds as much effect on blacks as on whites.[51]

Table 5.8 Effects of Parental Education on Children's Educational Attainment, by Race and Decade of Expected High School Graduation

Race and schooling	1940–49	1950–59	1960–69	1970–82
Percent not completing high school, by father's (or mother's) race and schooling				
White				
No high school	38.0	29.8	23.3	26.5
Some high school	23.2	17.1	13.9	17.4
High-school graduate	14.7	12.7	5.6	6.6
Attended college	6.7	4.5	2.4	2.6
Total	29.1	20.6	11.9	10.6
Black				
No high school	64.5	49.2	28.5	25.0
Some high school	41.0	26.5	29.5	18.9
High-school graduate	46.5	26.0	11.2	11.3
Attended college	22.7	17.2	7.2	6.3
Total	56.7	39.1	22.6	16.7
Regression of child's schooling on father's (or mother's) schooling				
Whites				
Regression coefficient	.326	.315	.324	.315
(Standard error)	(.014)	(.013)	(.010)	(.012)
Constant	9.445	9.788	10.016	9.778
R^2	.166	.179	.209	.220
Blacks				
Regression coefficient	.331	.260	.214	.199
(Standard error)	(.044)	(.033)	(.026)	(.024)
Constant	7.861	9.631	10.831	10.893
R^2	.142	.125	.104	.121

Source: General Social Survey, Cumulative File, 1972–1989. The dependent variable is the number of years of school completed by respondents over the age of 25 who were surveyed between 1972 and 1989. The independent variable is the education of the man who headed the respondent's family at age 15, or, when that is not available, the education of the woman who headed the respondent's household at age 15. Neither item is available for 12.7 percent of the sample. The white sample sizes for the cells of the top panel all exceed 275. The black sample sizes are as follows (by educational level): 1940–49 = 231/39/43/22; 1950–59 = 244/68/73/29; 1960–69 = 260/122/116/69; 1970–82 = 168/106/150/79. Among students who reached the age of 17 between 1970 and 1982, in other words, there were 168 black respondents whose father (or mother) had not attended high school and 79 whose father (or mother) had attended college.

The declining effect of family background on black educational attainment is precisely the opposite of what the underclass hypothesis predicts. Why class background counts for less among today's blacks than among today's whites or yesterday's blacks remains a puzzle.

Geographic distribution of dropouts. Mark Hughes examined the geographic distribution of dropouts in the eight metropolitan areas discussed earlier. He found that the proportion of sixteen- to nineteen-year-olds who had left high school without graduating fell from 22 percent in 1970 to 16 percent in 1980. The absolute decline was greatest in tracts with high initial rates. Thus, if we are concerned with the social consequences of dropping out, there was more improvement in underclass areas. The proportional decline was greatest in tracts with low dropout rates, however, so a larger fraction of young dropouts lived in bad neighborhoods in 1980 than in 1970.[52]

Cognitive skills. Just as everyone knows that dropout rates have risen in inner-city schools, so too everyone knows that academic standards have fallen. News stories about illiterate inner-city valedictorians reinforce this conviction, and so does the widely reported decline in SAT scores. SAT scores are not very useful for estimating the size of the educational underclass, however, because students do not take the SAT unless they plan to attend college. If we want to know whether high schools are losing the battle with illiteracy, we need data on *all* high-school students, not just the college-bound. The National Assessment of Educational Progress (NAEP), begun in 1970, is the best source of such data.

Table 5.9 shows the percentage of seventeen-year-old high-school students reading at various levels. More than half of all nine-year-olds can read at what NAEP calls the basic level.[53] A teenager who cannot read at this level comes close to being illiterate in the traditional sense of the term. Yet 18 percent of the black seventeen-year-olds who were still in school and 2 percent of the whites could not read at this level in 1971. By 1988 all but 2.9 percent of the blacks and 0.5 percent of the whites could read at the basic level. The proportion unable to read at what NAEP calls the intermediate level had also fallen (from 60 to 24 percent among blacks and from 16 to 11 percent among whites).[54]

NAEP did not test seventeen-year-olds who had left school until the late 1970s, and it still excludes dropouts from trend statistics. As a result, Table 5.9 overstates the percentage of all seventeen-year-olds who can read at any given level. The proportion of black seventeen-year-olds who were not in school fell between 1970–71 and 1987–88.[55] It

Table 5.9   Percent of 17-Year-Old High School Students Reading at or above
Selected Levels, by Race, 1970–1988

Reading skill level	1970–71	1974–75	1979–80	1983–84	1987–88
"Basic"					
White	97.7	98.6	99.1	99.1	99.5
Black	82.0	81.1	84.9	95.8	97.1
"Intermediate"					
White	83.5	86.1	87.3	87.9	89.3
Black	39.7	42.4	43.9	66.0	76.0
"Adept"					
White	43.3	44.0	44.1	46.3	46.3
Black	7.5	7.9	6.7	16.3	25.8
"Advanced"					
White	7.5	7.0	6.3	6.5	5.7
Black	.3	.3	.2	.9	1.9

Source: Ina Mullis and Lunn Jenkins, *The Reading Report Card, 1971–88* (Princeton:
Educational Testing Service, 1990), pp. 63–64.

Table 5.10   Percent of 17-Year-Old High School Students with Math Skills at or
above Selected Levels, by Race, 1970–1988

Math skill level	1977–78	1981–82	1985–86
"Basic Operations and Beginning Problem Solving"			
White	95.8	96.3	98.3
Black	70.0	75.3	86.0
"Moderately Complex Procedures and Reasoning"			
White	57.3	54.5	58.0
Black	18.0	17.3	21.7
"Multi-Step Problem Solving and Algebra"			
White	8.6	6.3	7.6
Black	.4	.6	.3

Source: John Dossey, Ina Mullis, Mary Lindquist, and Donald Chambers, *The Mathematics
Report Card* (Princeton: Educational Testing Service, 1988), pp. 141–142.

follows that seventeen-year-old blacks' reading scores probably improved even more than the table implies.[56]

The first NAEP mathematics tests were administered in 1972–73,
but the results are not available in the form shown in Table 5.10. Ques-
tion-by-question comparisons show little change between 1973 and

1978, however, so trends from 1978 to 1986 are probably good indicators of trends from 1973 to 1986. There is not much improvement in whites' skills during this period, but the proportion of blacks who could do basic mathematical operations rose sharply.

Social background and reading skills. NAEP also reports trend data for students whose parents had different amounts of education. Among those whose parents had not completed high school, the proportion reading at the basic or intermediate level rose, while the proportion reading at the adept or advanced level fell. This same pattern of homogenization recurs among seventeen-year-olds with college-educated parents, although the changes are smaller. These findings lead me to two conclusions:

- The performance of the worst readers improved between 1971 and 1988, regardless of family background. The biggest gains were made by children whose parents had very little education, presumably because they were the worst off to begin with.

- The performance of the best readers, which looks roughly stable in Table 5.9, deteriorated when we hold parental education constant. This could mean that parents with college (or high-school) diplomas were a less elite group in 1988 than in 1971. Or it could mean that schools did less to challenge good readers in the 1980s than they had done earlier.

Since both children of high-school dropouts and children of blacks improved their performance during this period, it would be astonishing if the children of black dropouts had not improved. The inference that black children whose parents had very little education were making significant gains during these years is also consistent with Table 5.8, which shows that the children of black dropouts stayed in school somewhat longer after 1970 than before.

Geographic distribution of reading gains. Lyle Jones used NAEP data to analyze trends in reading scores among blacks in poor inner-city schools. He found that the reading scores of black seventeen-year-olds in these schools rose substantially between 1971 and 1984.[57] These findings are obviously at odds with the widespread view that inner-city schools have deteriorated over the past generation. But the conflict between Jones's findings and the conventional wisdom may be more apparent than real. Despite sizable gains, blacks still do far worse than whites on reading and math tests. This means that when a predominantly white school becomes predominantly black, as many inner-city schools have, its reading scores are likely to fall. Our concern here, however, is not with the fate of specific schools but with the fate of demographic groups. That means we need to compare schools that were already all black or Hispanic in 1970 to similar schools today. Jones's data suggest that if we make this kind of comparison, test scores went up, not down. The widespread conviction that inner-city schools got worse may also reflect a revolution of rising expectations about what schools serving poor nonwhites should be able to accomplish.

Inequality and the educational underclass. The skills an individual needs to get a steady job, understand a tax form, or put together a "partially assembled" item from a mail-order catalogue are not fixed for all time. Nor do they depend on some impersonal technological imperative. They depend on the skills that other members of the society have. When most people are illiterate, society organizes itself on that assumption. Work is arranged so that very few workers have to read instructions, taxes are levied on the assumption that ordinary citizens cannot be expected to fill out forms, and Sears does not sell items that only a Swiss watchmaker can put together. When most people can read relatively complicated material, society reorganizes itself to take advantage of this fact, and those who cannot read such material are left behind.

It follows that if most citizens improve their reading and math skills a lot, while the least adept improve only a little, the least adept may become more of an underclass, even if they are more skillful than their counterparts were a generation earlier. Likewise, if college graduation replaces high-school graduation as the normal level of educational attainment, the fact that more youngsters are finishing high school may not be enough to prevent the growth of an underclass. Reducing the size of the educational underclass may, in short, depend not just on raising the competence of those at the bottom but on making competence more equal.

The available evidence suggests that even by this demanding standard America made progress between 1970 and 1988. Table 5.7, for example, shows college graduation rates among twenty-five- to twenty-nine-year-olds in various years. Both black and white college graduation rates leveled off around 1970. Since black high-school dropout rates declined a lot after 1970, and white dropout rates declined a little, inequality in years of schooling declined.

The same pattern holds for reading skills of seventeen-year-olds.

Table 5.9 shows that the number of "advanced" white readers declined slightly between 1971 and 1988, which is what we would expect given the decline in SAT verbal scores. The number of "advanced" black readers rose, but even among blacks the proportion of good readers grew less than the proportion of poor ones fell. As a result, the distribution of reading skills among seventeen-year-olds was more equal in 1988 than in 1971.[58]

The Violent Underclass

Journalists, politicians, cab drivers, and graduate students are all convinced that violent crime has increased over the past generation, especially in poor black areas. Indeed, one reason the underclass hypothesis appeals to many Americans is that it seems to explain the breakdown of law and order in these areas.

The federal government collects three kinds of statistics on the level of violence in the United States. The National Center for Health Statistics (NCHS) uses statistics provided by state and local health departments to estimate the proportion of individuals murdered each year. The Bureau of Justice Statistics uses the Census Bureau's on-going victimization survey to estimate the number of individuals who were raped, robbed, or assaulted in a given year. And the Federal Bureau of Investigation (FBI) uses data provided by state and local police departments to estimate the number of violent crimes "known to the police." I will take up these three sources of evidence in turn.

Homicide. Homicide rates have several advantages as indicators of the overall level of violence.[59] Unlike other forms of violence, homicide is relatively easy to define and hard to conceal. When a husband assaults his wife, neither she nor anyone else is likely to report the incident either to the police or to a victimization survey. If he kills her, her death will almost always be discovered, and the fact that she was murdered will usually be obvious even if the identity of the killer remains uncertain. The same logic often applies to violence between strangers. If two teenage gangs get in a fight, they usually try to conceal it. If one of the teenagers is killed, the others may want to conceal the fact, but they are unlikely to succeed. Furthermore, the incentives to conceal homicides have been fairly stable over time. Thus there is no obvious reason for supposing that the authorities' chances of detecting a homicide have changed.

Table 5.11 Murder Rate per 100,000 Persons, by Race, Sex, and Age, 1950–1988

Population	1950	1960	1965	1970	1975	1980	1985	1988
Total	5.2	4.7	5.5	8.3	10.0	10.7	8.3	9.0
Whites								
Male	3.8	3.6	4.4	6.8	9.1	10.9	8.2	7.9
Female	1.4	1.4	1.6	2.1	2.9	3.2	2.9	2.9
Blacks								
Male	47.3	36.6	n.a.	67.6	69.6	66.6	48.4	58.0
Female	11.5	10.4	n.a.	13.3	15.1	13.5	11.0	13.2
Black males								
Age 15–24	58.9	46.4	n.a.	102.5	n.a.	84.3	66.1	101.8
Age 25–34	110.5	92.0	n.a.	158.5	n.a.	145.1	94.3	108.8
Age 35–44	83.7	77.5	n.a.	126.2	n.a.	110.3	76.3	79.2
Age 45–54	54.6	54.8	n.a.	100.5	n.a.	83.8	51.1	45.2
Age 55–64	35.7	31.8	n.a.	59.8	n.a.	55.6	37.8	29.1

Note: Rates include deaths from executions as well as murder, but the effect of this is trivial. The data come from National Center for Health Statistics, *Health United States, 1990*, table 34, and *Statistical Abstract of the United States, 1979*, p. 181.

Table 5.11 shows NCHS estimates of the homicide rate from 1950 to 1987. Homicides declined slightly during the 1950s, rose dramatically during the 1960s, rose more moderately during the 1970s, and fell during the early 1980s. The 1988 rate was only 5 percent higher than the 1970 rate. FBI estimates suggest that the overall murder rate rose another 4 percent in 1989.[60] Nonetheless, the 1989 rate was below the 1980 rate and only slightly above the 1970 rate. The rough stability of the overall homicide rate since 1970 could, of course, conceal an increase among nonwhites offset by a decline among whites. But Table 5.11 shows precisely the opposite pattern. The white homicide rate rose during the 1970s, while the black rate remained constant. After 1980, both the black and white rates declined sharply. (NCHS does not report separate rates for Hispanics.)

The crack cocaine epidemic became national news in 1986. Both the police and the news media believe that crack unleashed an unprecedented wave of violence in poor neighborhoods. Table 5.11 suggests, however, that this increase in lethal violence was confined to black men between the ages of fifteen and twenty-four, whose chances of dying violently rose by more than 50 percent between 1985 and 1987. Homicide rates did not increase systematically among older black men, and they declined among white men. Since selling crack is mostly an adolescent occupation, the fact that homicides increased mainly among fifteen- to twenty-four-year-olds is not surprising.

Table 5.11 shows the race of homicide victims, not that of murderers. If the violent black underclass mostly murdered whites, its growth might not have had much impact on blacks' chances of dying violently. In reality, however, about 90 percent of those arrested for murder are of the same race as their alleged victim. Furthermore, while the proportion of interracial murders appears to have increased slightly since 1976, when the FBI first reported such data, the change has not been large.[61] Changes in the race of homicide victims therefore provide a fairly reliable index of changes in the race of murderers.

Robbery and aggravated assault. The Census Bureau began its National Crime Survey (NCS) in 1973. Every month the NCS asks roughly 8000 teenagers and adults whether they have been victims of various crimes during the previous six months. The Bureau of Justice Statistics (BJS) uses these data to estimate the number of persons over the age of twelve who were raped, robbed, and assaulted each year. There are too few rapes for the NCS to yield reliable data about their frequency. But

Table 5.12 Aggravated Assault and Robbery Rates per 100,000 Persons, by Race of Assailant and Year

Assault/Robbery	1973–75	1976–78	1979–81	1982–84	1985–86	1987–89
Aggravated assaults	792	792	782	712	656	677
White assailant	515	531	532	470	427	NA
Black assailant	226	198	188	185	168	NA
Other, mixed, or unknown assailants	63	65	66	57	61	NA
Robberies	544	498	549	511	415	432
White assailant	180	204	198	179	158	NA
Black assailant	305	239	285	276	208	NA
Other, mixed, or unknown assailants	60	55	66	56	49	NA
FBI estimate of murder rate	9.6	8.9	9.9	8.3	8.3	8.5

Sources: All rates are numbers of victims per 100,000 persons (including children). The population estimates and the estimates of the number of aggravated assaults and robberies for 1973 through 1986 are taken from U.S. Bureau of Justice Statistics, *Sourcebook of Criminal Justice Statistics, 1988* (Government Printing Office, 1989), pp. 283 and 427. The 1987 and 1988 victimization estimates are from Bureau of Justice Statistics, "Bulletin: Criminal Victimization, 1988" (Washington, 1989). The proportions of offenses committed by whites, blacks, and others in the relevant year were estimated from Bureau of Justice Statistics, *Criminal Victimization in the United States*, issued annually. The estimated racial mix of assailants combines data on offenses involving a single assailant and offenses involving multiple assailants. The category "other, mixed, or unknown" includes offenses in which the victim reported that the assailant was neither white nor black, that the assailant's race was impossible to determine, or that there were several assailants of different races. Offenses committed by white, black, and other assailants may not add to the total number of offenses because of rounding error. The number of murders known to the police is taken from FBI data (*Sourcebook of Criminal Justice Statistics, 1988*, p. 427, and Federal Bureau of Investigation, *Crime in the United States, 1988*, p. 9).

if murder data are reliable indicator of long-term trends in violence, as I have argued, the NCS should find much the same trend for robbery and aggravated assault between 1973 and 1988 that NCHS finds for homicide.[62]

Table 5.12 shows how the aggravated assault and robbery rates changed from 1973 to 1988, pooling adjacent years to minimize the effects of sampling error. For comparison, it also shows the FBI estimate of the murder rate in these years.[63] There was no clear trend in murder, aggravated assault, or robbery from 1973–1975 through 1979–1981. After 1981 all three forms of violence declined significantly. In 1987–88 both the murder and aggravated assault rates were 14 percent lower than they had been in 1973–1975, and the robbery rate was 21 percent lower.[64]

Table 5.12 also estimates the likelihood of being assaulted or robbed by offenders of different races. The risk of being assaulted or robbed by a black person fell fairly steadily from 1973 to 1986. If black violence has increased since 1973, the victims have not noticed it.

The Census Bureau's victimization surveys tell the same story as the NCHS and FBI estimates of homicide. Taken together, these data suggest five conclusions:

- Violence increased dramatically among both blacks and whites between about 1964 and 1974.

- Violence declined significantly among both blacks and whites after 1980.

- Violence increased again among fifteen- to twenty-four-year-old blacks from 1985 to 1988, but it did not increase much for other groups.

- Blacks are still far more likely than whites to engage in murder, aggravated assault, and robbery.

- Nonetheless, both the absolute and the proportional difference between black and white levels of violence declined between 1970 and 1987.

Police estimates of violent crime. Every year most local police departments try to count the number of crimes committed within their jurisdiction. Such estimates get a lot of attention from the local news media. Most police departments also forward their estimates to the FBI, which uses them to estimate the national crime rate. These FBI statistics suggest that violent crime rose by a factor of four between 1960 and 1988. They also suggest that while the increase slowed after 1980, it did not stop. Since the FBI estimates have helped shape both popular and scholarly beliefs about crime, it is important to understand how they are generated and why they are misleading.

The FBI index of violent crime (which is also widely used by local police departments) is the unweighted sum of the number of murders, rapes, robberies, and aggravated assaults occurring in a given year. Since murder and rape are relatively rare, trends in this index depend largely on trends in robbery and aggravated assault. In order to be included in the FBI count, a robbery or aggravated assault must come to the attention of the police, either because someone reports it or because the police see it occurring. The police must then investigate, conclude that a crime really occurred, and record the allegation as "founded" rather than "unfounded."

FBI estimates of robbery and aggravated assault differ from estimates based on victimization surveys for two main reasons. First, citizens do not report every robbery or aggravated assault to the police. Second, the police do not record all the crimes that citizens report. The NCS asks robbery and assault victims whether they reported the crime to the police. Victims were slightly more likely to report robberies and assaults in the late 1980s than in the early 1970s, but the change was not large.[65] NCS and FBI estimates of change over time appear to differ mainly because local police departments have changed the way they handle victims' complaints.

NCS data imply, for example, that citizens reported about 565,000 robberies to the police in 1973. The police reported about two thirds that number of robberies to the FBI. By 1987, NCS data indicate that a larger population reported about 578,000 robberies to the police. The police, however, reported 90 percent of these robberies to the FBI. Much the same story recurs for aggravated assault. In 1973, citizens reported twice as many aggravated assaults to the police as the police reported to the FBI. By 1987, citizens reported only 8 percent more aggravated assaults to the police than the police reported to the FBI.[66]

The reason for these changes in police reporting practice is not obscure. The Justice Department initiated the NCS in response to a widespread belief that local police departments were recording far fewer crimes than really occurred. The first NCS confirmed this suspicion. Partly as a result, the Justice Department spent a lot of money helping local departments improve their record keeping. Records were computerized, completing each record became a higher priority, and police officers spent more time on paperwork. As a result, most local police departments recorded big increases in most crimes. The exception was homicide, which was already well recorded.

The contrast between FBI and NCS estimates of trends in violent crime also raises serious doubts about FBI estimates of violent crime before 1973. The question is not whether the FBI estimates were too low—everyone agrees that that was the case—but whether the FBI overestimated the *increase* in crime between 1960 and 1973. The FBI's index of violent crime rose 159 percent between 1960 and 1973. The FBI's estimate of the murder rate rose only 84 percent during this period. This contrast suggests that some police departments were improving their record-keeping arrangements for nonlethal crime between 1960 and 1973.

The moral of this story seems clear. If we want to understand trends in violence, we should ignore local police estimates of nonlethal crime and rely instead on murder statistics and victimization surveys. These two measures offer no support for the hypothesis that violence in general or black violence in particular has become appreciably more common since the early 1970s. On the contrary, they suggest that violence has declined somewhat.

Who commits violent crimes? While violence was less common in America in the late 1980s than it had been in 1980 and hardly more common than in 1970, violence could conceivably have increased among members of the underclass while declining among more advantaged groups. Unfortunately, we have no reliable data on changes in the economic background of violent criminals.

Violence could also have increased in poor inner-city neighborhoods while declining elsewhere. It should be possible to test this hypothesis using data from victimization surveys, but BJS does not report victimization rates for census tracts with different characteristics.[67] Most big-city police departments report homicides by geographic area, but so far as I know, nobody has used these data to see whether homicide rose faster in poor neighborhoods than in rich ones after 1970.

Drug-related violence did increase dramatically in some poor nonwhite neighborhoods during the late 1980s. But turf wars among drug dealers do not necessarily imply any change in the size of the criminal underclass. When new drug markets open up, as the market for crack did in the late 1980s, the hierarchy that controls the trade is likely to be disrupted and violence is likely to increase. In due course, a new hierarchy is likely to emerge, and drug-related violence is likely to decline. We should not mistake changes of this kind for changes in the underlying class structure of American society.

Age and crime. Men between the ages of fifteen and twenty-four are about three times as likely as men over twenty-five to be arrested for violent crimes. Thus, when the proportion of men between the ages of fifteen and twenty-four increases, as it did during the 1960s, violent crime is likely to increase. When the proportion of fifteen- to twenty-four-year-olds declines, as it did in the 1980s, violent crime is likely to decline. But while demographic change certainly contributed to increased violence between 1964 and 1974 and reduced violence after 1980, age-specific crime rates also changed in both periods.

Among men over the age of fifteen, the fraction who were under the age of twenty-four rose from 19.7 percent in 1960 to 25.3 percent in 1975 and then fell back to 20.1 percent in 1987.[68] If age-specific rates of violence had remained constant, and if they were three times as high for fifteen- to twenty-four-year-olds as for older men and women, violent crime would have risen about 8 percent between 1960 and 1975 and would then have fallen about 7 percent between 1975 and 1987.[69]

Judging by the homicide rate, violence actually increased by more than 100 percent between 1960 and 1975. Changes in age-specific rates of violence therefore appear to have accounted for something like 92 percent of this change. Homicide and aggravated assault fell 14 percent between 1973–1975 and 1987–1988, while robbery fell 21 percent. Declines in the proportion of men between the ages of fifteen and twenty-four could account for between one third and one half of this change. The rest must have been due to declines in age-specific rates of violence.

Demographic changes may, however, also affect age-specific rates of violence. When the baby boomers reached adolescence, their sheer numbers may have shifted the balance of power between those who supported authority and those who resisted it. This shift may have made angry young men readier to express their feelings in violent ways. The graying of the baby boomers after 1980 may, in turn, have made violence less socially acceptable.

Incarceration and crime. The likelihood that violence will lead to imprisonment has also changed. Changes in the murder rate suggest that violent crime rates doubled between 1950 and 1975. Yet the fraction of the nation's population in federal and state prisons hardly changed during these years, averaging 0.11 percent.[70] Assuming that violent felons accounted for about the same fraction of the prison population in both years, the time served per offense must have fallen by about half.[71]

The prison population began to rise after 1975, largely because sentences became longer. By 1980, 0.14 percent of the population was in state or federal prisons, and by 1987 the proportion had reached 0.23 percent. Since violent crime rates did not increase between 1975 and 1987—indeed, they fell somewhat—the time served per offense must have more than doubled (although the great majority of violent offenders still served no time at all).

Changes in the prison population can affect the incidence of violent crime in three ways. First, incarceration obviously prevents inmates from murdering, raping, robbing, or assaulting noninmates. A panel convened by the National Academy of Sciences estimated that because of this "incapacitation effect," doubling the prison population might reduce the crime rate by about 10 percent.[72] Second, serving time in prison puts a violent offender in touch with many other violent offenders, while also making it harder to find a legitimate job after release. As a result, imprisonment may increase the number of crimes that felons commit after they are released. Third, increasing the time violent criminals can expect to spend behind bars is likely to have some effect on the number of offenses they commit. The magnitude of this deterrent effect is uncertain and controversial.

Whatever the cause, violence shows no clear trend since the early 1970s. Indeed, the black homicide rate was about the same in 1985 as in 1950. Robberies and aggravated assaults involving black assailants were less common in 1987–1988 than they had been in 1973 when the NCS began. These facts do not quite suffice to prove that the violent underclass was getting smaller, but they certainly do not support the commonplace view that it has grown.

The Reproductive Underclass

Middle-class Americans have always believed that adults should refrain from having children unless they can care for them properly. Until the 1960s this general principle led most Americans to espouse three norms regarding childbearing:

Couples were not supposed to have children unless they were prepared to get married. Conceiving a child out of wedlock was viewed as irresponsible. Not marrying before the child was born was even more irresponsible.

Couples were not supposed to have children unless the prospective father could support them. Since teenage boys could seldom earn enough to support a family, teenage fatherhood was irresponsible. Teenage motherhood was acceptable so long as the father was old enough to support a family.

Couples with modest incomes were supposed to limit their fertility. This norm was never generally accepted by the working or lower classes. Children had been an economic asset on farms. Small families became advantageous once America became an urban nation, but this fact did not become widely understood for several generations.

After 1960, these three norms changed in important ways. American women cut their fertility in half, so we stopped worrying about married couples having too many children. College enrollments soared, so we began to think of adolescence as continuing until people were in their early twenties and became increasingly dubious about teenage girls' readiness for parenthood. Concern about teenage motherhood ("children having children") was exacerbated by the fact that fewer teenage mothers had sexual partners old enough to marry and support them. And while Americans continued to believe that children were better off when they lived with both their natural parents, we became considerably more tolerant of unwed motherhood than we had been earlier in the century.

As a result of these changes, America entered the 1980s with only two widely accepted norms about parenthood:

- Adults should not have children until they are in their twenties.

- Parents should not have children out of wedlock unless they can support them, and probably not even then.

The reproductive underclass is composed of couples who violate these behavioral norms. Almost everyone assumes that such violations have become more common. In reality, however, teenage motherhood has become less common, teenage fatherhood remains rare, and out-of-wedlock births have increased only a little. The big change is that married couples are having far fewer children.

Teenage parenthood. There was a lot of talk during the 1980s about an epidemic of teenage childbearing in urban ghettos. In reality, however, teenage girls were having fewer babies than at any time since 1940. Black teenagers were having more babies than white teenagers, but the gap was narrowing rather than widening. Table 5.13 shows that back in 1960 a representative sample of 100 black girls would have had 80 babies by the time they reached the age of twenty. In the mid-1980s they would have had only 51 babies. Among whites, the number fell from 40 to 21.[73]

Most teenage mothers become pregnant by older men. As a result, teenage fatherhood has never been as common as teenage motherhood. In 1986, for example, only 1.9 percent of fifteen- to nineteen-year-old boys became parents, compared to 5.1 percent of girls that

Table 5.13 Expected Fertility by Age, Marital Status, Race, and Sex, 1960–1986

Births	1960	1965	1970	1975	1980	1986
Children born prior to age 20 per 100 persons						
White women	40	30	29	24	23	21
Black women	80	74	73	58	52	51
White men	9	8	11	9	8	7
Black men	22[a]	23[a]	29	23	20	21
Percent of lifetime births prior to age 20						
White women	11.3	10.8	12.1	14.2	13.1	12.1
Black women	17.6	19.3	23.5	25.9	22.9	22.9
White men	2.6	2.8	3.9	4.3	3.6	3.4
Black men	4.0[a]	4.8[a]	6.8	6.9	6.0	7.0
Out-of-wedlock births as percent of all births to women aged 15 to 19						
White	n.a.	n.a.	17.1	22.9	33.0	48.1
Black	n.a.	n.a.	62.7	76.9	85.2	90.0

Source: National Center for Health Statistics, *Vital Statistics of the United States, 1986, Vol. 1—Natality* (Government Printing Office, 1988), tables 1-6 and 1-7.

a. Estimated from data on all nonwhites, on the assumption that the fertility of black 15-to-19 year-old males increased at the same rate between 1960 and 1970 as the fertility of nonwhite 15-to-19-year-old males.

age. The age difference between teenage mothers and their sexual partners appears to be diminishing, however. In 1960, there were four times as many teenage mothers as teenage fathers. By 1986, there were less than three times as many.[74]

Teenage boys have never been able to earn enough to support a family, so they have seldom married.[75] When teenage girls started dating younger men, therefore, two changes occurred: fewer teenage girls had babies, but when they did, they were less likely to marry before the baby's birth (see rows 9 and 10 of Table 5.13).

The first big drop in teenage girls' fertility came between 1960 and 1965, when oral contraceptives were introduced and other forms of contraception became more readily available. The second big drop came between 1970 and 1975, when abortion became legal. The proportion of teenage pregnancies ended by abortion continued to rise after 1975, so the number of live births to teenagers continued to fall in the late 1970s.[76]

Births to teenagers are seldom intentional, whereas births to adults often are. If all else were equal, therefore, improvements in contraception and easier access to abortion should have lowered teenage fertility more than adult fertility. Between 1960 and 1975, however, adult fertility fell not just because contraception and abortion became more available but also because adults wanted fewer children. Since teenagers seldom wanted children even in 1960, the gap between teenage and adult preferences narrowed, and teenagers accounted for a rising fraction of all births.

After 1975, adult fertility leveled off, while teenage fertility continued to fall. As a result, the proportion of all babies born to teenagers began to fall. This decline was apparent among boys as well as girls, and among blacks as well as whites.

I have not been able to find trend data on births to poor teenagers or on births to teenagers in poor neighborhoods. But it is hard to see how births to black teenagers could have fallen by 37 percent between 1960 and 1986 if the decline were confined to affluent blacks.

Out-of-wedlock births. Unlike teenagers, unmarried adults are having more babies. The best (though not the most common) way of estimating trends in out-of-wedlock births is to ask how many children a woman could expect to have while unmarried if the age-specific birth rates observed in a given year persisted throughout her childbearing years. Table 5.14 shows that in 1960 the typical black woman could

Table 5.14 Expected Fertility by Marital Status, Race, and Sex, 1960–1987

Births	1960	1965	1970	1975	1980	1987
Expected lifetime births while unmarried						
White	.08	.11	.14	.12	.18	.29
Black	1.05	1.08	1.16	1.09	1.25	1.43
Expected lifetime births while married						
White	3.45	2.67	2.25	1.56	1.57	1.47
Black	3.49	2.75	1.93	1.15	1.01	.87
Total expected lifetime births						
White	3.53	2.78	2.39	1.69	1.75	1.77
Black	4.54	3.83	3.10	2.24	2.27	2.29
Births while unmarried as a percent of lifetime births						
White	2.3	4.0	5.7	7.3	10.2	16.7
Black	23.2	28.2	37.6	48.8	55.5	62.2

Source: National Center for Health Statistics, *Vital Statistics of the United States, 1987*, tables 1-6, 1-7, and 1-31. Expected births while married and unmarried assume that age-specific birth rates in the relevant year continue and that the percentage of births to unmarried women in that year continues. Expected births while married and unmarried may not add to total births because of rounding error. The ratio of marital to nonmarital births in 1960 and 1965 for blacks is estimated on the assumption that the trend from 1960 to 1969 was the same for blacks as for all nonwhites.

expect to have 1.05 out-of-wedlock births over her lifetime.[77] By 1987 the figure had risen to 1.42. The typical white woman could have expected 0.08 out-of-wedlock births over her lifetime in 1960 and 0.29 in 1987—a huge percentage increase but a small absolute increase.

These increases in out-of-wedlock childbearing would not have attracted much attention if married women had continued to have as many children as they had in 1960. In 1960, for example, a black woman could expect to have 3.49 children while she was married. Had black women continued to have that many children while married, the proportion of black babies born out of wedlock would only have risen from 23 percent in 1960 to 29 percent by 1987. A change of this kind would have passed almost unnoticed. In reality, however, births to married women plummeted, and the proportion of all black children born out of wedlock (which I will call the "illegitimacy ratio") rose from 23 to 62 percent. Among whites, it rose from 2 to 17 percent.[78]

These changes have probably had an adverse effect on children's life chances, but the effect has almost certainly been far smaller than most commentators assume. All else equal, growing up in a single-parent family is a handicap.[79] But having a lot of brothers and sisters is also a handicap, for many of the same economic and psychological reasons. Since unwed mothers have fewer children than mothers who marry, the adverse effect of unwed motherhood on children is likely to be quite small.[80]

Class differences in the spread of unwed motherhood. The illegitimacy ratio has risen in all strata of American society. The underclass hypothesis implies, however, that the increase was especially marked in the economic or educational underclass. I have not been able to find trend data on the economic background of unwed mothers, but Table 5.15 shows how the illegitimacy ratio has changed for women with different amounts of schooling.

- The illegitimacy ratio is much higher among blacks than among whites with the same amount of schooling. Among college graduates, for example, the illegitimacy ratio in 1986 was 2 percent for whites but 21 percent for blacks.

- Education also has a big effect on the illegitimacy ratio, regardless of race. Among black women the ratio in 1986 was 21 percent among college graduates compared to 83 percent among high-school dropouts. The corresponding figures for white women were 2 and 38 percent.

- The absolute increase in the illegitimacy ratio has been greater among blacks than among whites and greatest of all among blacks without high-school diplomas. This is consistent with the underclass hypothesis.

- The proportional increase has been greatest among whites without high-school diplomas. Their illegitimacy ratio increased by a factor of 4.3 between 1969 and 1986.

- College-educated whites are the only group that remains strongly committed to marrying before they have children. In 1986, 98 percent of the white college graduates who had babies were married.

Why has unwed motherhood become more acceptable? Wilson and Neckerman have argued that the two-parent family lost its appeal to blacks partly because fewer black men earned enough to support a family.[81] But as Chapter 4 showed, the decline in black marriage rates has been far too large for male joblessness alone to explain it.

Most conservatives believe that the generosity of the welfare system

Table 5.15 Percent of Women Having Children out of Wedlock and Percent of Women with Children under 18 Not Living with a Husband, by Education and Race, 1960 to 1987

Race and years of school	Percent of mothers unmarried when baby was born		Percent of female heads with children under 18 not living with husband			Percent of mothers with children under 18 not living with husband	
	1969	1986	1960 Census	1970 Census	1980 Census	1980 CPS	1987 CPS
White							
0 to 8	7.9	34.8	10.1	15.7	20.6	22.2	24.3
9 to 11	8.8	38.2	5.7	10.5	16.8	20.3	27.7
12	4.1	13.9	4.1	6.7	12.7	12.3	15.3
13 to 15	4.1	7.2	4.6	7.8	12.9	14.0	16.6
16 or more	1.2	2.2	4.9	5.5	8.9	9.0	11.0
Total	5.1	14.5	5.8	8.7	13.5	13.9	16.5
Black							
0 to 8	41.9	79.4	28.6	40.1	50.3	55.9	55.7
9 to 11	43.3	82.9	17.9	33.4	51.7	57.3	66.7
12	28.0	61.9	12.9	27.7	41.1	46.2	51.9
13 to 15	21.5	45.5	10.5	21.4	43.6	44.9	42.7
16 or more	6.6	20.8	14.3	18.4	20.7	29.8	28.3
Total	35.1	62.6	21.7	32.3	44.3	48.1	50.3

Sources: Columns 1 and 2 are from National Center for Health Statistics, *Vital Statistics of the United States, 1969*, table 1-69, and *Vital Statistics of the United States, 1986*, table 1-78. The 1969 data cover 31 states, while the 1986 data cover 47 states and District of Columbia. Totals include mothers whose education was unknown. These mothers' illegitimacy ratios typically fall between those of high school dropouts and high school graduates.

Columns 3 to 5 are from Census 1/1000 public use samples, while columns 6 and 7 are from March CPS samples. The female head of a family in which there is a child under 18 is not always the mother. Female heads are classified as not living with a husband if they are never married, separated, or divorced. This procedure leads to classification errors when the woman in question is the grandmother, aunt, or sister of the relevant children rather than their mother. In the Census data, all white percentages are based on cell sizes of more than 1000, while black percentages are based on samples of more than 500 except for women with 12 or more years of schooling in 1960, 13 or more in 1970, and 16 or more in 1980. The only Census cell with less than 100 cases is black college graduates in 1987. The CPS estimates for black college graduates in 1980 and 1987, and for blacks with less than 9 years of schooling in 1987 are based on 60 to 75 cases.

has contributed to the increase in unwed motherhood. The purchasing power of AFDC plus food stamps did rise between 1964 and 1976. But Table 5.14 shows that while births to married women fell during this period, out-of-wedlock births hardly increased at all. The number of out-of-wedlock births did rise after 1975, but by then real welfare benefits were falling. This history hardly suggests that raising benefits encourages out-of-wedlock births. Nor do unmarried women in high-benefit states have appreciably more babies than those in low-benefit states.[82] Welfare benefit levels do not, therefore, provide a very convincing explanation for the spread of unwed motherhood.

Yet changes in men and women's economic situations may have encouraged out-of-wedlock births indirectly, by altering broader cultural assumptions about relations between the sexes. The moral norm that a man should marry a woman if he has gotten her pregnant lost much of its force between 1960 and 1990. That norm rested on the assumption that since women could not support themselves or their children without male help, men had to assume economic responsibility for their children. As women's earning power rose, more of them were able to get along without male help. Most women who supported families without male help were highly skilled and had small families, but their existence still undermined the idea that marriage was the only way to keep children from going hungry. Wishful thinking did the rest.

Women's growing ability to control their own fertility may also have weakened men's feeling that they were morally obligated to marry a woman who was about to have their baby. When the pill replaced the condom as the contraceptive of choice, contraception was redefined as a woman's responsibility. When the Supreme Court legalized abortion and defined it as a procedure that only a woman could initiate, an even larger share of the responsibility for having a baby ended up in women's hands. If a woman can get a legal abortion but chooses not to, her boyfriend is unlikely to feel that her pregnancy is his responsibility and that he has an obligation to marry her (except, perhaps, when he is strongly opposed to abortion himself).

Improved contraception and abortion also lowered the economic cost of not marrying. In 1960, a sexually active woman could expect to have four or five children. Then as now, a woman with four or five children had almost no chance of earning enough to keep herself and her children out of poverty. By 1975, most married women had only two children and many unwed mothers had only one. A woman's chances of earning enough to avoid poverty were therefore considerably better, and her need for a husband was reduced. Knowing this, we may all have become more tolerant of men who decided not to marry a woman they had gotten pregnant.

Single parenthood. Up to this point I have implicitly accepted the traditional view that unwed parenthood is bad for children, and that society's ability to prevent out-of-wedlock births is a measure of its ability to protect the interests of the next generation. Some feminists reject this assumption on the grounds that women should not have to marry men in order to have babies. But if all else is equal, children surely benefit from having strong economic and emotional claims on two adults rather than just one. And on the average children raised by single mothers do somewhat worse on most measures of success than children raised by married couples.

But if our concern about unwed parenthood derives from its effect on children, we must worry not only about whether couples marry before they have children but also about whether they stay married after having children. It is not obvious that anyone benefits when teenagers who conceive a child out of wedlock marry for a year or two and then divorce—especially if, as often happens, they conceive a second child before divorcing. Divorced fathers tend to have somewhat stronger emotional and economic ties to their children than never-married fathers do. But neither group contributes much to the children's economic support, and neither is in a good position to give the children the supervision and attention they need.

While out-of-wedlock births are far more likely in lower-class than in middle-class families, divorce is more evenly distributed across social classes. This means that children's class backgrounds have far more impact on their chances of being born into a single-parent family than on their chances of living in such a family when they are teenagers. It also means that if we want to look at the class distribution of family breakdown, we need to consider not only out-of-wedlock births but the proportion of all children living with single mothers. Table 5.15 does this.

A woman's chance of having a child out of wedlock is lower than her chance of being a single mother later on. Only 6 percent of the white women who had babies in 1970 were unmarried, for example. Ten years later, 14 percent of white mothers with children under eighteen were unmarried. Among black women who had babies in 1970, 28 percent were unmarried. Ten years later, 48 percent of black mothers with children under eighteen were unmarried. Not only does the proportion of mothers who are unmarried increase as the children get older, but the absolute size of this increase is largely independent of the mother's education and race. It follows that the proportionate increase is much larger for groups with low illegitimacy ratios. (To verify this claim, the reader should compare the illegitimacy ratios for 1969 to the proportions of mothers with children under eighteen who were unmarried in 1980.)

Table 5.15 does not distinguish mothers who are still married to their child's father from those who have divorced and remarried. It therefore underestimates the degree to which children are exposed to marital disruption. But even if we had trend data on the proportion of children living with their natural father, we would surely find large class differences. We would probably also find that the absolute size of these differences had grown since the 1960s. Thus we would probably still conclude that the glue holding families together had weakened more in the underclass than in the middle class.

But while class differences in family structure have probably widened over the past generation, this trend may not continue, at least among blacks. Among black high-school dropouts, to take an extreme case, 83 percent of all babies were born out of wedlock in 1986. As a result, the illegitimacy ratio for black dropouts could not go much higher. Among black college dropouts, in contrast, the illegitimacy ratio was only 46 percent in 1986. That ratio could rise a lot, and past experience suggests that it will. If the trends that prevailed from 1969 to 1986 continue, something like 70 percent of black college dropouts who have babies in the year 2003 will be unmarried. If that were to happen, the gap between college dropouts and high-school dropouts would be somewhat smaller than it is today.

This point dramatizes the difficulties that arise when we think of family breakdown as a mark of membership in the underclass. The two-parent family is becoming less common at almost all levels of American society. Until now, the rate of change has been fastest in the underclass, but no group has been immune. The cost of the change has also been greatest for the underclass, because its members have fewer resources for coping with every form of adversity. In the long run, however, single parenthood will prove to be an American problem, not just an underclass problem.

Is the Underclass a Useful Idea?

Americans started talking about the underclass during the 1980s because they sensed that their society was becoming more unequal. The rich were getting richer, but the poor were as numerous as ever. Skilled professionals and business executives commanded ever higher salaries, but a growing fraction of working-age men had no job at all. At the same time, the fabric of lower-class society seemed to be unraveling. Poor couples were having more of their babies without marrying, and millions of single mothers were trying to live on welfare checks that paid less than the rich spent every year on vacations. Crime was rampant in many poor neighborhoods. Inner-city schools seemed unable to teach most of their students even basic skills. As a result, poor children no longer seemed to have much chance of escaping from poverty, as earlier generations had.

If all these problems had arisen more or less simultaneously, the claim that shinking economic opportunities were creating a new underclass would be hard to resist. In reality, however, while economic conditions began to deteriorate for less skilled workers in the 1970s, most of the other problems that led Americans to start talking about an underclass followed different trajectories. Some had been getting worse for a long time. Some had gotten worse between 1965 and 1975 but then leveled off. Some never got worse. Some were actually getting better. Thus, when we try to link changes in family structure, welfare use, school enrollment, academic achievement, or criminal violence to changes in economic opportunity, the connections prove elusive. To see why, it is helpful to compare the timing of changes in different areas.

Which problems have gotten steadily worse? Long-term joblessness is somewhat sensitive to the business cycle, but the underlying rate among twenty-five- to fifty-four-year-old men rose during both the 1970s and the 1980s.

The number of babies born to unmarried women did not rise much from 1960 to 1975, but the number of babies born to married women fell a lot, so the proportion of babies born out of wedlock rose. After 1975, the number of babies born to women while they were unmarried began to rise. Since divorce has also become more common, the fraction of women raising children without male help has risen steadily.

Which problems have stopped getting worse? While single motherhood increased steadily after 1960, the proportion of single mothers collecting welfare rose only between 1964 and 1974. After that, it began to decline again. As a result, the proportion of all mothers collecting welfare rose dramatically between 1964 and 1974 but then leveled off.

Violent crime doubled between 1964 and 1974, remained roughly constant during the late 1970s, declined significantly in the early 1980s, and edged up in the late 1980s. As a result, violence was somewhat less common in the late 1980s than in 1980 or 1970. This was especially true among blacks.

Which problems have gotten steadily better? Both non-Hispanic whites and blacks were more likely to earn a high-school diploma or GED certificate in the late 1980s than at any time in the past. The disparity between blacks and whites was also smaller. Improvements on these indices were, however, somewhat slower in the 1980s than in the 1960s or 1970s.

The proportion of seventeen-year-olds with basic reading skills rose steadily during the 1970s and 1980s, especially among blacks. The increase among whites was much smaller. Disparities between the best and worst readers, while still huge, diminished significantly. The proportion of seventeen-year-old blacks with basic math skills also rose during the 1980s.

Among blacks, educational attainment became less dependent on family background between 1940 and 1980. As a result, black children from disadvantaged backgrounds had better educational prospects in the 1980s than in 1970. Among whites, there was little change after 1970. I found no evidence on whether disadvantaged children's chances of growing up to be poor, jobless, or dependent on welfare have changed over time.

Which problems have stopped getting better? Teenage motherhood declined during the 1960s and 1970s. There was no clear trend during the 1980s. Teenage fatherhood rose during the 1960s, declined during the 1970s, and was roughly constant during the 1980s.

The proportion of individuals with family incomes below the poverty line, which had fallen steadily from 1940 to 1970, has not changed much since 1970. Only the character of poverty has changed. It has become less common among the elderly and more common among children. Poverty has also become more concentrated among families in which the head does not work regularly.

Which problems have I ignored? Drug use is a persistent problem, especially among the underclass. I have not discussed it because I have not been able to find any convincing quantitative evidence about the prevalence or severity of the problem. Surveys of high-school students show dramatic declines in almost all forms of drug use during the 1980s. Yet people who spend time in poor communities are convinced that drugs became a more serious problem during the 1980s. Both claims may be correct.

The trends I have described do not fit together in any simple or obvious way. Those who think that everything has gotten worse for people at the bottom of the social pyramid since 1970 are clearly wrong. Economic conditions have deteriorated for workers without higher education, and two-parent families have become scarcer, but welfare dependency has not increased since the early 1970s, and illiteracy, teenage motherhood, and violence have declined somewhat.

So far as I can see, the claim that America has a growing underclass does not help us understand complex changes of the kind I have described. On the contrary, arguments that use class as their central explanatory idea obscure what is going on. The reasons for this deserve brief discussion.

We use terms such as "middle class" and "underclass" because we know that occupation, income, educational credentials, cognitive skills, a criminal record, out-of-wedlock childbearing, and other personal characteristics are somewhat correlated with one another. Class labels provide a short-hand device for describing people who differ along many of these dimensions simultaneously. The term "middle class," for example, evokes someone who has attended college, holds a steady job, earns an adequate income, got married before having children, and has never murdered, raped, robbed, or assaulted anyone. The term "underclass," in contrast, conjures up a chronically jobless high-school dropout who has had two or three children out of wedlock, has very little money to support them, and probably has either a criminal record or a history of welfare dependence.

Relatively few people fit either of these stereotypes perfectly. Many people are middle class in some respects, working class in others, and underclass in still others. But those who use class labels always assume that everyone is a member of some class or other. In order to assign everyone to a class, they allow their classes to be internally heterogeneous. If they assign people to classes on the basis of how they make their living, they allow the members of these classes to differ with regard to income, educational credentials, cognitive skills, family structure, and arrest record. Everyone who stops to think recognizes that the world is untidy in this sense. We use class labels precisely because we want to make the world seem tidier than it is. The purpose of labels is to draw attention to the differences between classes. But by emphasizing differences between classes, such labels inevitably encourage us to forget about the much larger differences that exist *within* classes.

The illusion of class homogeneity does no harm in some contexts, but it encourages two kinds of logical error when we try to describe social change. First, whenever we observe an increase in behavior that has traditionally been correlated with membership in a particular class, we tend to assume that the class in question must be getting bigger. If more working-age men are jobless, we assume that the underclass must be getting bigger, without stopping to ask whether the men who have become jobless have other attributes that might make them part of the underclass. The second error is a mirror image of the first. Once we decide that a class is growing, we tend to assume that every form of behavior associated with membership in that class is becoming more common. Having concluded that the underclass is getting bigger, we assume that dropout rates, crime, and teenage parenthood must also be rising. The underlying logic here is that if one correlate of membership in the underclass is rising, all must be rising.

If we want to understand what is happening to those at the bottom of American society, we need to examine their problems one at a time, asking how each has changed and what has caused the change. Instead of assuming that the problems are closely linked to one another, we need to treat their interrelationships as a matter for empirical investigation. When we do that, the relationships are seldom as strong as class stereotypes lead us to expect. As a result, some problems can become more common while others become less so.

Exaggerating the correlations among social problems can have political costs as well. Portraying poverty, joblessness, illiteracy, violence, unwed motherhood, and drug abuse as symptoms of a larger meta-problem, such as the underclass, encourages people to look for meta-solutions. We are frequently told, for example, that piecemeal reform is pointless and that we need a comprehensive approach to the problems of the underclass. Some even believe we need a revolutionary change, although revolutions are so out of favor at the moment that few favor them publicly.

Our most pressing need, it seems to me, is for schools, employers, police forces, churches, health maintenance organizations, and welfare offices that can deal with poor people's problems in more realistic ways—ways that build on people's strengths without ignoring their weaknesses. Changes of this kind require an immense amount of trial and error. Unfortunately, America has never been very good at learning from its mistakes. Instead of looking for ways of improving our institutions, we tend to blame some politician for every failure and look for a replacement. Politicians therefore become specialists in avoiding blame, not in solving problems. This may be unavoidable in a large, diverse society. But if we cannot manage piecemeal reforms, looking for metasolutions is almost certain to be time wasted so far as the American underclass is concerned. If we want to reduce poverty, joblessness, illiteracy, violence, or despair, we will surely need to change our institutions and attitudes in hundreds of small ways, not in one big way.

= 6 =

Welfare

By Kathryn Edin and Christopher Jencks

T he Family Support Act of 1988, America's most recent effort at
welfare reform, is supposed to move single mothers off welfare
through a combination of job training, work requirements, childcare
subsidies, and child-support enforcement.[1] Cutting the welfare rolls is,
in turn, supposed to save the taxpayer money while enhancing the self-
respect of single mothers and their children. The main effects of the
Family Support Act will not become apparent until the mid-1990s.
Judging by the experience of states that have already established com-
pulsory training programs and work requirements, however, the act
will not save taxpayers much money. Nor will it move many single
mothers off the welfare rolls. The reason is simple: single mothers do
not turn to welfare because they are pathologically dependent on handouts or unusually reluctant to work—they do so because they cannot
get jobs that pay better than welfare. The new law will not do much to
change this fact.

Meanwhile, the nation's 3.7 million welfare families confront an ur-
gent problem: they do not get enough money from welfare to pay their
bills. Nor can most single mothers earn enough to pay the bills. Unless
they get a lot of help from a parent or boyfriend, the only way most
unskilled single mothers can keep their families together is to combine
work and welfare. Yet telling the welfare department they are working
will soon reduce their welfare check by almost the full amount of their
earnings, leaving them as poor as before.[2] The only way most welfare
recipients can make ends meet, therefore, is to supplement their welfare checks without telling the department.

Welfare benefits have always been low, but their purchasing power
has fallen steadily since the mid-1970s. Most people assume that, when

benefits fall, recipients just live more frugally. But low benefits have another, more sinister effect that neither conservatives nor liberals like to acknowledge: they force most welfare recipients to lie and cheat in order to survive. Conservatives ignore this problem because admitting that welfare recipients cannot survive without cheating would weaken the case for cutting benefits. Liberals ignore the problem because admitting that welfare recipients cheat for any reason whatever reduces public sympathy for their plight.

Yet welfare mothers operate on the same moral principles as most other Americans. They believe that their first obligation is to care for their children, and they assume this means providing food, shelter, heat, electricity, furniture, clothing, and an occasional treat. Since the welfare system seldom gives mothers who follow its rules enough money to pay for such necessities, they feel entitled to break the rules. Welfare mothers also feel that working ought to make them better off. Since the welfare system does not allow them to keep what they earn if they report their earnings, they feel entitled to ignore the reporting requirement.

We have, in short, created a welfare system whose rules have no moral legitimacy in recipients' eyes. This feeling is not confined to second-generation welfare recipients in poor neighborhoods—the so-called underclass. It is shared by mainstream women who have finished high school, held jobs, married, had children, and ended up on welfare only when their husbands left them. It is a feeling bred by a system whose rules are incompatible with everyday American morality, not by the peculiar characteristics of welfare recipients.

How Welfare Mothers Survive in Illinois

When we began studying the Illinois welfare system in 1988, Aid to Families with Dependent Children (AFDC) paid a single mother with one child and no outside income $250 per month. She also got $149 per month in food stamps, plus a Medicaid card that entitled her to free medical care and prescription drugs. Since food stamps are virtually the same as cash, a mother with one child ended up with $399 a month, or roughly $4800 per year. Her annual income (including food stamps) rose to $6700 if she had two children, $7900 if she had three, and $9300 if she had four. These benefit levels were 60 to 75 percent of the federal poverty line.

To see how families got by on so little money, Edin conducted intensive interviews with twenty-five welfare families in Cook County (which includes both Chicago and its nearby suburbs) during 1988 and with another twenty-five early in 1990. Previous experience suggested that if she simply drew a random sample of welfare recipients, went to their homes, and asked them to describe their income and expenditures, she would get a lot of refusals, a lot of evasion, and a lot of budgets that did not include enough income to cover the family's expenditures. She therefore took a different tack, asking acquaintances who knew welfare recipients in different capacities to introduce her to one or two recipients and tell them she was trustworthy.[3] All but nine of the fifty-nine mothers she contacted in this way agreed to be interviewed.[4]

Cook County is obviously not representative of the nation as a whole. Its AFDC benefit levels are close to the national average, but rents in Chicago, while lower than in New York or Los Angeles, are higher than in most small cities. Cook County probably has more subsidized housing than most smaller metropolitan areas, but much of this housing is extremely dangerous and many welfare mothers are unwilling to live in it.[5]

Because Edin used personal contacts to locate her sample, she could not make it perfectly representative of Cook County, and she did not try to do so.[6] Since 77 percent of Cook County recipients are black, she had to oversample white recipients in order to get enough whites for racial comparisons. Her final sample was 46 percent African American, 38 percent European, 10 percent Latin American, and 6 percent Asian. National figures are quite similar.[7] Because Edin oversampled whites, she also oversampled the Chicago suburbs relative to the city.[8] In order to maximize her chances of finding recipients who lived on what they got from the welfare department, she drew 44 percent of her sample from subsidized housing. In the nation as a whole, only 18 percent of all recipients live in subsidized housing.[9] Oversampling recipients in subsidized housing reduces the discrepancy between the rents her mothers paid and the rent that the average American welfare mother pays.

Not one of Edin's fifty mothers claimed that she lived exclusively on her welfare check, and only two even came close.[10] In this respect Edin's mothers are, as we shall see, much like welfare mothers in larger national samples. But unlike the welfare mothers interviewed in national surveys, almost all of Edin's mothers reported enough income, both legal and illegal, to cover their expenses.[11] Every single mother supplemented her check in some way, either by doing unreported work, by getting money from friends and relatives, or by persuading someone else to pay a lot of her expenses.

Not one of these fifty mothers reported all her extra income to the welfare department, and only four reported any of it. Not reporting outside income is illegal, but the chances of being caught are low. Furthermore, even if a recipient is caught, she cannot be cut off the rolls or prosecuted for fraud unless the state can show that she *intended* to break the law, which it seldom can. A recipient who gets caught cheating is supposed to repay her excess benefits, but so long as she remains on welfare, the state can reduce her monthly check only by 10 percent.[12]

Once we look at these mothers' monthly budgets, it is easy to see why they all supplemented their AFDC checks. Unless a welfare mother lived in subsidized housing, her check was seldom enough to pay even her rent and utility bills, much less her other expenses. Edin interviewed twenty-eight mothers who lived in unsubsidized housing. (Seventeen had their own apartments, while eleven shared an apartment with another adult.) These twenty-eight mothers' AFDC checks averaged $327 per month. They paid an average of $364 a month for rent, gas (the principal source of heat in Chicago), and electricity. On the average, therefore, rent and utilities cost them $37 more than AFDC provided.

The twenty-two mothers who lived in subsidized housing were in a much better position. They got an average of $320 a month from AFDC and spent only $123 on rent and utilities. This left them with $197 in cash to get through the month. None managed on this amount, but they came closer than mothers in private housing.

Where did the money go? Almost all welfare mothers get food stamps, but very few can feed their family for an entire month on stamps alone. Edin's fifty mothers received stamps worth $14 per person per week. They spent about $18 per person per week on food. Their families averaged just over three members, so they needed about $50 in cash during an average month for groceries. For the sample as a whole, cash expenditures on food, rent, gas, and electricity averaged $314 a month. Since the average recipient got only $324 a month in cash from the welfare department, she had only $10 left for other expenses.

Welfare mothers are not miracle workers. Like everyone else, they must pay for clothing, laundry, cleaning supplies, school supplies, trans-portation, furniture, appliances, and so on. Edin's welfare mothers spent only a third of what the average midwestern mother spent on items of this kind. Nonetheless, by the end of the month expenses other than food, rent, and utilities had cost the average mother $351.[13] Almost all this money came from unreported income.

Figure 6.1 shows where these fifty mothers got the money to pay their bills. Only 58 percent of their income came from food stamps and AFDC. Of the remaining 42 percent, just over half came from absent fathers, boyfriends, parents, siblings, and student loans, while just under half came from unreported work of various kinds. Seven moth-ers held regular jobs under another name, earning an average of $5 an hour. Twenty-two worked part time at off-the-books jobs such as bar-tending, catering, babysitting, and sewing, earning an average of $3 an hour. Four sold marijuana, but even they earned only $3 to $5 an hour. A fifth sold crack as well as marijuana and earned something like $10 an hour, but she was murdered soon after Edin interviewed her, apparently because she had not repaid her supplier. The only mothers who earned a lot on an hourly basis were the five who worked occa-sionally as prostitutes. They earned something like $40 an hour.

Figure 6.1

Income Sources of 50 Chicago-Area Welfare Recipients

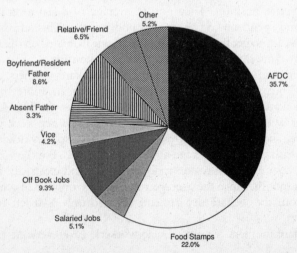

How Well Do Chicago Welfare Mothers Live?

Edin's welfare families averaged just over three members.[14] Those who lived in private housing reported total incomes, including both cash and food stamps, averaging $940 a month. Those who lived in subsidized housing reported total incomes averaging $840 a month, but if we allow for the fact that their housing subsidies saved them about $240 a month, their cash-equivalent incomes averaged about $1080 a month.[15] Taken together, therefore, Edin's fifty mothers were consuming goods and services worth at least $1000 a month.[16]

The federal poverty line for a family of three was only $9435 when Edin started interviewing in 1988 and was no more than $10,000 when she finished her interviewing early in 1990. Since Edin's mothers were consuming goods and services worth an average of $12,000 a year, relatively few of them were poor by the federal standard. The federal poverty line is not a very good benchmark, however, because it is not based on the cost of the goods and services that poor people really consume. It is merely an arbitrary line, drawn in 1964 so as to divide the richest four fifths of the population from the poorest one fifth.[17]

Public-opinion surveys show that the average American now thinks a family needs an income well above the official poverty line to escape from poverty. In 1989, the Gallup survey asked 3511 American adults the following question: "People who have income below a certain level can be considered poor. That level is called the 'poverty line.' What amount of weekly income would you use as a poverty line for a family of four (husband, wife, and two children) in this community?" Respondents' answers averaged $303 a week ($15,700 a year) which was 24 percent higher than the official poverty line for a family of four ($12,675). Respondents in cities of one million or more set the figure about 12 percent higher, at about $17,600 a year.[18]

Most of Edin's mothers lived in families of two or three, so they presumably needed less than $17,600 a year to escape poverty. How much less is unclear. The official poverty line for a family of three is 22 percent less than that for a family of four. But when survey researchers have asked the public how much money families of different sizes need to maintain any given standard of living, the answers do not vary much by size. The best available evidence suggests that the public would probably set the poverty threshold for a family of three only 8 or 9 percent below the threshold for a family of four.[19] In a city the size of Chicago, therefore, the public would probably set the poverty line for a family of three at about $16,000. For a family of two, the figure would probably be about $14,400. Using this standard, all but one of Edin's fifty welfare families was poor.

Another way of characterizing Chicago welfare recipients' standard of living is to ask how many lacked the material comforts that most Americans regard as necessities. It is hard to answer this question precisely, but Edin's judgment was that forty-four of her fifty mothers lacked at least some of the things most Americans take for granted. One of the six mothers who seemed relatively comfortable had recently received $7000 from an insurance company after being hit by a car. Another worked full time caring for Alzheimer's patients, earning $8 an hour. A third had an unusually generous rent subsidy and supplemented her income by stealing large quantities of meat from grocery stores. A fourth headed a large family of Asian refugees and had two grown sons who lived elsewhere but covertly paid the rent on the family's $600-a-month apartment. A fifth mother had a live-in boyfriend who held a steady job as a bus driver. The sixth was the sample's only successful drug dealer, who also held a regular job under an assumed name and lived with her mother. Not even these six families lived especially well, but they were not deprived by conventional standards.

The remaining forty-four families did without things that almost everyone regards as essential. Half lived in very bad neighborhoods. Half lived in badly run-down apartments, where the heat and hot water were frequently out of order, the roof leaked, plaster was falling off the walls, or windows fitted so badly that the wind blew through the apartment in the winter. One in four did without a telephone, and one in three reported spending nothing whatever on entertainment. Many said their food budgets were too tight for fresh fruit or vegetables. Only two of the Chicago residents had a working automobile. (Nine of the thirteen suburbanites had automobiles, since they lived in areas without public transportation.)

It is true that all fifty families had color television sets, and that a quarter had video recorders—"extravagances" that often offend intellectuals who rely on books for entertainment. But because both TV sets and video recorders last a long time, they cost only a few dollars a month. Since they provided both the mothers and their children with cheap entertainment, the mothers were willing to forgo almost any other comfort (such as reliable hot water or fresh vegetables) to ensure that they had a working television. Without one, their lives would have been extraordinarily bleak.

These mothers also bought a few other things that would raise conservative eyebrows. More than half occasionally rented a video tape or took the children to McDonald's for dinner. More than half used cigarettes or alcohol. Three spent $20 to $40 a month on the lottery. From an economic viewpoint, however, these luxuries were of minor importance. Taken together, they accounted for only 6 percent of the sample's total expenditures.

More important than these small extravagances, at least from an economic viewpoint, was the fact that half these welfare mothers were unwilling to live in Chicago's worst neighborhoods. If we set aside those in public housing, mothers who lived in very bad neighborhoods paid $180 to $265 a month in rent, whereas those who lived in average neighborhoods usually paid $325 to $425 a month. Mothers who lived in average neighborhoods could therefore have cut their monthly expenditures by something like $150 if they had moved to bad neighborhoods. It is important to remember, however, that bad neighborhoods are not just run-down, dirty, and short on amenities. They are also dangerous. White, Asian, and Mexican welfare mothers are particularly reluctant to live in these neighborhoods, which are overwhelmingly black. But some black mothers also paid higher rent to live in better neighborhoods.

Most of the Chicago residents could have cut their expenses even further if they had been willing to move into one of Chicago's large public housing projects, such as Cabrini Green or Robert Taylor Homes. But living in "the projects"—and especially exposing their children to this environment—was an appalling prospect to all the whites and Asians whom Edin interviewed and to many of the blacks. These mothers were willing to do almost anything to avoid such a fate.

How Typical Are Our Chicago Welfare Families?

Edin also interviewed twenty-five Cook County case workers who dealt with AFDC recipients on a daily basis. Case workers periodically review each recipient's rent and utility bills in order to calculate her food-stamp entitlement. The case workers all agreed that when an

AFDC recipient lived in private housing, her rent consumed most of her check and her utility bills consumed the rest. They therefore assumed that she must have additional unreported income.

Case workers all turned a blind eye to such indirect evidence of cheating, because investigating a recipient's unreported income would have required extra work and would not have earned them any credit with their superiors. Many case workers also felt moral scruples about preventing welfare recipients from supplementing their checks, since they believed it was impossible to live on what welfare paid. Perhaps because case workers habitually ignored all but the most flagrant evidence of cheating, officials farther up in the welfare hierarchy all believed (or at least claimed to believe) that welfare recipients had little unreported income.

While we are confident that almost all Cook County welfare mothers supplement their AFDC checks, we have less evidence about recipients in other cities. The only other in-depth study of urban welfare recipients' nonwelfare income is Jagna Sharff's field study of a Puerto Rican neighborhood in New York.[20] After two years of studying this neighborhood, Sharff concluded that "almost every man, woman, and older child" participated in the underground economy and that no welfare recipient reported such income to the welfare department. Unfortunately, Sharff did not collect data on how much income welfare families derived from the underground economy.

We have no direct evidence regarding welfare recipients in cities other than New York and Chicago, but circumstantial evidence suggests that their situation is usually quite similar to that of Chicago mothers. The cost of food, clothing, laundry, appliances, furniture, and transportation does not vary much from one major city to another, and even rent varies less than many people imagine. In 1980, for example, the United States had six metropolitan areas with more than 4 million residents: New York, Philadelphia, Chicago, Detroit, Los Angeles, and the San Francisco Bay Area. In 1984–85 monthly rents for low-budget families averaged $240 a month in the Bay Area and Los Angeles, $220 a month in New York and Philadelphia, and $175 a month in Chicago and Detroit.[21] The same regional pattern recurred in metropolitan areas with 1.5 to 4 million residents, but rents in these cities were $15 to $90 a month less than in the largest cities. Low-budget families spent more for rent in big southern cities like Atlanta and Houston than in eastern or midwestern cities of comparable size.

Edin's Chicago recipients reported receiving $900 a month in cash and food stamps. They would probably have needed another $100 a month to maintain the same standard of living in the Bay Area, Los Angeles, or New York. They might have been able to get by on $100 a month less in a smaller midwestern city like Cleveland or Milwaukee. If these estimates are even approximately correct, no major American city gave welfare mothers enough money to buy what Edin's mothers regarded as the bare necessities of life. In 1988, a single mother with two children got cash and food stamps worth $750 a month in California, $701 in New York City, $699 in Detroit, $589 in Philadelphia, $552 in Chicago, $491 in Atlanta, $412 in Houston, and $342 in Birmingham.[22] These figures suggest that welfare mothers who lived at the same level as Edin's respondents would not have needed quite as much unreported income in Los Angeles, New York, or Detroit as in Cook County but would have needed more in Atlanta, Houston, and Birmingham. Nowhere could they have gotten by on AFDC alone.

The situation may be different in small towns and rural areas. Edin interviewed a small number of welfare mothers in rural Minnesota, where the combined value of AFDC and food stamps is 25 percent higher than in Chicago and rent is typically about half as much as in Chicago. She found several Minnesota mothers who said they lived entirely on their AFDC checks. Those who supplemented their checks also earned far less than their Chicago counterparts. We would expect to find the same pattern in other depressed rural areas of high-benefit states.

Opportunities for supplementing AFDC are also likely to be more limited in rural areas than in big cities. If a welfare mother gets any kind of job in a rural area, her neighbors soon know about it, which probably means her case worker knows too. Case workers may look the other way if a welfare mother earns a little money from baby sitting or cleaning someone's house, but they are unlikely to tolerate her taking a regular job without reporting her earnings.

Nonetheless, many rural welfare mothers live in states where benefits are so low that no one could possibly survive on them without additional income. Alabama, Louisiana, Mississippi, Tennessee, and Texas, for example, gave welfare mothers with two children less than $200 a month in cash in 1988. Even if we assume rural recipients in these states paid very little rent, they surely could not have gotten by on $200 a month. Indeed, if it *were* possible to get by on $200 a

month in these states, their legislatures would almost certainly cut
benefits still further, because any benefit level adequate to support a
family would strike them as encouraging welfare dependency.

What Do National Surveys Show?

To check the validity of our claim that very few families make ends
meet on welfare alone, we looked at the Labor Department's Consumer Expenditure Survey (CES) for 1984–85. The CES sample is far
from perfect. Our best estimate suggests that more than half the welfare recipients in the target population either refused to participate
or failed to report their income from public assistance.[23] We assume
that welfare recipients with outside income were especially likely to refuse. Nonetheless, the data provided by those who participated are
remarkable.

Of the 267 households heads with children under eighteen who reported having received income from public assistance during the previous twelve months, 87 percent also reported income from other
sources.[24] Just over half these households included more than one
adult. The second adult in a household is seldom part of the AFDC "recipient unit," so his or her income seldom counts for the purpose of
calculating welfare benefits.[25] But even when we restrict our attention
to one-adult welfare households, 81 percent report outside income.
Some single mothers may have gotten welfare during one part of the
year and worked during a different part of the year. Others may have
gotten both welfare and nonwelfare income simultaneously and reported their nonwelfare income to the welfare department. But since
mothers who reported outside income to the CES got almost as much
money from public assistance as mothers who reported no outside income, we assume that most mothers with outside income were on the
rolls throughout the year and did not tell the welfare department about
their other income.[26]

Even when CES welfare mothers denied receiving any outside income, they seldom claimed to live solely on what they got from AFDC
and food stamps. Depending on how we calculate their expenses, between 73 and 82 percent of mothers who were the only adult in their
household and who reported no outside income also reported spending
more during 1984–85 than they got from AFDC and food stamps.[27]

Despite its many limitations, therefore, the Consumer Expenditure

Survey yields a picture that is broadly consistent with Edin's Chicago interviews. First, hardly anyone claims to live solely on AFDC and food stamps. Second, one-adult welfare families that participated in the CES reported spending about $6800, of which $4200 came from AFDC and food stamps, $1500 came from other sources, and $1100 was not accounted for. If we assume that the missing $1100 came from unreported income, these figures confirm Edin's finding that welfare mothers get only about three fifths of their income from AFDC and food stamps. The big difference between the 1984–85 CES and Edin's Chicago interviews in 1988–1990 is that, even after we adjust for inflation, CES welfare mothers who lived in one-adult households said they spent a lot less than Edin's mothers.

Underclass versus Mainstream Mothers

Many observers have argued that welfare recipients lie and cheat because they are part of a deviant subculture in which such behavior is acceptable. The boundaries of this subculture vary from one account to another. Oscar Lewis talks about a culture of poverty that the young imbibe from their parents by the time they are eight years old.[28] Any subculture absorbed during the first seven years of life must be mainly transmitted within the family. His account does not suggest that this subculture is restricted to poor families in poor neighborhoods. William Julius Wilson, in contrast, talks about a ghetto culture that flourishes only in neighborhoods with very high poverty rates, many jobless men, few intact families or strong churches, inadequate police protection, and understaffed schools.[29] A subculture that persists only in poor neighborhoods must be created and maintained primarily through public interactions among neighbors. Others have suggested, however, that racial antagonism makes blacks less law-abiding than whites who occupy similar economic positions.

Edin interviewed twenty-three black recipients, two Puerto Ricans, three Mexican-Americans, three Asians, and nineteen whites. Since the two Puerto Rican mothers clearly had some black ancestry, and since a growing body of evidence suggests that Puerto Ricans tend to have the same economic and social problems as American blacks, we grouped the two Puerto Ricans with the twenty-three blacks. We describe the remaining twenty-five mothers as nonblack.

In order to see whether family background influenced welfare moth-

Table 6.1 Income Sources and Expenses of 50 Chicago Welfare Families, by Family Background, Race, and Place of Residence

Category	Got welfare as a child[a]		Black or Puerto Rican	White, Asian, or Mexican	Lives in the ghetto[b]	
	Yes	No			Yes	No
Mean income by source						
AFDC and food stamps	$545	$509	$534	$517	$562	$510
Unreported	393	377	397	372	379	387
Total	938	886	931	889	941	897
Mean family size	3.5	2.9	3.3	3.0	3.6	3.0
Income per person (excluding rent and utilities)	$197	209	209	198	196	206
Unreported income as a percent of total	42	43	43	42	40	43
Percent with						
Legal job	52	52	48	52	53	49
Legal job under false social security number	13	15	20	8	13	14
Income from selling sex, drugs, or stolen goods	30	7	24	12	33	11
Percent of income derived from selling sex, drugs, or stolen goods	7	2	7	1	9	2
Number of interviews	22	28	25	25	15	35

a. Lived in a family that received welfare at any time while growing up.
b. Living in a predominantly black Chicago neighborhood with poverty rate of 40 percent or more in 1980.

ers' behavior, we compare the twenty-seven first-generation recipients to the twenty-three second-generation recipients. We call anyone who said her family had received welfare at any time while she was growing up as a second-generation recipient. Most first-generation recipients grew up in intact families.

To see whether living in a bad neighborhood influenced welfare mothers' behavior, we compared the fifteen mothers who lived in neighborhoods with poverty rates above 40 percent in 1980 to the thirty-five mothers who lived in less-impoverished neighborhoods. All the neighborhoods with poverty rates above 40 percent were overwhelmingly black, so we refer to the fifteen mothers who lived in them as ghetto residents. We call the other thirty-five mothers nonghetto residents. The fifteen ghetto residents Edin interviewed were all black or Puerto Rican, and they had all grown up on welfare.

Table 6.1 shows that those mothers who grew up on welfare, who were black, or who lived in the ghetto had more children than the average mother and therefore got slightly more income from AFDC and food stamps. These mothers also paid less rent because they lived in worse areas. Once we subtract rent and utility costs from a mother's income, family background, race, and location have little impact on a welfare family's per capita income. After paying their rent and utility bills, all groups of mothers had about $200 per person to get through the month.

All groups also got between 40 and 43 percent of their total income from sources other than AFDC and food stamps. At least in this small sample, therefore, neither family background nor race nor living in a bad neighborhood influenced a welfare recipient's willingness to break the rules by supplementing her check without telling the welfare department. The fact that all sorts of recipients broke the rules with equal abandon suggests that breaking the rules is a byproduct of being on welfare, not exposure to a deviant subculture.

Taking a job under a false social security number indicates greater indifference to the rules than other forms of cheating, since a recipient caught using a false number is more likely to be prosecuted for fraud than a recipient who merely fails to report income from her boyfriend or from off-the-books work. Table 6.1 shows that first- and second-generation welfare recipients are equally likely to use false social security cards. The same is true of mothers who live in the ghetto rather than better neighborhoods. Blacks in this sample are more likely than whites to use false social security cards, but the difference could easily be due to chance.

While all mothers seem ready to break rules governing their outside earnings, they are not all equally willing to break other rules. Table 6.1 shows that welfare mothers' willingness to sell sex, drugs, and stolen goods does vary by race, family background, and location. Many of these differences are statistically reliable by conventional standards. But the sample is too small to distinguish the effects of family background from the effects of current location.

Welfare mothers from disadvantaged groups (blacks, ghetto residents, and second-generation recipients) might earn more money from vice of various kinds because they have fewer opportunities to earn money in socially acceptable off-the-books jobs. At least in this small sample, however, this was not the case. Table 6.1 shows that roughly half of all mothers did some kind of legitimate off-the-books work. This figure did not vary much by family background, race, or place of residence.

Overall, we find no evidence that subcultural differences influence a welfare recipient's willingness to violate welfare regulations or take legitimate jobs. Family background, race, and location do correlate with willingness to sell sex, drugs, and stolen goods. But it is important to remember that even the fifteen welfare mothers who lived in the ghetto earned less than a tenth of their income this way.

What Happens to Mothers Who Can't Supplement Their Checks?

Finding several hundred dollars a month to supplement a welfare check requires a certain amount of skill. We must therefore ask what happens to welfare mothers who either cannot or will not supplement their checks. We have no direct evidence on this question because Edin found no Chicago mothers who tried to live exclusively on welfare. Simple arithmetic shows, however, that a Chicago mother who does not supplement her check cannot afford to rent her own apartment in the open market. This leaves her with three options: sharing a private apartment, finding subsidized housing, or breaking up her family.

Welfare recipients often share an apartment with their mother or with a grown daughter, and a few live with other relatives or girlfriends. Such arrangements often create conflict, but some single mothers make them work. Many single mothers also share their apartments with boyfriends, at least for short periods, but few of the mothers Edin interviewed saw their boyfriends as economic assets.

The eleven mothers who shared their apartments with another adult spent about $250 a month less on rent and utilities than those who lived on their own in unsubsidized housing. But sharing did not seem to affect their other living expenses. Except for the one teenager whose mother paid all her household bills, none of the eleven mothers who shared housing was able to live on her check. Indeed, these mothers' deficits averaged more than $300 a month. We therefore doubt that many big-city mothers can make ends meet simply by doubling up.

Subsidized housing cuts a family's rent even more than doubling up. Such housing come in two varieties: public housing run by the city and private housing in which the tenant receives a rent subsidy, usually under Section 8 of the federal housing act. Federal law limits rents in both public housing projects and Section 8 apartments to 30 percent of the tenant's reported income.

At least in Chicago, all tenants prefer Section 8 housing to public housing, because Section 8 units are located in economically mixed buildings that tend to be safer and better maintained than the housing projects. But in Chicago the waiting lists for Section 8 housing are so long that few mothers even bother to apply. In the suburbs, where welfare recipients are white rather than black, waiting lists are much shorter. Most suburban recipients said they had been assigned a Section 8 unit within a year of applying. A Chicago welfare recipient who wants an apartment within a year must apply to one of the big high-rise public housing projects, such as Cabrini Green or Robert Taylor Homes. The waiting lists for smaller, more desirable projects are much longer.

A Cook County welfare mother in subsidized housing might be able to survive on her check if she made her own clothes, fed her family a lot of beans and rice, never went anywhere beyond walking distance from the project, never smoked or drank, and entertained her children entirely with library books that she always returned on time. But a mother who could do all this would seldom be on welfare in the first place. If she were, she would almost certainly supplement her welfare check rather than force her children to live in Cabrini Green or Robert Taylor Homes.

In states like California, Michigan, and New York, where AFDC benefits are higher than in Illinois, single mothers in subsidized housing might find it easier to make ends meet on welfare alone. In some cities, moreover, public housing is far less dangerous and better maintained than it is in Chicago. Nonetheless, only 18 percent of the nation's welfare families live in subsidized housing, presumably because the supply is limited.

If a big-city welfare mother cannot supplement her check, get into subsidized housing, or find someone to share the rent, she will almost inevitably end up in a public shelter. This is not common: our best estimate is that no more than 2 percent of all AFDC families are living in shelters at any given moment.[30] Nonetheless, almost every major American city now has a significant number of such mothers. They all tell pretty much the same story: they fell behind on their rent, were evicted, and could not afford the security deposit and first month's rent for a new apartment. Some moved in with relatives but were unable to work out a permanent arrangement. Eventually they ended up in a shelter.

Since many homeless welfare mothers have histories of mental illness, alcoholism, or drug abuse, it is tempting to blame their plight on inept economic management.[31] But if incompetence were these mothers' only problem, a social worker should be able to find them housing they could afford, and welfare departments should be able to keep them housed by paying the rent directly to the landlord. Such arrangements have been tried and are sometimes helpful. But we have found no big city where those who deal with the homeless believe welfare recipients can make ends meet in private housing without supplementary income of some sort.

Confronted with a homeless family, welfare workers almost always assume that their job is to find the family some kind of housing subsidy. In many cities the welfare department can get homeless families into federally subsidized housing by moving them to the head of the waiting list. Where subsidized housing is scarce, or where its tenants have been able to prevent the welfare department from using it as a dumping ground for "undesirables," the welfare department may have to pay the family's rent in a hotel or private apartment. Either solution implicitly concedes that a single mother cannot make ends meet on AFDC alone.

If a welfare mother cannot find a permanent home, she is likely to conclude that she cannot care for her children properly. At that point she may ask her relatives to take the children, at least temporarily.

Faced with the possibility of losing her children, however, almost every mother is willing to ignore AFDC rules and supplement her check if she can.

We do not know how many welfare mothers have to break up their families. In 1988, 7 percent of black children, 4 percent of Hispanic children, and 2 percent of white children were not living with either their mother or their father.[32] Unfortunately, the Census Bureau does not ask *why* such children are not living with their parents. Some are orphans. Some of the rest are de facto orphans, who never had much contact with their father and whose mother is either dead, in prison, mentally or physically ill, or incapacitated by drugs or alcohol. We do not currently know how many of these children have mothers who could care for them if they had more money.

Our best estimate is that the proportion of white children separated from both parents has been almost constant since the early 1970s.[33] The proportion of black children separated from both parents probably averaged about 5.3 percent in 1968–1972, 4.4 percent in 1973–1976, 5.8 percent in 1977–1980, 6.1 percent in 1983–1985, and 6.9 percent in 1986–1988. These trends coincide loosely with trends in welfare benefits, which once we adjust properly for inflation rose from 1968 to 1976 and declined from 1976 to 1988.[34]

We created AFDC half a century ago to prevent single mothers from having to give up their children for economic reasons. At that time unwed mothers were still leaving newborns on doorsteps, and mothers whose husbands had died or deserted them were still putting children in orphanages. AFDC was supposed to end all this, and it certainly reduced the problem. What we created, however, was not a system that allowed all single mothers to keep their children but a system that allowed them to keep their children if they could supplement their welfare check in some way and conceal this fact from the welfare department. If conservative legislators were able to prevent such supplementation, as they keep trying to do, more mothers would have to give up their children.

How Much Can Single Mothers Earn If They Don't Collect Welfare?

If unwed motherhood, desertion, and divorce were confined to college graduates, most of whom can earn fairly good salaries, America would not need AFDC. But less than a quarter of all single mothers have spent any time in college, and a third have not even finished high school.[35] A single mother without higher education can seldom find a job that pays enough to support her family. When Charles Michalopoulos and Irwin Garfinkel studied single mothers who worked, they found that those who resembled welfare recipients in terms of education, labor-market experience, and other demographic attributes typically earned only $5.15 an hour (in 1989 dollars). Even mothers with high-school diplomas and ten years of work experience averaged only $6.55 an hour, while those who had no diploma and no previous work experience—a common situation among welfare mothers—averaged only $4.10 an hour.[36] The one piece of good news was that black mothers earned almost as much as white mothers with the same amount of schooling.[37]

American workers put in an average of thirty-five hours a week during the 1980s.[38] Working thirty-five hours a week at $5.15 an hour would yield $180 a week. Single mothers cannot expect to work every week, however, because the jobs open to them involve frequent layoffs and terminations. The official unemployment rate among single mothers averaged 10 percent during the 1980s.[39] If welfare mothers were employed 90 percent of the time and earned $180 a week, they would make an average of $8500 a year (in 1989 dollars).[40]

In an effort to increase welfare mothers' potential earnings, the Family Support Act encourages states to provide more job training. Congress authorized the first training programs for welfare mothers in 1967. Since then we have tried teaching welfare mothers to write resumés, pressuring them to apply for lots of jobs, giving them classroom instruction to improve their basic skills, and offering them temporary public-service jobs. Occasionally we have even given them on-the-job training in private-sector jobs. We have also produced countless evaluations of these efforts.

Gary Burtless of the Brookings Institution recently reviewed these evaluations.[41] Four conclusions stand out. First, most training programs for welfare mothers have been part-time, short-term, and inexpensive. Second, most programs raised welfare recipients' annual earnings enough to justify their modest cost. Third, while the programs were usually cost-effective, their absolute benefits were small. None of the programs that Burtless reviewed had raised welfare recipients' earnings by more than $2000 (in 1989 dollars), and in most cases the benefits were far smaller. Fourth, because their absolute benefits were small, low-cost training programs did not move many mothers off the welfare rolls.[42]

These findings do not mean we should abandon job training. We should, however, stop expecting low-cost programs to work miracles. If welfare mothers can currently earn $8500, we might plausibly expect a universal program of short-term training to raise the average to $9500. If we offered longer and more intensive programs, we might get the figure up to $10,500.

The big unanswered question is what would happen if we gave welfare mothers full-time, multiyear training, comparable in cost to a residential college. Some welfare recipients already use student loans to attend college. We have seen no evaluations of their postcollege experience. Nor do we know what happens to the earnings of welfare mothers exposed to other demanding, long-term training programs. Until we run such experiments, we should not write off job training as hopeless. But we should remember that when legislators talk about job training, they mean low-cost training, and low-cost training will not yield big increases in earnings.

Why Don't More Single Mothers Work?

Because most welfare mothers' potential earnings are so low, work seldom has much economic payoff for those who follow the rules. Table 6.2 illustrates the economic consequences of taking a full-time job in 1987 for a welfare mother with two children living in Pennsylvania (a fairly typical state with benefits similar to those in Illinois). If she did not work at all, her income from AFDC and food stamps would have been about $6500. If she earned $8000 and reported her earnings to the welfare department, she would have lost all her AFDC benefits and Medicaid coverage within a year, but she would have kept most of her food stamps. She would also have been eligible for the Earned Income Tax Credit, but this would merely have offset her social security and state income taxes. In the end, she would have grossed $3100 more by working than by staying on welfare.

In most cases, however, working would also have raised her expenses. Since she would eventually lose her Medicaid coverage, she would have to pay her own medical bills, which would have averaged about $800 in 1987.[43] She would also have needed different (and often

Table 6.2   Effects of Working on the Annual Income of a Welfare Mother
            with 2 Children in Pennsylvania, 1987

Income	Mother not employed	Mother employed 1633 hours at $4.90
AFDC benefits	$4824	–
Food stamps	1656	$1453
Earnings	–	8000
Earned income tax credit, less social security and state income taxes	–	105
Gross income after taxes	6480	9558
Less work-related expenses for		
Transportation (250 days at $2/day)		500
Clothing		300
Medical expenses		800
Net income after taxes	6480	7958
Less paid childcare if		
2 schoolage children ($1276)	6480	6682
2 preschool children ($2315)	6480	5643
Net income after taxes if father pays $1989 in child support		
Free childcare	7080	9947
Paid childcare, schoolage children	7080	8671
Paid childcare, preschool children	7080	7632

Sources: Lines 1 to 5: U.S. House of Representatives, Committee on Ways and Means, *Background Material and Data on Programs within the Jurisdiction of the Committee on Ways and Means* (Government Printing Office, 1988), p. 406. Food-Stamp benefits are calculated for a recipient with average rent. Benefits for a working mother are calculated after transitional benefits expire.

Lines 6 to 8: See notes to text.

Lines 10 to 14: Charles Michalopoulos and Irwin Garfinkel, "Reducing the Welfare Dependence and Poverty of Single Mothers by Means of Earnings and Child Support," Institute for Research on Poverty, Discussion Paper 882-89 (Madison: University of Wisconsin, 1989). Estimates are for the average AFDC family in the Survey of Income and Program Participation, which had 2.0 children.

better) clothing in most jobs, which would have raised her clothing bills by an average of $200 a year.[44] If she lived in a big city, she might have been able to take public transportation to work, which would have cost her about $500 a year. Otherwise, she would probably have needed a car, which would have cost more. Thus even if she got free childcare, working full time would have raised her net income only

$1500. If she had to pay for childcare, as roughly half of all working single mothers do, she would often have been worse off working than on welfare.[45] If she got no child support, even a job paying $10,000 a year would have left her with only $700 more than she got on welfare.[46]

The calculations in Table 6.2 make it quite easy to see why so many unskilled single mothers spend so much of their adult lives on welfare. The essence of the "welfare trap" is not that welfare warps women's personalities or makes them pathologically dependent, though that may occasionally happen. The essence of the trap is that, although welfare pays badly, low-wage jobs pay even worse. Most welfare mothers are quite willing to work if they end up with significantly more disposable income as a result. But they are not willing to work if working will leave them as poor as they were when they stayed home.

How Much Must a Welfare Mother Earn to Be Better Off?

In Edin's sample, welfare families consumed goods and services worth an average of at least $12,000 a year.[47] If these women had worked in legitimate jobs, our estimates suggest that they would have needed an additional $800 for medical bills, $300 for clothing, $500 for transportation, and $1200 for childcare.[48] They would therefore have needed $14,800 in cash, food stamps, and housing subsidies to maintain their current standard of living. When we add in taxes, the total rises to about $16,000 a year.[49] Interestingly, the Gallup survey suggests that the public would also have set the poverty threshold for these mothers at about $16,000.

A woman who worked thirty-five hours a week and was unemployed 10 percent of the time would have to earn almost $10 an hour to make $16,000 a year. By current American standards, $10 an hour is a lot of money. The average wage for all nonagricultural workers in the United States, male and female, skilled and unskilled, was only $9.66 in 1989.[50]

We can recast these calculations in a slightly different way by asking how many hours a week Edin's welfare mothers would have to work in order to earn $16,000. If they earned $6 an hour, which is a bit more than those with regular jobs actually earned, they would have to work 2667 hours a year. If they worked every week and took no vacation, they would have to put in fifty-one hours a week (50 percent more than the average American works) to maintain their current standard of living. If they were unemployed 10 percent of the time, they would have to put in fifty-seven hours during the weeks they worked.

These calculations lead inexorably to one conclusion. An unskilled single mother cannot expect to support herself and her children in to-day's labor market *either* by working *or* by collecting welfare. If she wants to make ends meet, she must get help from her parents, her boy-friend, the absent father, or the government. This help can take many forms: child-support payments, housing subsidies, food stamps, AFDC benefits, Medicaid, or sharing a residence. But without some kind of help, she cannot make ends meet.

If we make the plausible assumption that a single mother in Chicago can earn $5 an hour, work thirty-five hours a week, and expect to work forty-seven weeks a year, we can expect her to earn $8225 before taxes. That means she needs Medicaid, food stamps, housing subsidies, child-care subsidies, and child-support payments worth another $7000 to maintain the same modest standard of living as Edin's mothers. At present, her best hope of getting that much money is to collect AFDC and to work without telling the welfare department. If we want her to work more and cheat less, we need policy changes that make this practical.

"Make 'em suffer" as a Strategy for Cutting the Rolls

Between 1964 and 1972, when liberals shaped American social policy, the combined purchasing power of AFDC and food stamps for a family of four rose 40 percent. During these years court decisions and admin-istrative changes also made it easier for single mothers to get on the welfare rolls and eliminated some of the more humiliating features of welfare receipt, such as midnight raids to check on recipients' sexual behavior. As a result, the fraction of all single mothers receiving AFDC rose from 29 percent in 1964 to 63 percent in 1972.[51] State-to-state comparisons suggest that this increase was largely due to changes in administrative practice and in the way people felt about being on wel-fare rather than changes in cash benefits, but it is hard to be sure.[52]

Conservative legislators have long believed that single mothers should work rather than collect welfare. Since conservatives do not want to spend public money to make work more attractive, their strategy has been to make welfare less attractive. We can call this the "make 'em suffer" strategy for cutting the rolls. Since the mid-1970s, conservatives have been moderately successful in implementing this strategy.

Between 1976 and 1988 the typical welfare recipient's purchasing power fell about 16 percent.[53] Getting on welfare also became harder, and staying on took more time and effort. As New York City discovered during its fiscal crisis in the mid-1970s, a welfare department can cut its rolls substantially by hassling recipients. If a department asks applicants to fill out long forms requiring extensive documentation, rejects applications that are incomplete or contain errors, and forces rejected applicants to appeal or reapply, some will give up. The same methods can drive some current recipients off the rolls. As concern about cutting costs and catching cheaters increased during the late 1970s and 1980s, hassling recipients became increasingly common

A welfare department can also cut its rolls by closing offices, which forces single mothers to travel farther to meet their case worker. Understaffing offices, so recipients must wait all day to do their business, can also cut the rolls. If welfare recipients must spend a lot of time in training programs they believe to be worthless, this too will cut the rolls—though recipients like training programs that they think will lead to a good job. Forcing recipients to do unpaid community service can also make welfare less attractive.

Some combination of declining real benefits and increasing hassles cut the fraction of single mothers collecting AFDC from over 60 percent in the mid-1970s to about 45 percent in 1988. The absolute number of recipients has not dropped, however, because the number of single mothers keeps rising.

Conservatives used to argue that a less generous welfare system would discourage single motherhood by making it more financially painful. This plausible hypothesis proved false. For reasons nobody fully understands, single motherhood has spread steadily since 1960, no matter what we did to welfare benefits. Among families with children, the proportion headed by unmarried women rose between 1960 and 1964, when welfare benefits were almost constant. It kept rising between 1964 and 1976, when real benefits were rising. And it continued to rise from 1976 to 1988, when real benefits were falling.[54] Comparisons between states with high and low benefits tell the same story: the generosity or stinginess of the welfare system has almost no effect on a state's illegitimacy rate and only a modest effect on the number of single mothers.[55] If the goal of the "make 'em suffer" strategy is to discourage single motherhood, it must be judged a failure.

Defenders of the strategy could argue, of course, that it has never had a fair trial. The purchasing power of the overall benefit package has fallen only 16 percent since the mid-1970s, and the rules conservatives invented to make welfare less attractive have not all been implemented. In particular, the rule that recipients must report their outside income so the welfare department can deduct it from their AFDC check has never been well enforced. If conservatives were prepared to spend a lot more money spying on welfare recipients and prosecuting fraud, they could presumably make failure to report outside income somewhat riskier. Such a change would probably drive somewhat more single mothers off the rolls. But the monetary costs of such spying would almost certainly outweigh the savings, and the political costs would also be high. If this strategy were to succeed, moreover, it would substantially increase material hardship among single mothers and their children.

Can Welfare Benefits Be Raised?

The traditional liberal response to single mothers' economic problems has been to push for higher AFDC benefits. In our view this is a mistake. The only politically viable strategy for significantly improving the economic position of single mothers and their children over the next generation, we would argue, is to concentrate on helping those who work at low-wage jobs.

American liberals have a habit of trying to help the neediest. Because AFDC benefits have always been low, welfare mothers look like the neediest of the needy. As a result, liberals have fought hard to help welfare recipients, while largely ignoring single mothers with low-wage jobs. Welfare recipients have always gotten Medicaid, for example, while equally impoverished working mothers seldom have.

Legislators' failure to help single mothers with low-wage jobs has turned the American welfare system into a political and moral disaster. To begin with, it has made "welfare" synonymous with helping people who do nothing to help themselves. In addition, it has created a system in which unskilled single mothers cannot improve their situation by working harder—a situation that violates deeply held American ideals cutting across all partisan divisions. Such a system will never have many political supporters, even among hard-core liberals. If we try to prop it up, we will fail. Welfare benefits will remain low, single mothers will remain poor, and we will turn another generation of recipients into welfare cheaters.

By now most liberal legislators have accepted the conservative view that we should encourage single mothers to work. This shift reflects a pervasive change in public attitudes toward working mothers. Even affluent mothers are now going out to work in unprecedented numbers. This change has made it increasingly difficult to argue, as liberals once did, that single mothers should have a right to stay home with their children at the taxpayer's expense. Most Americans now see becoming a full-time homemaker not as a right or a necessity but a luxury. Few see any reason why they should pay higher taxes in order to make this luxury available to the poor.

In today's political climate, the only convincing argument for paying poor mothers to stay home would be that having a full-time mother at home helps children escape from poverty. This was a plausible claim in the 1950s, when most Americans saw working mothers as child abusers. Now, when more than half of all married mothers work, the idea that they are doing their children irreparable damage is less popular. It is also incompatible with the evidence. Comparisons between children whose mothers do and don't work offer little support for the idea that staying home does children much good. Some studies show benefits, some show costs, and most show no effect at all. If working outside the home does harm a mother's children, the effect is too small to be of much social importance.[56]

Defenders of welfare can still argue, of course, that it is cheaper to pay unskilled women to care for their children than to provide their children with high-quality daycare at public expense. For very young children, this argument is correct. As a result, almost everyone who has thought about the problem agrees that we need some variant of welfare for single mothers with infants. But once children are toilet-trained, they require less attention. From a strictly economic viewpoint, it seldom makes sense to pay mothers to stay home with young children, especially after they enter kindergarten.

If a mother does not have a God-given right to stay home with her children, if paying her to do so does not make economic sense, and if it does not do her children much good, the case for welfare collapses. At the moment, most liberal legislators still assume that welfare mothers are needier than single mothers with jobs, so they feel some moral obligation to improve welfare benefits. But as we saw in Table 6.2, most northern states provide welfare packages as generous as those that employers offer unskilled workers. The moral case for helping welfare mothers rather than working mothers therefore rests on a factual mistake. As the number of working mothers increases, the political case for helping them will become ever more compelling. Eventually, liberal legislators will figure this out.

Strategies for Helping Single Mothers Who Work

Most legislators, both liberal and conservative, already agree that we should try to make work pay for single mothers. Conservatives want to do this by cutting welfare benefits, while liberals want to increase the benefits of work. Thus far, liberal attempts to make work more rewarding have taken three forms: job training, raising the minimum wage, and tougher enforcement of absent fathers' child-support obligations. Each of these strategies helps single mothers who work, but even if we pushed each strategy to its limits we would not solve single working mothers' economic problems.

Job training. As we have seen, even universal job training would probably not raise the average welfare mother's potential earnings by more than $1000 or $2000.

Minimum wage. The minimum wage rose to $4.25 in 1991. Yet even if every welfare mother could find steady work at $4.25 an hour, her expected earnings would be less than $8000 a year. If we make realistic assumptions about unemployment rates, the figure would be more like $7000.

If we wanted to ensure that every employed single mother could support herself and two children from her earnings alone, we would have needed a minimum wage of at least $9 an hour in 1988. Political difficulties aside, raising the minimum wage to $9 an hour would be an economic disaster. Most American communities already have more unskilled workers than unskilled jobs. Anything that raises the cost of hiring unskilled workers will further reduce demand for their services. If McDonald's had to pay its workers $9 an hour, a Big Mac would cost twice what it now costs, and more working people would make their lunches at home, reducing the number of fast-food jobs. Likewise, if manufacturers had to pay unskilled workers $9 an hour, they would buy more machines to replace unskilled workers and would move more plants overseas, where unskilled workers are cheaper and often more reliable. This is not a promising way of solving single mothers' problems.

Child support. Better child-support enforcement makes work more attractive because the law allows a working mother to keep whatever the absent father contributes. A welfare mother, in contrast, can keep only the first $50 of the father's monthly contribution. The more the father pays, therefore, the bigger the advantage to the mother of working rather than collecting welfare.

But the absent fathers of children on welfare are mostly young, poorly educated, and poorly paid. Furthermore, judges and legislators seldom expect absent fathers to allocate more than 30 percent of their income to their children. As a result, their support payments seldom amount to much, even when they make them. Under the widely used "Wisconsin standard," for example, the typical absent father would have owed only $2000 in 1987.[57] Since many absent fathers now pay nothing at all and many others pay only part of what they owe, collecting even $2000 would represent a substantial improvement over the present situation. But a big-city mother with two children who got $2000 from an absent father would still need about $13,000 from other sources to make ends meet. Relatively few single mothers will be able to earn that much in the near future.

Liberals clearly need a new strategy for helping single mothers. In trying to formulate such a strategy they can afford to be flexible about details so long as they keep in mind three basic principles:

- Urban families with children can seldom make ends meet on incomes below the poverty line. Any policy that pretends families can somehow "make do" on the sums that welfare currently gives them is a fraud and will force welfare recipients to engage in fraud. If mothers work, they will need incomes substantially above the poverty line, since they have to pay for medical care, childcare, transportation, and taxes.

- Single mothers without higher education can seldom earn enough to support themselves and their families. This will remain true even if we raise the minimum wage to $5 or $6 an hour, get more welfare mothers to return to school, and provide more and better job training.

- While child-support enforcement can help single mothers with low-wage jobs make ends meet, such mothers also need direct help from the public treasury.

Broadly speaking, there are two ways of using public funds to help single mothers who work: we can modify the existing welfare system so it helps those who work, or we can gradually create a separate system of government-financed "fringe benefits" for all working men and women. Modifying the existing welfare system would be cheaper, at least in the short run. In the long run, however, a program of fringe benefits for all working families would win more political support, be more just, and do more good.

Transforming AFDC

The simplest way of helping single mothers who work is to let all single mothers collect AFDC, regardless of how much outside income they get. This approach would, in effect, convert AFDC into a child-support system for single mothers. Instead of seeing welfare as a program that ought to provide single mothers with a decent standard of living but doesn't, we would redefine it as a program that ought to provide a single mother with enough income so she can make ends meet if she also works, gets child support, or gets help from her boyfriend or family. This is the way welfare recipients already look at the program. By making their behavior legal, we would encourage their efforts at self-help instead of discouraging them.

If all single mothers were eligible for AFDC, the cost of AFDC in fiscal 1990 would have been about $35 billion instead of $20 billion.[58] Instead of accounting for roughly 0.5 percent of all personal income, AFDC would have accounted for almost 1 percent. Allowing all single mothers to collect AFDC would have at least three benefits. First, more single mothers would work in the official economy, where jobs usually provide more valuable experience and pay better than the off-the-books jobs that most welfare mothers now take. Second, single mothers would no longer have to choose between keeping their families together and breaking the law (though some would, no doubt, continue to lie about their living arrangements). Third, material hardship would decline among single mothers, and it would decline most among those who now obey the law and work in low-wage jobs.

Despite these advantages, making AFDC available to all single mothers is politically impossible. Setting aside the income tax, AFDC is America's least popular government program. Few politicians would want their name associated with a proposal that doubled the number of welfare recipients, even if the proposal also changed the meaning of being on welfare. Furthermore, if we eliminated restrictions on welfare recipients' outside income, legislators would soon cut welfare benefits, leaving single mothers unable to make ends meet even if they worked. Single mothers are a relatively small, unorganized, and unpopular group. A program aimed exclusively at them will never be generous.

Helping All Parents with Low-Wage Jobs

Given these political difficulties, liberals should probably follow Daniel Patrick Moynihan's advice to Richard Nixon on race and subject welfare to a protracted period of benign neglect. Instead of trying to reform a system that has resisted reform for as long as it has existed, liberals should try to construct a new system that concentrates on helping all parents who work in low-wage jobs. Rewarding work is consistent with current American values. And trying to help low-wage workers with families is consistent with widespread legislative concern about the current condition of children.

Fringe benefits for low-wage parents also seem a natural response to the steady decline in unskilled workers' purchasing power over the past generation. The average male worker's real earnings have hardly changed over the past two decades, but the real wages of the least educated have fallen, while the real wages of the best educated have risen. A national effort to help those at the bottom could, we suspect, win widespread support from the Democrats' traditional constituency.

In shaping a program of fringe benefits for working Americans, we should focus on workers who are trying to support children. Some obvious possibilities would be to:

- Provide extra cash to parents who work at low-wage jobs by increasing the Earned Income Tax Credit. We should also make the credit larger for families with more children.[59]

- Provide tax credits for childcare expenses if all the adults in a family have full-time jobs. Single mothers would get these credits if they worked. Two-parent families would get them if both parents worked.

- Allow all workers to buy Medicaid coverage for themselves and their family for, say, 5 percent of their earnings. (Or better yet, provide universal health insurance with premiums tied to income.)

- Give all parents who work a tax credit for housing expenses equivalent to the average value of a Section 8 housing certificate (or perhaps equivalent to what we now give the average home-owner).

- Provide mortgage subsidies for working parents who buy homes in low-income neighborhoods, helping to stabilize these neighbor-hoods.

Because Americans have such a strong prejudice against taxation, such benefits may have to decline as family income rises, but our goal should be to ensure that every working parent gets some benefit from every program. Except for medical care, however, none of these benefits should be defined as a universal right. They should be defined as rewards for work, as social security is. In America, social-welfare policy cannot afford to be seen as offering the indolent something for nothing.

If programs of this kind existed today, the great majority of welfare mothers would seek regular employment. Even in what passes for a full-employment economy, however, there are many communities in which unskilled women cannot find steady work. When the economy goes into recession, as it periodically does, such communities become more numerous. In areas where unemployment exceeds, say, 6 percent we should guarantee single mothers either a low-wage public-service job or paid job training. These positions should provide the fringe benefits we have already described.

Even in tight labor markets there will also be some single mothers whom nobody wants to hire. Some of these women ought to qualify for disability benefits. The remainder should stay in the existing AFDC system. But if we really made work pay for single mothers, the welfare rolls would shrink dramatically.

A program for making low-wage work economically attractive could win broad political support. Perhaps more important, it could retain such support over time, because it would be seen as reinforcing rather than subverting the work ethic. We cannot create such a system overnight. Indeed, we probably cannot create it in a decade. But what liberals need most today is not a program they can get through Congress next year. They need an agenda worth pursuing over the long run. The creation of an economic system that allows unskilled workers to support their families through some combination of wages and government benefits could and should be a central element in any such agenda.

Notes

Introduction

1. For a history of the struggle over eligibility, see Winifred Bell, *Aid to Dependent Children* (New York: Columbia University Press, 1965).
2. ADC also provided benefits to two-parent families in which the husband was disabled and had never contributed to the social-security system, but this part of the program has always been quite small and has never aroused much controversy.
3. Despite its name, the Economic Opportunity Act contained at least one provision that sought to do far more than just equalize opportunity. Title II authorized federal support for local "community action" agencies that many hoped would allow the poor to shape their own political and economic destinies. The act required these agencies to seek "maximum feasible participation" of the poor in their programs. But the Office of Economic Opportunity (OEO) soon diverted much of the community-action money to Headstart, and the Nixon administration cut off the rest. OEO's equal-opportunity programs, such as Headstart and Job Corps, proved more politically resilient than community action.
4. See James S. Coleman, Ernest Q. Campbell, Carol J. Hobson, James McPartland, Alexander M. Mood, Frederic D. Weinfeld, and Robert L. York, *Equality of Educational Opportunity* (Washington: U.S. Government Printing Office, 1966).
5. For additional evidence on this point, see both my own reanalysis of Coleman's original data and the other reanalyses in Frederick Mosteller and Daniel Patrick Moynihan, eds., *On Equality of Educational Opportunity* (New York: Random House, 1972).
6. Their joint work was summarized in Peter Blau and Otis Dudley Duncan, *The American Occupational Structure* (New York: Wiley, 1967).
7. Blau and Dundan did not study intergenerational mobility among women. Subsequent work has shown, however, that mobility patterns among employed women are broadly similar to those among men. See, for example, Donald Treiman and Kermit Terrell, "Sex and the Process of Status Attainment: A Comparison of Working Men and Women," *American Sociological Review,* 40 (April 1975), 174–200, and William Sewell,

Robert Hauser, and Wendy Wolf, "Sex, Schooling, and Occupational Status," *American Journal of Sociology,* 86 (November 1980), 551–583.

8. Coleman et al., *Equality of Educational Opportunity,* p. 300. The figures would have been somewhat higher if the authors had pooled blacks and whites from all over the country and if they had had more accurate background measures, but the basic point would not change.

9. In 1968 Duncan showed that income was even less dependent on family background than occupational standing was. ("Inheritance of Race or Inheritance of Poverty?" in Daniel Patrick Moynihan, ed., *On Understanding Poverty* (New York: Basic Books, 1968), pp. 85–110. Most subsequent studies suggested that family background explained more of the variation in mature men's incomes than Duncan's initial study of twenty-five- to thirty-four-year-olds had, but no national survey suggested that family background explained more than a fifth of the variation in annual income at any age. Mary Corcoran and I reanalyzed the data used by many of these studies in "The Effects of Family Background," in Christopher Jencks et al., *Who Gets Ahead?* (New York: Basic Books, 1979), pp. 50–84.

10. I remain extraordinarily indebted to C. Arnold Anderson of the University of Chicago for forcing me to deal with Blau and Duncan's work. Had he not done so, my subsequent career might have been quite different.

11. Along with Smith and myself, the authors were Henry Acland, Mary Jo Bane, David Cohen, Herbert Gintis, Barbara Heyns, and Stephan Michelson. *Inequality* was published by Basic Books.

12. While a large gap between those at the bottom and those in the middle is probably sufficient to produce widespread poverty in any society, it is not a necessary condition for widespread poverty. If a society is sufficiently poor, it can have widespread poverty without much inequality, because the average family has trouble meeting its basic material needs.

13. Elsewhere I have argued that equal opportunity won almost universal support precisely because the ideal was so incoherent that both liberals and conservatives could interpret it as mandating the kinds of programs they favored. (See "What Must be Equal for Educational Opportunity to Be Equal?" *Ethics,* 8 (April 1988), 518–533.

14. Robert Nozick, *Anarchy, State, and Utopia* (New York: Basic Books, 1974).

15. I have tried to correct factual errors in all three chapters. In Chapter 1, I have also added new material.

16. Both 1979 and 1989 fell near the peak of a business cycle, so they are good years for assessing long-term trends. Real per capita pretax income grew 17 percent between 1979 and 1989, and unemployment fell from 5.8 to 5.2 percent. Nonetheless, the proportion of the population reporting pretax incomes below the poverty line rose from 10.5 to 11.4 percent.

(These income and poverty figures come from U.S. Bureau of the Census, "Money Income and Poverty Status in the United States, 1989," *Current Population Reports,* Series P-60, no. 168, tables E-1 and E-8. They are adjusted for inflation using the CPI-U-X1 rather than the old CPI-U. The poverty rates do not take account of noncash benefits, but the value of such benefits did not change much between 1979 and 1989. Chapters 2 and 5 discuss poverty statistics in more detail.)

17. In April 1980, 52.8 percent of white eighteen- and nineteen-year-olds were enrolled in school, compared to 51.7 percent of blacks. Among twenty- and twenty-one-year-olds, the enrollment rates were 33.3 percent for whites versus 28.4 percent for blacks. Among twenty-two- to twenty-four-year-olds, the rates were 17.4 percent for whites versus 15.9 percent for blacks (U.S. Bureau of the Census, *1980 Census of Population, Vol. 1: Characteristics of the Population, General Social and Economic Characteristics, United States Summary,* PC80-1-C1, Government Printing Office, 1983, table 123). By October 1988 the gap was somewhat greater than it had been in 1980 but was still quite modest (U.S. Bureau of the Census, "School Enrollment—Social and Economic Characteristics of Students, October 1988 and 1987," *Current Population Reports,* Series P-20, no. 443, Government Printing Office, 1990, table 123). Official enrollment rates in both years slightly understate the true differences between blacks and whites, because sample surveys miss more young blacks than young whites, and most of those missed are not in school.

18. For data on high-school students' test scores, see Tables 4.2, 5.9, and 5.10 in this volume. No one tests national samples of college graduates, but racial differences among applicants to medical school, law school, and Ph.D. programs mirror those in Tables 4.2, 5.9, and 5.10.

19. For data on earnings by education and race through 1980, see Chapter 1. For more recent data, see Chinhui Juhn, Kevin Murphy, and Brooks Pierce, "Accounting for the Slowdown in Black-White Wage Convergence," University of Chicago, Graduate School of Business, 1989.

20. On patterns of residential segregation by income level, see Reynolds Farley and Walter Wallen, *The Color Line and the Quality of Life in America* (New York: Russell Sage, 1987), p. 149.

21. Some conservatives attribute such differences to heredity. For reasons I discuss at length in Chapter 3, this "explanation" turns out to be a non-explanation unless we can actually identify the relevant genes and show how they exert their influence.

22. We do not have direct measures of violent crime rates by race and educational attainment, but we have overwhelming evidence that young blacks are far more likely than young whites to commit such crimes (see Chapters 3 and 5). Since young blacks and whites now spend almost the same

length of time in school, we can safely infer that their violent crime rates differ even when their exposure to schooling is the same.

23. When Edin and I wrote Chapter 6, she had interviewed only welfare mothers. Since then, she has begun to interview single mothers with low-wage jobs. Like welfare recipients, all these mothers find they must supplement their regular earnings in some way. Some do additional work, some rely on boyfriends and relatives, some share expenses with a girlfriend, and some sell sex or drugs.

1. Affirmative Action

1. Parts of this chapter are reprinted with permission from *The New York Review of Books,* March 3 and March 17, 1983, Copyright © Nyrev, Inc. Certain parts also appeared in the *American Behavioral Scientist,* July–August 1985. I have substantially revised the present version to take account of developments during the 1980s and changes in my own views.

2. Sowell's *Ethnic America* and *Markets and Minorities* were both published by Basic Books (New York, 1981).

3. For descriptive data on the GSS, see James A. Davis and Tom W. Smith, *General Social Surveys, 1972–1989* (Storrs, Conn.: Roper Center for Public Opinion Research, 1989). The tabulations in the text were done by Richard Mrizek.

4. Tom Smith, National Opinion Research Center, personal communication, April 9, 1991.

5. By the late 1980s almost 2 percent of GSS respondents said that their ancestors were exclusively Native American. Another 5 percent reported some Native American ancestors. (Both proportions have risen over the past twenty years, apparently because Native American ancestry has become more socially acceptable and in some circles even glamorous.) Preliminary counts from the 1990 Census indicate that about 1.3 percent of the population gave its race as American Indian or Native American. Had significant numbers of individuals with both European and Native American ancestors reported their race as Native American, the 1990 Census count would presumably have been much higher than it was.

6. In 1980, 58 percent of Hispanics said they were white, 3 percent said they were black, less than 1 percent said they were Native American, and 38 percent said they were "other." See U.S. Bureau of the Census, *1980 Census of Population, General Social and Economic Characteristics, United States Summary,* PC80-1-C1 (Washington: U.S. Government Printing Office, 1983), table 74.

7. In addition to these two explanations, Sowell proposes two others that are less persuasive: age and geography. In *Markets and Minorities* he notes that

American blacks, Indians, and Hispanics have median ages between eighteen and twenty-two, while European groups have median ages between thirty-six and forty-six. He then reports that in 1974 families whose heads were between forty-five and fifty-four had incomes 93 percent higher than families whose heads were under twenty-five, leaving the reader with the impression that if the median black, Indian, or Hispanic were as old as the median European, he would be almost as affluent.

This argument is wrong. The main reason for the age differential between rich and poor ethnic groups is that poor groups have more children and die younger. These facts have almost no impact on family incomes, which depend on the age distribution of family heads. Such distributions vary little from one ethnic group to another and, contrary to Sowell, account for almost none of the income variation between groups. For all practical purposes, therefore, age is irrelevant to ethnic income differences.

Sowell also suggests that ethnic differences in family income arise partly because different ethnic groups live in different parts of the country. What he fails to mention is that most non-European groups live in relatively rich areas, not poor ones. The Japanese mostly live in California, for example, and the West Indians mostly live in New York City. Incomes in both places averaged about 15 percent higher than those in the nation as a whole during the year covered by Sowell's data (1969). Comparing the Japanese or West Indians to their neighbors would thus have reduced their apparent affluence, weaking Sowell's claim that nonwhites with the right traditions and values have been able to overcome the effects of discrimination.

Other Asians and Hispanics are also concentrated in big cities where both incomes and living costs are above the national average, so Table 1.1 overstates their relative affluence. American blacks are also disproportionately urban, but because they tend to live in southern rather than northern cities, their white neighbors' incomes are just about at the national average. Taking account of blacks' geographic location would therefore leave the picture in Table 1.1 almost unchanged. Like age, therefore, geography explains only a tiny fraction of the overall difference between black and white family incomes.

8. The 1980 Census found, for example, that Asians' per capita income averaged only 90.1 percent of white per capita income. Yet Asians' family incomes were 109.4 percent of the white average, and their household incomes were 111.8 percent of the white average. See *1980 Census of Population, U.S. Summary,* table 128.

9. For income comparisons between married and unmarried mothers with children living at home see U.S. Bureau of the Census, "Money Income of Households, Families, and Persons in the United States, 1987," *Current*

Population Reports, Series P-60, no. 162 (Government Printing Office, 1989), table 21.

10. Ibid., tables 17 and 33.

11. See *1980 Census of Population, U.S. Summary,* tables 120 and 127.

12. These estimates are based on tabulations by David Rhodes using CPS data tapes provided by Robert Mare and Christopher Winship. For a fuller picture of the trend, see Chapter 5.

13. For an analysis of young black and white workers' reservation wages that is broadly consistent with the story in the text see Harry Holzer, "Reservation Wages and their Labor Market Effects for Black and White Male Youth," *Journal of Human Resources,* 21 (Spring 1986), 157–177. For an analysis of the interplay between declines in real earnings among unskilled workers and declines in their rate of employment since 1967, see Chinhui Juhn, "The Decline of Male Labor Market Participation: The Role of Declining Market Opportunities," Department of Economics, University of Chicago, 1991.

14. *Markets and Minorities,* p. 23. Sowell presents a table from an article by Eric Hanushek to support his claim, but Hanushek's table does not in fact address the question of employer discrimination in pay. What Hanushek shows is that after making a somewhat tenuous adjustment for variation in what students learn in a given year of school, an extra year of elementary or secondary schooling increased both black and white men's earnings by about 5 percent in 1969, while an extra year of higher education increased both groups' earnings by about 9 percent. This does not mean that blacks and whites with comparable skills end up with comparable earnings, as Sowell implies. Since blacks with very little schooling earn less than whites with equally little schooling, increasing both groups' earnings by the same percentage each time they get an extra year of schooling ensures that blacks will earn less than whites at every educational level.

15. See James Crouse, "The Effects of Academic Ability," in Christopher Jencks et al., *Who Gets Ahead?* (New York: Basic Books, 1979), p. 118.

16. Calculated from Jencks et al., *Who Gets Ahead?,* tables A2.1, A2.5, and A2.7

17. "Why Doesn't Pay Have More Effect on Job Satisfaction?", Center for Urban Affairs and Policy Research, Northwestern University, Working Paper 83-3, 1982.

18. Citing Ernest van den Haag, Sowell claims that when one compares persons of the same age and socioeconomic group, blacks commit no more crimes than whites. Van den Haag does make this claim, but not on the basis of his own research; instead he cites three other studies, all of which show the opposite of what he says they show. For more recent estimates of racial differences in crime by educational level, see Richard Freeman,

"Crime and the Economic Status of Disadvantaged Young Men," (Department of Economics, Harvard University, 1991).

19. A 1/1000 sample of 1980 Census respondents yielded 131 Chinese and Japanese Americans with college degrees who worked 48 or more weeks in 1979. They earned 88 percent of what white college graduates earned. The sampling error of this estimate is about 6 percentage points.

20. Ethnic solidarity may still lead to a certain amount of principled discrimination by members of small ethnic minorities. Korean or Jewish businessmen may hire members of their own group out of a sense or loyalty, even when they think they could get a more satisfactory worker elsewhere for the same wage.

21. Edmund Phelps, "The Statistical Theory of Racism and Sexism," *American Economic Review,* 62 (September 1972), 659–661.

22. For evidence that even middle-class blacks still encounter a lot of racial prejudice in public places see Joe R. Feagin, "The Continuing Significance of Race: Anti-Black Discrimination in Public Places," *American Sociological Review,* 56 (February 1991), 101–116.

23. For a discussion of how employers perceive different kinds of black workers, see Joleen Kirschenman and Kathryn Neckerman, "'We'd Love to Hire Them, But . . .': The Meaning of Race to Employers," in Christopher Jencks and Paul Peterson, eds., *The Urban Underclass* (Washington: Brookings, 1991), pp. 203–232.

24. Measured in constant dollars, EEOC's budget quadrupled during the 1970s, and the number of cases it resolved grew tenfold. OFCC, which monitored federal contractors' affirmative action plans, was much smaller than EEOC, but it grew even faster during the 1970s. See James Smith and Finis Welch, "Affirmative Action and Labor Markets," *Journal of Labor Economics,* 2 (April 1984), 269–301.

25. See James P. Smith and Finis Welch, "Black Economic Progress after Myrdal," *Journal of Economic Literature,* 27 (June 1989), 519–564; Richard Freeman, "Black Economic Progress after 1964: Who Has Gained and Why?" in Sherwin Rosen, ed., *Studies in Labor Markets* (Chicago: University of Chicago press, 1981), pp. 247–294; and John Bound and Richard Freeman, "What Went Wrong? The Erosion of the Relative Earnings and Employment of Young Black Men in the 1980s," Department of Economics, University of Michigan, 1990.

26. Bound and Freeman, "What Went Wrong?"

27. With other characteristics controlled, the racial gap grew from 11 to 13 percent among high-school graduates and from 15 to 18 percent among those who had not completed high school.

28. Jonathan Leonard, "Affirmative Action as Earnings Redistribution: The Targeting of Compliance Reviews," *Journal of Labor Economics,* 3 (July 1985), 363–384.

244 Notes to Pages 55–74

29. Figures 1.1 and 1.2 are restricted to men in the civilian labor force who were between the ages of twenty and sixty-four at the time of the survey and who were estimated to have had at least one and no more than forty years of potential labor force experience since leaving school. Potential experience was estimated as (Age–18) for men with twelve or fewer years of school and as (Age–Highest Grade Completed–6) for men with more than twelve years of school. Since the number of black college graduates interviewed in any one year is quite small, I show three-year moving averages.

30. In the small sample of young black college graduates covered by Figures 1.1 to 1.3, there is no decline in the ratio of black to white weekly earnings after 1976 of the kind that Bound and Freeman report. This is probably a matter of measurement or sampling error.

31. See James P. Smith and Finis Welch, "Black Economic Progress after Myrdal," *Journal of Economic Literature,* 27 (June 1989), 519–564, as well as Smith and Welch, "Affirmative Action and Labor Markets," *Journal of Labor Economics,* 2 (April 1984), 269–301. See also Jonathan Leonard, "The Impact of Affirmative Action on Employment," *Journal of Labor Economics,* 2 (October 1984), 439–463, and "Employment and Occupational Advance Under Affirmative Action," *Review of Economics and Statistics,* 66 (August 1984), 377–385. Leonard provides references to earlier studies covering the years 1967–1974.

32. For a discussion of the politically popular but fallacious doctrine that a test must be separately validated by every firm that uses it, see Frank Schmidt and John Hunter, "Employment Testing: Old Theories and New Research Findings," *American Psychologist,* 36 (October 1981), 1128–1137.

2. The Safety Net

1. Reprinted with permission from *The New York Review Books,* May 9, 1985, Copyright © 1985, Nyrev, Inc. I have made a few alterations in the original text to correct minor errors.

2. Murray's *Losing Ground* was published by Basic Books (New York, 1984).

3. In a letter Murray denied that he used 1965 as a "turning point." For his letter and my response see *New York Review of Books,* October 24, 1985, pp. 55–56.

4. Until 1980 the thresholds were lower for farm families and for families headed by women. A widow living alone, for example, was supposed to need about 7 percent less than a widower living alone.

5. U.S. Bureau of the Census, "Estimates of Poverty Including the Value of Noncash Benefits, 1979–1982," Technical Paper 51 (Washington: U.S. Government Printing Office, 1984).

6. Ibid.

7. Murray presents a different set of estimates for "net" poverty, taken from the work of Timothy Smeeding. Unlike the Census Bureau's estimates, Smeeding's estimates are corrected for underreporting of income. Smeeding's estimates for years prior to 1979 are also corrected for underreporting of noncash benefits. But Smeeding's 1979 estimate, on which Murray places great emphasis, is not corrected for such underreporting. As a result, Smeeding's series underestimates the decline in net poverty during the 1970s.

8. U.S. Public Health Service, *Health, United States, 1983*, pp. 126, 127, 137.

9. Hope Corman and Michael Grossman examine the effect of Medicaid on infant mortality in "Determinants of Neonatal Mortality Rates in the United States: A Reduced-Form Model," *Journal of Health Economics*, 4 (1985), 213–236.

10. From 1950 to 1980 the correlation between the official poverty rate and the logarithm of real median family income is 0.995.

11. As Murray notes, GNP *per person* also grew quite rapidly during the 1970s because the number of workers grew as the number of children fell. But this change did not reduce poverty because family size did not decline appreciably among those with incomes below $10,000 in 1980 dollars. See U.S. Bureau of the Census, *Current Population Reports*, Series P-60, no. 80, p. 17, and no. 132, p. 61 (Government Printing Office, 1971 and 1982).

12. U.S. Bureau of the Census, *Statistical Abstract of the United States, 1984*, pp. 368, 371.

13. Murray's figures show even more rapid growth in both "public aid" and "public assistance" after 1965 because he concentrates exclusively on *federal* spending, ignoring state and local expenditures. I find it hard to see how a writer who sees rising AFDC benefits as a major source of social decline can focus entirely on federal spending. It is the states, after all, that set AFDC benefit levels.

14. For details see Table 5.5 (Chapter 5).

15. See note 5 above.

16. *Statistical Abstract of the United States, 1984*, p. 371.

17. House Committee on Ways and Means, "Background Material and Data on Programs within the Jurisdiction of the Committee on Ways and Means" (Government Printing Office, 1985). The drop is even larger using the conventional inflation adjustment based on the CPI instead of the PCE deflator.

18. The percentage of *families* on the rolls stabilized after 1975. The percentage of *persons* on the rolls declined after 1975 because AFDC families shrank faster than non-AFDC families.

19. David Ellwood and Mary Jo Bane, "The Impact of AFDC on Family

Structure and Living Arrangements," *Research in Labor Economics,* 7 (1985), 137–207.

20. Ibid.

21. Rereading this passage in 1991, the argument strikes me as exaggerated. Illegitimacy rates rose by a large *percentage* among white college graduates, but the *absolute* increase was small (see Chapter 5, Table 5.15).

22. *Economic Report of the President, 1985,* pp. 269, 274.

23. In discussing the effects of rising black school enrollment on black unemployment rates, Murray completely ignores the fact that those who enrolled in school were abler than those who dropped out. Because of this "creaming" process, the unemployment rate would have risen among black teenagers who were not in school even if nothing else had changed. Robert Mare and Christopher Winship analyze this and related issues in "The Paradox of Lessening Racial Inequality and Joblessness among Black Youth," *American Sociological Review,* 49 (February 1984), 39–55.

24. Chapter 6 discusses the relative rewards of work and welfare in more detail, using data from the late 1980s.

3. Crime

1. Reprinted with permission from *The New York Review of Books,* February 12, 1987, Copyright © 1987, Nyrev, Inc.

2. New York: Simon and Schuster, 1985.

3. Michael Bohman et all., "Predisposition of Petty Criminality in Swedish Adoptees," *Archives of General Psychiatry,* 39 (November 1982), 1234.

4. Wilson and Herrnstein also present data from the Danish study suggesting that having biological parents with a criminal record exerts more influence on a son's behavior than having adoptive parents with a criminal record. This comparison is misleading, however, because natural parents with criminal records had usually committed far more crimes than adoptive parents with criminal records.

5. See the correspondence between Leon Kamin and Sarnoff Mednick, William Gabrielli and Barry Hutchings in *Science,* 225 (March 1, 1985), 983–989.

6. Wilson and Herrnstein also summarize a number of studies comparing small samples of identical twins, who share all their genes, with fraternal twins, who share roughly half their genes. These studies show that identical twins' criminal records are more alike than fraternal twins' records. This evidence is not very convincing, however, because identical twins are also likely to have more influence on one another than fraternal twins.

7. This estimate is derived from data presented by Sarnoff Mednick et al. in

Science, 224 (May 25, 1984), 891–894. The estimate in the text is for the zero-order correlation of phenotypes. The implied heritability is higher.

8. See Edmund McGarrell and Timothy Flanagan, eds., *Sourcebook of Criminal Justice Statistics, 1984,* U.S. Department of Justice (Washington: U.S. Government Printing Office, 1985).

9. "How Much Can We Boost IQ and Scholastic Achievement?" *Harvard Educational Review,* 39 (Winter 1969, 1–123.

10. Richard Herrnstein, "I.Q.," *Atlantic Monthly,* September 1971, pp. 43–64.

11. For a more technical discussion of these issues see my paper "Heredity, Environment, and Public Policy Reconsidered," *American Sociological Review,* 45 (October 1980), 723–736.

12. The most representative data on social background and adolescent IQ scores are probably those in William Sewell, Robert Hauser, and Wendy Wolf, "Sex, Schooling, and Occupational Status," *American Journal of Sociology,* 86 (November 1980), 551–583. Background explains somewhat more of the variation in IQ scores among younger children than among adolescents.

13. See Travis Hirschi, *Causes of Delinquency* (Berkeley: University of California Press, 1969), or Albert Reiss and Albert Lewis Rhodes, "The Distribution of Juvenile Delinquency in the Social Class Structure," *American Sociological Review,* 26 (October 1961), 720–732.

14. Michael Bohman, "Some Genetic Aspects of Alcoholism and Criminality," *Archives of General Psychiatry,* 35 (March 1978), 269–276.

15. New York: Pantheon, 1986.

16. Marvin Wolfgang, Robert Figlio, and Thorsten Sellin, *Delinquency in a Birth Cohort* (Chicago: University of Chicago Press, 1972), p. 119.

17. See the paper by Reiss and Rhodes cited in note 13. The studies reviewed by Charles Tittle, Wayne Villemez, and Douglas Smith in "The Myth of Social Class and Criminality," *American Sociological Review,* 43 (October 1978), 643–656, mostly seem to show the same thing, though the authors do not interpret them in the same way that I do.

18. Judith and Peter Blau, "The Cost of Inequality: Metropolitan Structure and Violent Crime," *American Sociological Review,* 47 (February 1982), 114–129.

19. Steven Messner, "Societal Development, Social Equality, and Homicide: A Cross-National Test of a Durkheimian Model," *Social Forces,* 61 (September 1982), 225–240. See also John and Valerie Braithwaite, "The Effect of Income Inequality and Social Democracy on Homicide," *British Journal of Criminology,* 20 (January 1980), 45–53.

20. Data on the distribution of family income in different countries are seldom comparable, so statistical comparisons are likely to be wrong. Felix

Paukert, in "Income Distribution at Different Levels of Development: A Survey of Evidence," *International Labor Review,* 108 (August-September 1973), 97–126, reports that the distribution of family income was more equal in India than in either the United States or other affluent countries, largely because the Indian poor received a significantly higher fraction of national income than the poor in more affluent countries. No one who has spent time in India believes this.

21. The paper by Paukert cited in note 20 reports *more* inequality in most European countries than in the United States during the 1960s, which contradicts Currie's argument and my own. Malcom Sawyer provides somewhat more recent and probably better data on Europe in his "Income Distribution in OECD Countries," *OECD Economic Outlook, Occasional Studies* (Paris: Organization for Economic Cooperation and Development, 1976). These data show more inequality in the United States than in almost any European country.

22. For a more detailed treatment of crime trends in the United States, see Chapter 5.

23. For unemployment statistics, see *Economic Report of the President* (Government Printing Office, 1991). For murder rates since 1900, see Bureau of Justice Statistics, "Violent Crime in the United States" (Government Printing Office, 1991), p. 6.

24. Roger Lane, *The Roots of Violence in Black Philadelphia, 1860–1900* (Cambridge: Harvard University Press, 1985).

4. The Ghetto

1. This chapter originally appeared in *The New Republic,* June 13, 1988, but without the notes and tables included here.

2. Compare Elliot Liebow, *Tally's Corner* (Boston: Little, Brown, 1967), or Oscar Lewis, *La Vida* (New York: Random House, 1965), to Ken Auletta, *The Underclass* (New York: Random House, 1982), or to Leon Dash, "At Risk: Chronicles of Teenage Pregnancy," *Washington Post,* January 6–31, 1986, or to Nicholas Lemann, "The Origins of the Underclass," *Atlantic Monthly,* June and July 1986.

3. Chicago: University of Chicago Press, 1987, p. 6.

4. See Robert Mare and Christopher Winship, "The Paradox of Lessening Racial Inequality and Joblessness among Black Youth: Enrollment, Enlistment, and Employment, 1964–1981," *American Sociological Review,* 49 (February 1984), 39–55. The averages in the text are derived from annual estimates that appear in Figure 5.6 of Chapter 5.

5. "Housing Segregation, Negro Employment, and Metropolitan Decentralization," *Quarterly Journal of Economics,* 82 (1968), 175–197.

6. See for example Joleen Kirschenman and Kathryn Neckerman, "'We'd

Love to Hire Them But . . .': The Meaning of Race for Employers," in Christopher Jencks and Paul Peterson, eds., *The Urban Underclass* (Washington: Brookings, 1991), pp. 203–232.

7. For a detailed review of the evidence on this point, see Christopher Jencks and Susan E. Mayer, "Residential Segregation, Job Proximity, and Black Job Opportunities," in Laurence Lynn and Michael McGeary, eds., *Inner-City Poverty in the United States* (Washington: National Academy Press, 1990), pp. 187–222.

8. For estimates of unemployment by educational attainment and race since 1959, see U.S. Department of Labor, *Handbook of Labor Statistics* (Washington: U.S. Government Printing Office, 1983), table 66. For data on the overall rate of joblessness by race, see Chapter 5.

9. For an effort to estimate the contribution of urbanization to rising black teenage joblessness, see John Cogan, "The Decline in Black Teenage Employment, 1950–1970," *American Economic Review,* 72 (September 1982), 621–638.

10. See Richard Freeman, "Employment and Earnings of Disadvantaged Young Men in a Labor Shortage Economy," in Jencks and Peterson, eds., *The Urban Underclass,* pp. 103–122.

11. See Neal Rosenthal, "The Shrinking Middle Class: Myth or Reality," *Monthly Labor Review,* March 1985, pp. 3–10, and Patrick McMahon and John Tschetter, "The Declining Middle Class: A Further Analysis." *Monthly Labor Review,* September 1986, pp. 22–27.

12. See, for example, *Economic Report of the President, 1988* (Government Printing Office), tables B44-B46.

13. See U.S. Bureau of the Census, "Income in 1967 of Persons in the United States," *Current Population Reports,* Series P-60, no. 60, table 4, and "Money Income of Households, Families, and Persons in the United States: 1987," ibid., no. 162, table 35. The estimates in the text are adjusted for inflation using the fixed-weight price index for personal consumption expenditures from the National Income and Product Accounts. They include men reporting no income whatever.

14. *Handbook of Labor Statistics, 1983,* table 66.

15. Richard Freeman and Harry Holzer, "Young Blacks and Jobs—What We Now Know," *Public Interest,* Winter 1985, pp. 18–31.

16. Harry Holzer, "Reservation Wages and their Labor Market Effects for Black and White Male Youth," *Journal of Human Resources,* 21 (Spring 1986), 157–177.

17. For a discussion of trends in what Americans think it takes to get along at various levels, see Lee Rainwater, *What Money Buys* (New York: Basic Books, 1974).

18. See Table 5.7 in Chapter 5.

19. Bureau of the Census, "Marital Status and Living Arrangements, March

1985," *Current Population Reports,* Series P-20, no. 410 (Government Printing Office, 1986), p. 71.

20. Bureau of the Census, "Child Support and Alimony, 1978," *Current Population Reports,* Series P-23, no. 112 (Government Printing Office, 1981), p. 5.

21. I estimated the 1960 figures from National Center for Health Statistics, *Vital Statistics of the United States, 1981: vol. 1, Natality* (Government Printing Office, 1985), table 31, assuming that the nonwhite illegitimacy rate exceeded the black rate by the same percentage in 1960 as in 1968, which is the first year for which the black rate is reported separately. The 1985 figure is from *Statistical Abstract of the United States, 1988,* table 87. Both figures underestimate the proportion of children born to single mothers, since a significant fraction of married mothers are separated from their husbands by the time the child is born.

22. Larry Bumpass estimates that, among children born in the late 1970s, 42 percent of whites and 86 percent of blacks will spend some time in a single-parent family. See "Children and Marital Disruption: A Replication and Update," *Demography* 21 (Feburary 1984), 71–82. Projections of this kind may be off by a few points either way. See also Sandra Hoffreth, "Updating Children's Life Course," *Journal of Marriage and the Family,* 47 (February 1985), 93–116.

23. For a summary of what we do know, see Sara McLanahan, "The Consequences of Single Parenthood for Subsequent Generations." *Focus* (Institute for Research on Poverty, University of Wisconsin), 11 (Fall 1988), 16–24.

24. Bureau of the Census, "Money Income and Poverty Status of Families and Persons in the United States, 1986," *Current Population Reports,* Series P-60, no. 157 (Government Printing Office, 1987), table 16. As I emphasize in Chapter 1, marriage would not raise these families' incomes unless the father worked. Marriage does, however, encourage fathers to work more regularly.

25. See Table 5.5 in Chapter 5.

26. See David Ellwood and Mary Jo Bane, "The Impact of AFDC on Family Structure and Living Arrangements," *Research in Labor Economics,* 7 (1985), 137–207.

27. For more recent and carefully controlled studies that reach the same conclusion see Robert D. Mare and Christopher Winship, "Economic Opportunities and Trends in Marriage for Blacks and Whites," in Jencks and Peterson, eds., *The Urban Underclass* pp. 175–202, and David Ellwood and David Rodda, "The Hazards of Work and Marriage: The Influence of Male Employment on Marriage Rates" (Cambridge: Kennedy School of Government, Harvard University, 1989).

28. Bureau of the Census, *1980 Census of Population: Low Income Areas in Large Cities,* PC-2-8D (Government Printing Office, 1985).

29. The rates for central-city whites were 13.8 percent in 1959, 9.7 percent in 1969, 10.7 percent in 1979, and 13.2 percent in 1989. See Bureau of the Census, "Characteristics of the Population Below the Poverty Level, 1979," and "Money Income and Poverty Status in the United States, 1989," *Current Population Reports,* Series P-60, nos. 130, table 4, and 168, table 18 (Government Printing Office, 1981 and 1991).

30. For data on trends in racial segregation, see Douglas Massey and Nancy Denton, "Trends in Residential Segregation of Blacks, Hispanics, and Asians," *American Sociological Review,* 52 (1987), 802–825, and the sources cited there. For data on economic segregation, see Douglas Massey and Mitchell Eggers, "The Ecology of Inequality: Minorities and the Concentration of Poverty," *American Journal of Sociology,* 95 (March 1990), 1153–1188, and Reynolds Farley, "Residential Segregation of Social and Economic Groups among Blacks, 1970–1980," in Jencks and Peterson, eds., *The Urban Underclass,* pp. 274–298.

31. Other things equal, if flight had been confined to middle-income blacks, economic segregation would have increased within the black community. The sources cited in note 30 suggest that this did not happen.

32. Dennis Hogan and Evelyn Kitagawa, "The Impact of Social Status, Family Structure, and Neighborhood on the Fertility of Black Adolescents," *American Journal of Sociology,* 90 (1985), 825–855. See also Jonathan Crane, "Effects of Neighborhoods on Dropping Out of School and Teenage Childbearing," in Jencks and Peterson, eds., *The Urban Underclass,* pp. 299–320.

33. See Mary Corcoran, Roger Gordon, Deborah Laren, and Gary Solon, "Intergenerational Transmission of Education, Income, and Earnings" (Ann Arbor: University of Michigan, Institute for Social Research, 1987), and Linda Datcher, "Effects of Community and Family Background on Achievement," *Review of Economics and Statistics,* 64 (1982), 32–41.

34. "Social Class, Social Areas and Delinquency," *Sociology and Social Research,* 63 (1978), 49–72.

35. For a detailed review of the literature on neighborhood effects, see Christopher Jencks and Susan E. Mayer, "The Social Consequences of Growing Up in a Poor Neighborhood," in Lynn and McGeary, eds., *Inner-City Poverty,* pp. 111–186.

5. The Underclass

1. I am indebted to Mary Corcoran, Sheldon Danziger, Jane Mansbridge, Susan Mayer, Paul Peterson, and Elizabeth Uhr for helpful comments on

earlier versions of this chapter, and to the Center for Urban Affairs and Policy Research, the Russell Sage Foundation, the Sloan Foundation, and the Ford Foundation for support while working on these issues. Earlier versions of this essay were presented at a conference on "The Truly Disadvantaged" held at Northwestern University in 1989 and published in Christopher Jencks and Paul Peterson, eds., *The Urban Underclass* (Washington: Brookings, 1991).

2. For a history of the term, see Robert Aponte, "Definitions of the Underclass: A Critical Analysis," in Herbert Gans, ed., *Sociology in America* (Newbury Park: Sage Publications, 1990), pp. 117–137.

3. The original articles were published on November 16–30, 1981. They are available in book form in Ken Auletta, *The Underclass* (New York: Random House, 1982).

4. See Ronald Mincey, "Is There a White Underclass?" (Washington: Urban Institute, 1988). The city with the largest concentration of such white underclass neighborhoods seems to be Columbus, Ohio, which attracts many immigrants from West Virginia, eastern Kentucky, and eastern Tennessee, the heartland of white poverty in America.

5. Wilson's definition of the underclass, though formally color-blind, also implies that it is largely nonwhite. He sees the underclass as having two crucial features: chronic joblessness and social isolation. He then equates social isolation with living in a neighborhood where most of the residents are lower class. As a result, members of the white lower class are seldom part of his underclass while members of the black lower class often are.

6. The great majority of Latinos now living in the United States came here from Mexico. Most probably have both European and Native American ancestors. Many Puerto Ricans, in contrast, are of mixed European and African ancestry. When the 1980 Census asked respondents to classify each member of their household as white, black, Native American, Asian, or "other," non-Hispanics almost all used one of the first four categories. Only a little over half of all Hispanics used these four categories, and almost all of these said they were white. Most of the rest classified themselves as "other." I have not been able to find any data on whether Hispanics who say they are white differ in appearance or ancestry from those who say they are "other." Nor do Census publications distinguish Hispanics who say they are white from those who say they are "other."

7. The first such study, which predated Auletta's popularization of the term, was Frank Levy, "How Big Is the American Underclass?" (Washington: Urban Institute, 1977). For a more recent study that equates membership in the underclass with persistent poverty, see Patricia Ruggles and William Marton, "Measuring the Size and Characteristics of the Underclass: How Much Do We Know?" (Washington: Urban Institute, 1986).

8. See Mollie Orshansky, "Counting the Poor: Another Look at the Poverty Profile," *Social Security Bulletin,* 28 (January 1965), 3–29.

9. For evidence that there is no sharp break in the prevalence of material hardship near the poverty line, see Susan E. Mayer and Christopher Jencks, "Poverty and the Distribution of Material Hardship," *Journal of Human Resources,* 24 (Winter 1989), 88–113.

10. For evidence that the poverty line does not, in fact, represent a constant level of material well-being, see both Chapter 2 of this book and Susan E. Mayer, "Recent Trends in Economic Inequality in the United States: Income vs. Expenditures vs. Material Well-Being," Graduate School of Public Policy Studies, University of Chicago, 1991.

11. The official rate adjusts the poverty threshold for inflation using the Consumer Price index for urban consumers (CPI-U). Before 1983, the CPI-U exaggerated the rate of inflation because of the way it treated the costs of home ownership. The rates in row 3 of Table 5.1 adjust for inflation using the CPI-U-X1, which estimates changes in housing costs from changes in rents. Because the CPI-U and CPI-U-X1 both use 1967 as their benchmark year, the CPI-U-X1 yields higher poverty rates than the CPI-U before 1967, the same rate in 1967, and lower rates after 1967.

12. The choice of years in Table 5.1 was dictated by the availability of data. At the time this essay was written, poverty counts using the CPI-U-X1 were only available for 1974 through 1988. To extend the CPI-U-X1 series back in time, I exploited the fact that 1967 was the benchmark year for the CPI-U-X1, making poverty rates using the CPI-U and CPI-U-X1 the same in that year.

13. Before the advent of Medicare and Medicaid in 1965, the poor seldom had health insurance. In many cases they got free care. In other cases they did without care. The Labor Department's Consumer Expenditure Survey (CES) shows that in 1960–61 families with total expenditures below the poverty line spent 7.2 percent of their money on medical care. This figure fell to 6.6 percent in 1972–73 and remained constant from 1972–73 to 1984–85. (All these estimates are based on tabulations by Larry Radbill using the original CES "interview" surveys for the relevant years. They all exclude nonprescription durgs.)

14. For a detailed analysis of the changing distribution of earnings, see Chinhui Juhn, Kevin Murphy, and Brooks Pierce, "Wage Inequality and the Rise in Returns to Skill" (Chicago: University of Chicago Graduate School of Business, 1988). On trends in per capital family income, see Sheldon Danziger, "Economic Growth, Poverty, and Inequality in an Advanced Economy" (Madison: University of Wisconsin, Institute for Research on Poverty, Discussion Paper 862-88, 1988), table 2.

15. See Paul Peterson, "The Urban Underclass and the Poverty Paradox," in

Christopher Jencks and Paul Peterson, eds., *The Urban Underclass* (Washington: Brookings, 1991).

16. Terry Adams, Greg Duncan, and Willard Rogers, "The Persistence of Poverty," in Fred R. Harris and Roger Wilkins, eds., *Quiet Riots: Race and Poverty in the United States* (New York: Pantheon, 1988), pp. 78–99, fig. 5.2.

17. See Greg Duncan and Willard Rogers, "Has Children's Poverty Become More Persistent?" (Ann Arbor: University of Michigan, Institute for Social Research, 1991). The data come from the Panel Study of Income Dynamics.

18. Since blacks' share of the total population rose from 11.0 percent in 1967 to 12.3 percent in 1988, the fact that they constituted a constant fraction of the poverty population implies that racial disparities in poverty rates narrowed slightly. Blacks also constituted a slightly smaller fraction of all poor *children* in 1988 than in 1974, but this was because more poor children were Hispanic.

19. Because Table 5.2 uses the official poverty thresholds, it understates the decline in poverty between 1968 and 1987. The demographic characteristics of the poor do not change much when we lower the threshold by 5 or 10 percent, however, so the characteristics of the poor would not change much if we substituted the CPI-U-X1 for the CPI-U and included noncash benefits.

20. *The Truly Disadvantaged* (Chicago: University of Chicago Press), p. 8. See also Martha Van Haitsma, "A Contextual Definition of the Underclass," *Focus,* 12 (Summer 1989), 27–31.

21. Estimates of weekly joblessness using retrospective data from the March CPS differ from official estimates covering the same year for a variety of technical reasons. Official estimates of weekly joblessness are based on men's reports of their employment status in the week the CPS interviews them. BLS averages these estimates to get annual figures. Because the CPS rotates households in and out of its sample, retrospective estimates based on the March CPS come from a somewhat different sample than the monthly estimates collected during the previous year. Retrospective estimates are also subject to different sorts of reporting error and cover a slightly different population from the monthly estimates. The March survey misses men who were interviewed during the previous year but subsequently died, were institutionalized, joined the armed forces, or left the country. It includes men who were not interviewed during the previous year because they were living in a foreign country, were in the armed forces, or were inmates of institutions.

22. The poverty thresholds used in Figure 5.3 are identical to the official thresholds in 1979 but differ in other years because I used the fixed-

weight price index for Personal Consumption Expenditures (PCE) from the National Income and Product Accounts rather than the CPI-U to adjust for inflation. Because the PCE price index rose less than the CPI-U in the 1970s, this procedure yields higher poverty rates for years prior to 1979 and slightly lower rates after 1979 than the official thresholds would.

23. I used a 1/1000 sample of decennial Census records to calculate the fraction of all twenty-five- to fifty-four-year-old men who were inmates. For whites, the figures were 0.9 percent in 1960, 0.6 percent in 1970, and 0.6 percent in 1980. For blacks, they were 2.4 percent in 1960, 2.5 percent in 1970, and 2.3 percent in 1980.

24. The proportional increase in long-term joblessness appears to be higher for black college graduates than for any other group, but this is probably a byproduct of sampling error. The CPS sample of black males between the ages of twenty-five and fifty-four included an average of 65 college graduates per year and 70 men with one to three years of college per year from 1963 through 1968. Table 5.3 shows separate estimates for 1963–1965 and 1966–1968 as well as for black college graduates and dropouts. The differences between these four estimates do not have any obvious explanation and are not statistically reliable. I therefore assume that the four values differ largely by chance. If one pools all four values, the best estimate of long-term joblessness from 1963 through 1968 for black men who had attended college is 1.9 ± 0.5 percent. The best estimate for 1985–1987 is 8.4 ± 0.7 percent. This fourfold increase is roughly comparable to the increase for less-educated black males over the same period.

25. Chinhui Juhn, "The Decline of Male Labor Force Participation: The Role of Declining Market Opportunities," Department of Economics, University of Chicago, 1991.

26. Ibid.

27. Juhn estimates the effects of changes in real wages on the implicit assumption that men's reservation wages rise at the same rate as prices. She shows that if this assumption is correct, wage changes explain much of the decline in employment after 1970. Unfortunately, wage changes cannot explain trends prior to 1970, when real wages were rising but nonparticipation was also rising. Nor can her assumption explain why the rate of employment among men was lower in 1987 than in 1959, given that unskilled workers' real wages were higher in 1987 than in 1959.

Wage inequality did not increase during the 1960s. Thus if one alters Juhn's model to assume that reservation wages rise in tandem with the median wage rather than prices, it becomes easier to explain why trends after 1970 are not a mirror image of trends during the 1960s.

28. See Donald Parsons, "The Decline in Male Labor Force Participation,"

Journal of Political Economy, 88 (February 1980), 117–134, as well as the exchange between Parsons and Robert Haveman and Barbara Wolfe in the *Journal of Political Economy,* 92 (June 1984), 532–549. Parsons argues that since men must be jobless for at least a year in order to qualify for disability benefits, significant numbers of men leave the labor force hoping to qualify and are later turned down. But rejected applicants seldom return to the labor force: see John Bound, "The Health and Earnings of Rejected Disability Insurance Applicants," *American Economic Review,* 79 (June 1989), 482–503. This fact makes it hard to argue that large numbers of men leave the labor force for purely strategic reasons.

29. Mark Alan Hughes, "Concentrated Deviance or Isolated Deprivation? The 'Underclass' Idea Reconsidered," Woodrow Wilson School, Princeton University, 1988. This paper appeared in *Journal of Policy Analysis and Management,* 8 (1989), 274–282, but without the tables I discuss here.

30. The estimates in the text are unweighted means for all eight metropolitan areas. The estimates for the best and worst fifth of all census tracts assume that the distribution of tract means was normal in both 1969 and 1979, so that the best and worst fifth of all tracts averaged 1.4 standard deviations above and below the mean for their metropolitan area. Because the estimates of protracted joblessness include all men over the age of sixteen, the absolute level is much higher than it would be for twenty-five- to fifty-four-year-old men. The absolute increase is also greater, because more men over fifty-five had retired in 1979 than in 1969.

31. Averaging over all eight areas, the proportional increase in joblessness was slightly larger in better neighborhoods, but the difference was small and did not recur in all eight metropolitan areas. In the absence of other evidence, one might treat Hughes's findings as evidence that economic segregation declined slightly in the 1970s, but larger studies that focus on income do not support this conclusion. Douglas Massey and Mitchel Eggers found no trend in income segregation among whites and a small increase among blacks in large cities: "The Ecology of Inequality: Minorities and the Concentration of Poverty," *American Journal of Sociology* 95, (March, 1990), 1153–1188. Reynolds Farley found almost no change in income segregation among blacks: "Trends in the Residential Segregation of Social and Economic Groups among Blacks: 1970 to 1980," in Jencks and Peterson, eds., *The Urban Underclass.* I therefore doubt that Hughes would have found any decline in segregation of the jobless if he had had a larger sample of cities.

32. Hughes believes that his findings contradict Wilson's argument that the underclass grew. Hughes construes Wilson's argument as requiring that joblessness rise proportionally faster in bad neighborhoods, which it did not do. I read Wilson's argument as requiring only that the subjective cost

of being jobless declined more in bad neighborhoods. Neither Hughes nor Wilson offers any evidence regarding the functional form of the relationship between the rate of joblessness and the strength of the norms forbidding it.

Wilson does argue in *The Truly Disadvantaged* that middle-class blacks fled from poor neighborhoods during the 1970s, and that their flight increased economic segregation within the black community. But this claim is not critical to his main argument about the growth of a geographically concentrated urban underclass. That argument requires only that the norms prohibiting joblessness weaken more in the ghetto than elsewhere.

33. The percentage point difference between blacks and whites with the same amount of schooling grew at all educational levels. The proportional increase was also greater for blacks than for whites at all educational levels except high-school graduation.

34. Chinhui Juhn, "The Decline of Male Labor Force Participation."

35. Blacks accounted for 27.0 percent of all arrests in 1971, 26.4 percent in 1978, 24.5 percent in 1980, 27.0 percent in 1985, and 29.6 percent in 1988. See Bureau of Justice Statistics, *Sourcebook of Criminal Justice Statistics,* issued annually. The statistics cited come from the issues dated 1973 (p. 272), 1980 (p. 344), 1982 (p. 403), 1985 (p. 376), and 1989 (p. 430).

36. For a review of the evidence for and against the spatial mismatch theory, see Christopher Jencks and Susan E. Mayer, "Residential Segregation, Job Proximity, and Black Job Opportunities," in Laurence E. Lynn and Michael McGeary, eds., *Inner-City Poverty in the United States* (Washington: National Academy Press, 1990), pp. 187–252.

37. *Economic Report of the President* (Government Printing Office, 1990), p. 339.

38. For a description of the way they constructed this series, see their "The Paradox of Lessening Racial Inequality and Joblessness among Black Youth: Enrollment, Enlistment, and Employment, 1964–1981," *American Sociological Review,* 49 (February 1984), 39–55.

39. The estimates in Figures 5.6 and 5.7 are not strictly comparable, because Figure 5.7 includes a few students over the age or twenty-five and excludes members of the armed forces from both its numerator and denominator. These differences should not have much effect, however.

40. Bureau of Labor Statistics, *Handbook of Labor Statistics,* table 48.

41. Although the text refers to "single mothers," the data in Table 5.5 actually cover all families with children under eighteen in which the head was a woman. Bureau of the Census, "Household and Family Characteristics," *Current Population Reports,* Series P-20, no. 437 (Government Printing Office, 1989), table 1, shows that only 88 percent of these families are actually headed by the child's mother. The remaining families are mostly

headed by the child's grandmother or grandfather but include the child's mother.

42. Table 5.5 uses CPS data to estimate the employment rate among women who head households with children under eighteen. It does not use CPS data to estimate the proportion who collect welfare or who combine work and welfare, because welfare receipt is seriously underreported in the CPS. We do not know whether welfare recipients have unusually high refusal rates (perhaps because they are cheating and fear detection) or simply fail to report that they are on welfare. Table 5.5 estimates the rate of welfare receipt by comparing the number of women heading families with children under eighteen to administrative estimates of the number collecting welfare in a given month.

We do not know how many women combined work and welfare in an average month during 1960, but the figure was presumably low, since working had no economic benefits for welfare recipients who reported their earnings to the welfare department. If 52 percent of single women who headed households with children under eighteen worked and 27 percent collected welfare in an average month, 21 percent must have survived without either working or collecting welfare. In 1968, the figure was $100-52-(37-6)=17$ percent. By 1972, such women had vanished, since 53 percent collected welfare without working and 49 percent worked. (Totals can exceed 100 percent because of sampling error, because the numerator and denominator of the welfare rate do not cover precisely the same universe, or because some welfare mothers tell the CPS but not the welfare department that they worked.) After 1972 all single mothers appear to be either working, collecting welfare, or both.

43. U.S. House of Representative, Committee on Ways and Means, "Background Material and Data on Programs within the Jurisdiction of the Committee on Ways and Means," (Government Printing Office, 1989), p. 564.

44. For counts of female heads with children under eighteen from 1971 through 1988, see Bureau of the Census, "Money Income and Poverty Status in the United States, 1988," *Current Population Reports,* Series P-60, no. 166 (Government Printing Office, 1989), table 20. Blacks constituted 34 percent of all female-headed families with children in both 1971 and 1987, so I assumed the same was true in 1969. Counts of female heads with children under eighteen are not identical to counts of single mothers with children under eighteen, but almost all such households include a single mother.

45. Mark Alan Hughes, "Concentrated Deviance and the Underclass Hypothesis," (Princeton: Woodrow Wilson School, 1988). Note that public

assistance includes those receiving General Assistance as well as AFDC. Because of underreporting and misunderstandings about what constitutes public assistance, these data are not very accurate.

46. Although the United States has a reputation for not placing much emphasis on the "right" accent (at least as compared to Britain), Americans can estimate an individual's social class quite accurately on the basis of the way he or she talks. In the late 1960s, Dean Ellis reported a series of studies in which panels of undergraduates listened to tape recordings of different people retelling Aesop's fables: "Speech and Social Status in America," *Social Forces* 45 (March 1967), 431–437. A panel's estimate of the speaker's social class correlated 0.8 with the speaker's score on the Hollingshead Index of social status, which is based on education and occupation. Even when all the speakers were college freshmen who had graduated in the upper third of their high-school class, their father's Hollingshead score correlated 0.8 with the panel's estimate of their social class. When Ellis told speakers to make themselves sound as "upper class" as possible, the correlation between the panel's estimates and the Hollingshead Index fell from 0.8 to about 0.65. When he told speakers to count from one to twenty instead of reading a story aloud, the correlation also fell to 0.65. White panels judged the social class of blacks about as accurately as they judged the class of whites. Unfortunately, Ellis did not report the inter-rater reliability of individual judgments.

47. Because high-school graduates are often eighteen or nineteen years old, comparing the number of graduates in a given year to the number of persons who were seventeen years old in that year can somewhat understate or overstate the graduation rate in years when the number of seventeen-year-olds differs substantially from the number of eighteen- and nineteen-year-olds. Table 5.6 uses five-year averages to minimize this problem. The ratio of high school graduates to seventeen-year-olds exceeded 76 percent between 1966 and 1970. It was less than 72 percent in 1980 and 1981.

48. The estimates in row 3 come from different sources and cover different populations from the estimates in rows 1 and 2, so rows 1 and 2 need not add up to row 3. The numerators of rows 1 and 2 come from administrative data, which are likely to be incomplete. Row 3 comes from the CPS, which misses a disproportionate number of young male dropouts but may elicit exaggerated estimates of educational attainment from those it interviews. Row 3 includes individuals who attended school in other countries and subsequently immigrated to the United States, so if all else were equal it would be slightly lower than the sum of rows 1 and 2. But row 3 also excludes those who are in the armed forces or in institutions, which probably has the opposite effect.

49. Unlike the 1980 Census, the CPS classifies almost all Hispanics as white.

50. Results not shown here indicate that the coefficient was significantly higher for whites who reached the age of seventeen before 1930.

51. Results not shown here indicate that before 1940 the effect of parental education on children's education was even larger among blacks than among whites. Among blacks who would have finished high school in the 1920s and 1930s, an extra year of parental education boosted children's expected attainment by 0.43 years.

52. The standard deviation of tract means fell in all eight metropolitan areas, from an average of .167 to an average of .145. Since the grand means for all eight metropolitan areas fell from .217 to .155, the coefficient of variation rose in all eight areas.

53. The labels that NAEP gives the four reading levels shown in Table 5.9 have no intrinsic meaning. To construct these cutoff points, NAEP sets the mean for the combined sample of nine-, thirteen-, and seventeen-year-olds at 250 and sets the standard deviation at 50. The labels in Table 5.9 then represent scores above 200, 250, 300, and 350.

55. The gains in Table 5.9 look steadier than they should because the Educational Testing Service and the U.S. Department of Education have suppressed the results of a 1985–86 reading assessment that showed a large, inexplicable, one-time drop in reading skills. The reasons for this drop remain murky, but the fact that the 1987–88 results are in line with the long-term upward trend convinces me that 1985–86 was indeed an aberration.

55. The proportion of sixteen- and seventeen-year-old whites enrolled in school was 90.6 percent in October 1970 and 91.8 percent in October 1987. For blacks, the proportions were 85.7 percent in 1970 and 91.5 percent in 1987 (Bureau of the Census, "School Enrollment—Social and Economic Characteristics of Students, October 1988 and 1987," *Current Population Reports,* Series P-20, no. 443, table A-3). I could not find trend data for seventeen-year-olds alone, but in October 1987 the enrollment rate for seventeen-year-olds was 88.0 percent among whites and 88.2 percent among blacks (table 22). It is not clear how these figures change between fall and spring, when NAEP does most of its testing. NAEP also misses seventeen-year-olds who are already enrolled in college. But while 5 percent of all seventeen-year-olds are enrolled in college in October of a typical year, most of them have probably turned eighteen by the time NAEP does its testing.

56. One way to check this conclusion is to look at thirteen-year-olds, almost all of whom are in school. The proportion of black thirteen-year-olds reading above both the basic and the intermediate levels rose dramatically

between 1971 and 1988, but there was no comparable increase among white thirteen-year-olds.

57. Jones reports that NAEP only samples about 250 blacks per year in poor inner-city schools. The sampling errors of his trend estimates are therefore likely to be quite large. See Lyle Jones, "Achievement Trends for Black School Children, 1970–84," and "Trends in School Achievement of Black Children," Department of Psychology, University of North Carolina, Chapel Hill, 1987.

58. The standard deviation of seventeen-year-olds' reading scores fell from 42 to 36 points among whites and from 44 to 36 points among blacks. The black-white differential fell from 1.15 standard deviations in 1971 to 0.55 standard deviations in 1988. See Ina Mullis and Lunn Jenkins, *The Reading Report Card,* 1971–88 (Princeton: National Assessment of Educational Progress, 1990), p. 65.

59. Here and throughout, I use the term "homicide" to include both murder and nonnegligent manslaughter. I also use the term "murderer" to describe those who engage in nonnegligent manslaughter. For a more detailed discussion of the advantages and disadvantages of using homicide rates as evidence of changes in the level of violence, see Dane Archer and Rosemary Gartner, *Violence and Crime in Cross-National Perspective* (New Haven: Yale University Press, 1984).

60. FBI press release, dated April 8, 1990.

61. Roughly 70 percent of all homicides result in an arrest, so arrest data are a fairly good guide to the characteristics of suspected murderers. For data on the race of those arrested by race of victim, see for example FBI, *Crime in the United States* (Government Printing Office, 1976 and 1986).

62. An aggravated assault is one involving a weapon or resulting in serious injury. A robbery is a theft from a person that is carried out by means of force or threat of force.

63. The FBI's estimate of the homicide rate is always slightly lower than the NCHS estimate, but they show essentially the same trend.

64. The NCS also shows a decline in rape after 1981.

65. Among those telling the NCS that they were victims of an aggravated assault, for example, 57 percent claimed they had reported it to the police in 1987–88, compared to 53 percent in 1973–1975. For robbery, the reporting rate was 56 percent in 1987–88, compared to 53 percent in 1973–1975. (See U.S. Bureau of Justice Statistics, "Bulletin: Criminal Victimization, 1988" (Washington, 1989), p. 5.

66. Compare U.S. Bureau of Justice Statistics, *Sourcebook of Criminal Justice Statistics, 1988* (Government Printing Office, 1989, pp. 283, 427, and "Bulletin: Criminal Victimization 1988," p. 5.

67. Early in the 1980s BJS did release data tapes that included some information on the characteristics of the neighborhoods in which NCS respondents lived. The neighborhoods were not census tracts, however, and some of the data appears to have been erroneous. Using these data, Samuel Myers and William Sabol concluded that the fraction of all black victims living in neighborhoods with poverty rates above 25 percent in 1970 had fallen from 27 percent in 1973 to 20 percent in 1981 ("Crime and the Black Community: Issues in the Understanding of Race and Crime in America," Department of Economics, University of Maryland, College Park, no date). This decline is hard to interpret, since the neighborhoods in question were losing population during the 1970s. What we need are changes in victimization *rates* for rich and poor neighborhoods.

68. *Statistical Abstract of the United States, 1989,* p. 13. In a crude effort to adjust for the undercount of young males, the estimates in the text are based on data for both sexes combined.

69. If the violent crime rate for men twenty-five and over is R and the rate for men fifteen to twenty-four is 3R, the overall rate in 1960 would be $(.197)(3R)+(.803)(R)=1.394R$. The analogous rates would be 1.506R in 1975 and 1.402R in 1987.

70. *Statistical Abstract of the United States, 1989,* table 318.

71. Because of plea bargaining it is quite difficult to determine what percentage of prisoners actually committed violent crimes.

72. Alfred Blumstein, Jacqueline Cohen, Jeffrey Roth, and Christy Visher, eds., *Criminal Careers and "Career Criminals"* (Washington: National Academy Press, 1986), p. 123.

73. The estimates in Table 5.13 are not in fact based on the experience of women who turned twenty in a given year. Instead, the estimates are projections of what would happen if the age-specific birth rates in a given year were to continue indefinitely.

74. *Vital Statistics of the United States, 1986. Vol. 1—Natality* (Government Printing Office, 1989), table 1–7. My estimates assume that no teenage father or mother had more than one child per year.

75. For statistics on marriage rates by age, see Robert D. Mare and Christopher Winship, "Economic Opportunities and Trends in Marriage for Blacks and Whites," in Jencks and Peterson, *The Urban Underclass.*

76. We do not know how many illegal abortions there were before 1973. The "abortion ratio" among fifteen- to nineteen-year-olds (that is, the ratio of legal abortions to the sum of legal abortions and live births) was .283 in 1973, .364 in 1975, .451 in 1980, and .462 in 1985 (see, *Statistical Abstract of the United States, 1983,* pp. 61 and 68, and *1990,* p. 71). If there were no spontaneous miscarriages, these ratios would imply 8.1 pregnancies per 100 girls aged fifteen to nineteen in 1973, 8.7 in 1975, 9.7 in

1980, and 9.5 in 1985. These estimates probably overstate the increase in the pregnancy rate, however, since some pregnancies now ended by abortion would previously have been ended by miscarriage.

77. I estimated marital and nonmarital fertility by dividing expected lifetime fertility between marital and nonmarital births in the same way that actual births were divided in the relevant year.

78. Although the term "illegitimacy ratio" implies a moral judgment that now seems outmoded, alternative phrases, such as "the ratio of babies born out of wedlock to all babies," are so cumbersome that no reader should be expected to put up with them.

79. For a summary of recent evidence regarding the impact on children of growing up in a mother-only family, see Sara McLanahan, "The Consequences of Single Parenthood for Subsequent Generations," *Focus,* Madison, Institute for Research on Poverty, Fall 1988, pp. 16–21.

80. David L. Featherman and Robert M. Hauser, in *Opportunity and Change* (New York: Academic Press, 1978), tables 5.9, 6.9, and 6.19, present regression equations predicting years of school completed, occupational status, and earnings for national samples of men in 1962 and 1973. The independent variables are the education and occupational status of the head of the respondent's family when the respondent was sixteen years old, number of siblings, and dummies for race, farm origins, and "living with both your parents most of the time up to age 16." The coefficient of growing up in a broken family is typically two to four times the coefficient of siblings. If this pattern also holds for sons born out of wedlock, the positive effects of declining family size would outweigh the negative effects of the increase in out-of-wedlock births between 1960 and 1987.

81. William Julius Wilson and Kathryn M. Neckerman, "Poverty and Family Structure: The Widening Gap between Evidence and Public Policy Issues," in Sheldon Danziger and Daniel Weinberg, eds., *Fighting Poverty* (Cambridge: Harvard University Press, 1986), pp. 232–259.

82. The best analysis of welfare benefit levels and out-of-wedlock births is still David Ellwood and Mary Jo Bane, "The Impact of AFDC on Family Structure and Living Arrangements," in R. Ehrenberg, ed., *Research in Labor Economics,* (JAI Press, 1985), 137–207. See also the review in Irwin Garfinkel and Sara McLanahan, *Single Mothers and Their Children* (Washington: Urban Institute Press, 1986), pp. 55–63. For contrary evidence, see Robert Plotnick, "Determinants of Out-of-Wedlock Childbearing: Evidence from the National Longitudinal Survey of Youth," *Journal of Marriage and the Family,* 52 (August 1990), 735–746.

6. Welfare

1. An earlier version of this chapter, based on Edin's first twenty-five interviews, appeared in *American Prospect,* Winter 1990. David Ellwood, Irwin Garfinkel, Jane Mansbridge, Susan Mayer, Paul Starr, and members of the "underclass workshop" at Northwestern University's Center for Urban Affairs and Policy Research all made helpful comments on earlier drafts.

2. In April 1991 federal law allowed welfare recipients who worked full-time to keep $90 a month for work-related expenses and $175 per child per month for documented childcare expenses. During the first twelve months after a welfare recipient starts working, she can also keep some additional earnings. After that, her AFDC check is reduced by the full amount of her earnings (less allowable work-related expenses and childcare). Mothers can also keep the first $50 of any child support the welfare department extracts from the absent father.

3. Edin also promised all her recipients anonymity and recorded the interviews using fictitious names.

4. Edin actually contacted sixty mothers, but we dropped one of them because she cared for her children only two days a week.

5. We were not able to obtain data on the proportion of Cook County AFDC recipients in subsidized housing, so our judgment about the availability of subsidized housing is impressionistic. We discuss comparative housing costs in more detail later.

6. Edin's method almost inevitably oversamples welfare recipients with a lot of friends and undersamples short-term recipients. For a more detailed description of the way in which the initial sample of twenty-five was drawn, see Kathryn Edin, "There's a Lot of Month Left at the end of the Money: How Welfare Recipients in Chicago Make Ends Meet," Ph.D. diss. (Department of Sociology, Northwestern University, 1989).

7. According to the Illinois Department of Public Aid, Cook County recipients are 77 percent black and 10 percent non-Hispanic white. In the nation as a whole, recipients are roughly 40 percent black and 39 percent non-Hispanic white. U.S. House of Representatives, Committee on Ways and Means, "Background Material and Data on Programs within the Jurisdiction of the Committee on Ways and Means" (Washington: U.S. Government Printing Office, 1989), p. 564.

8. Roughly 17 percent of Cook County recipients live in the suburbs, compared to 26 percent of Edin's recipients.

9. In the nation as a whole, 9 percent of all AFDC recipients lived in public housing in 1987, while another 9 percent lived in other forms of subsidized housing ("Background Material and Data on Programs within the Jurisdiction of the Committee on Ways and Means," 1989, p. 564).

In Edin's sample, 20 percent lived in public housing, and 24 percent lived in other forms of subsidized housing. Almost all the mothers in public housing lived in Chicago's two largest projects (Cabrini Green and Robert Taylor Homes). All but one of the twelve mothers in other forms of subsidized housing lived in the suburbs.

10. The two mothers who came close to living on their checks ran deficits of $26 and $54 a month. A third teenage mother ran a cash surplus because she lived with her own mother, who paid her rent, utilities, and groceries. This allowed the teenager to use most of her $250 AFDC check for personal expenses. She saved the balance (about $60 a month) in order to attend college. The value of the food, rent, and utilities this teenage recipient received from her mother substantially exceeded her monthly savings, so without her mother's help she would have had a deficit.

11. When national surveys ask welfare mothers about their income and expenses, most mothers report spending far more than they take in. Economists have traditionally explained such puzzles by arguing that the families in question were only temporarily poor and were either drawing down their savings or borrowing against future income. (The classic formulation of this argument is Milton Friedman, *A Theory of the Consumption Function*, Princeton University Press, 1957.) This explanation of excess consumption among low-income families makes sense when applied to farmers or small businessmen who have had a bad year. It does not make much sense for welfare mothers, since mothers with savings are not eligible for welfare and very few have access to long-term credit. Only two of Edin's respondents had sufficient assets to support expenditures in excess of income for more than a month or two. (Both had received insurance settlements after going on welfare.) None had significant debts other than student loans, which they (and we) treated as ordinary income. A few had bought furniture or appliances on time, but they (and we) treated these as equivalent to renting the item in question.

Edin's respondents reported substantial month-to-month income fluctuations, which they dealt with by small-scale saving and borrowing. To eliminate this source of noise, Edin asked about "average" monthly income and expenditures. Using this approach, most respondents' estimates of their monthly income and expenditures came very close to balancing. A few respondents reported average monthly income significantly higher than their average expenditure. Since only one respondent reported saving anything, we infer that most respondents with "surplus" income were overestimating their income, underestimating their expenditures, or both. (Such optimism is common at all income levels.) For the sample as a whole, monthly income (including food stamps but no other in-kind income) exceeded expenditure by an average of 4.8 percent.

12. If a recipient has not repaid her excess benefits by the time she leaves the rolls, she must in theory make a lump-sum repayment.

13. To estimate the average midwestern family's expenditure on items other than food, shelter, and utilities in 1988–1990, we used data from the Consumer Expenditure Survey for the first quarter of 1989 (see U.S. Bureau of Labor Statistics, "Consumer Expenditure Survey: Quarterly Data from the Interview Survey," Report 784, 1990, table 4). Since welfare mothers get Medicaid, we excluded health-care expenditures from the comparison. Edin's fifty mothers reported cash expenditures averaging $664 a month, of which $50 went for food, $203 for rent, $30 for gas, $30 for electricity, and $13 for health care. That left $339 for everything else. The average midwestern family spent $1022 a month on items other than food, shelter, utilities, and health care.

14. The AFDC recipient unit—usually the mother and those of her children under eighteen—averaged 3.14 in Edin's sample, which is almost exactly the national average. The recipient unit is often smaller than the household, which may include the recipient's mother, a girlfriend, a boyfriend, an unreported husband, or grown children. Most mothers saw themselves as financially separate entities within their household and described budgets that covered only themselves and their children. When this was not the case, Edin had to make somewhat arbitrary allocations.

15. The monetary value of housing subsidies is a vexed question. If all the subsidized housing in which Edin's welfare mothers lived were rented at its market value, the ten apartments in public housing projects would rent for less than the twenty-eight unsubsidized apartments, while the twelve subsidized units in private buildings (eleven of which were in the suburbs) would rent for considerably more than the unsubsidized private units. Averaging over all subsidized units, their market value was probably not very different from that of the unsubsidized units. We therefore estimated the market value of the subsidy by calculating the difference between what subsidized and unsubsidized tenants paid for rent and utilities ($240 a month). The actual cost to the taxpayer is undoubtedly higher than this.

16. When Edin estimated the value of all noncash income, including all gifts provided by relatives and boyfriends, the fifty mothers' total income rose another $100 a month, to $1126. This estimate is conservative, in the sense that Edin tried to err on the low side when valuing gifts.

17. For details on how the original line was constructed, see Mollie Orshansky, "Counting the Poor: Another Look at the Poverty Profile," *Social Security Bulletin,* 28 (January 1965), 3–29.

18. The Gallup results are reported in William O'Hare, Taynia Mann, Kathryn Porter, and Robert Greenstein, *Real Life Poverty in America: Where the American Public Would Set the Poverty Line* (Washington: Center on Bud-

get and Policy Priorities, 1990). Families with incomes below $10,000 set the line somewhat lower than more affluent families. The published Gallup data suggest that poor families in cities of one million or more would probably set the poverty line for a family of four at about $16,000 (in 1989 dollars).

19. Lee Rainwater, in *What Money Buys* (New York: Basic Books, 1974), showed that survey respondents' estimates of how much money it took to achieve a given standard of living ("not poor," "getting along," "comfortable") all had about the same elasticity with respect to family size, regardless of which adjective he used to define the level of living. The elasticity of the poverty line with respect to family size was 0.29. The poverty threshold for a family of three should therefore be about $(3/4)^{.29}=92$ percent of that for a family of four, while the threshold for a family of two should be $(2/4)^{.29}=82$ percent of that for a family of four. Averaging across all five of the living levels that Rainwater investigated, the elasticity of respondents' estimates with respect to family size averaged 0.32. Since differences between living levels appear to be random, one could argue for using this figure rather than 0.29. In that case the poverty line for a family of three would be 91 percent of that for a family of four, and the line for a family of two would be 80 percent of that for a family of four.

20. Jagna Sharff, "The Underground Economy of a Poor Neighborhood," in Leith Mullings, ed., *Cities of the United States* (New York: Columbia University Press, 1987).

21. These estimates come from the 1984–85 Consumer Expenditure Surveys. All the numerical estimates from the CES presented here differ from those presented in earlier versions of this essay because earlier versions were not properly weighted. The CES does not identify specific metropolitan areas, but it does identify metropolitan areas of 4 million or more. Combining this information with data on region yields the groupings in the text. The estimates cover all families that rented their homes and reported total expenditures below $4000 per person. The CES does not allow us to determine how much of the city-to-city variation in rent is attributable to variation in housing subsidies.

22. U.S. House of Representatives, Committee on Ways and Means, *Background Material and Data on Programs within the Jurisdiction of the Committee on Ways and Means* (Government Printing Office, 1988), pp. 408ff.

23. The Bureau of Labor Statistics estimates that 15.5 percent of all target households refused to participate (*Consumer Expenditure Interview Survey: Quarterly Data, 1984–87,* Bulletin 2332, Government Printing Office, 1989). Among participants on our data tape, 10 percent failed to answer one or more of the income questions. The overall refusal rate for our purposes is thus $.155 + (.10)(1-.155)=24$ percent.

There were 86.8 million households in the United States in 1985 (*Statistical Abstract, 1989,* table 58). The 1985 CES data tapes indicate that there are about 3.7 percent more "consumer units" than households in the United States, for a total of 90.0 million consumer units in 1985. (In order to define a consumer unit, the CES divides expenses into three categories: rent, food, and "other." Individuals are members of the same consumer unit if they report sharing at least two of these three kinds of expenses.)

The AFDC caseload averaged 3.72 million families in 1985 (*Statistical Abstract, 1989,* table 604). Data from the Survey of Income and Program Participation (SIPP) and other sources suggest that something like 30 percent of those who are on the rolls at any given moment will leave within twelve months, to be replaced by an equal number of new entrants (see John Fitzgerald, "The Effects of the Marriage Market and AFDC Benefits on Exit Rates from AFDC," University of Wisconsin, Institute for Research on Poverty, Discussion Paper 878–89, 1989). This estimate implies that at least 4.8 million families received AFDC at some time during 1985. It follows that roughly 4.8/90.0=5.33 percent of all consumer units must have received income from AFDC. In our weighted 1984–85 CES sample, 2.65 percent of all consumer units included children under eighteen and reported that they had received income from "public assistance" during the previous twelve months. (For reasons that elude us, the unweighted percentage was 3.15, implying that on this dimension the CES weighting scheme makes the sample less representative.) Almost all these families presumably got income from AFDC. The estimated response rate among AFDC families was thus about 2.65/5.33=50 percent of the overall response rate. The overall response rate for welfare families must therefore have been about. (.50)(.845)(.90) = 38 percent.

24. The number of welfare recipients given in the text is from the unweighted sample. All other values are weighted. We assumed that a family received income from AFDC if it included children under the age of eighteen and reported income from public assistance during the past twelve months. This assumption could lead to classification errors in households where an adult who was not a parent of the children collected General Assistance, or where a married couple was receiving other benefits they classified as "public assistance." Most of our analyses therefore focused on one-adult households, where such classification errors should not be a serious problem.

25. Official AFDC data indicate that 37 percent of all AFDC families shared living quarters with one or more nonrecipients in 1984. These household members' incomes are not counted when calculating AFDC benefits unless they contribute to the AFDC mother's living expenses. In addition, 12 percent of all AFDC "recipient units" included two parents, one of whom was either unemployed or disabled. Overall, therefore, nearly half

of all households with income from AFDC included more than one adult in 1984 (Committee on Ways and Means, "Background Materials," 1989, p. 564). This is also true in the CES sample.

Official data imply, however, that only a quarter of all two-adult AFDC households included a married couple in 1984. In the CES, 56 percent of all two-adult households with children and income from public assistance included a married couple. Some of these couples may have told the CES they were married while telling the welfare department they were not. Others may have misclassified income from other sources as coming from public assistance. Either way, it seemed best to concentrate on one-adult AFDC households.

26. If the turnover in the AFDC caseload averages 30 percent annually, roughly $(1.0-.3)/(1.0+.3) = 54$ percent of those on the rolls at some point during a year are on for the entire year. On the average, part-year recipients should receive about half as much AFDC income as full-year recipients. Recipients who reported their outside income to the welfare department should also have received less from welfare than recipients with no outside income. Yet one-adult households with outside income got only 1 percent less from public assistance than one-adult households with no other income. Among households with two or more adults, those with outside income got only 5 percent less from public assistance than those with no other income.

27. We worked with what the Labor Department calls the "Interview Survey," which does not include detailed data on expenditures at grocery stores, drug stores, laundries, or dry cleaners. This information is collected from a different sample in the "Diary Survey," which covers a shorter period. The Interview Survey asked only one question about food expenditures. Some respondents said they spent far less on food than they got from food stamps. While a few of these respondents may have been selling their food stamps, most reported food expenditures so low that they could not possibly have fed the family for a month. We suspect that these respondents misunderstood the question about grocery expenditures and reported only their *cash* expenditures on food, ignoring the value of their food stamps. If we assume that all those who reported spending less on food than they got in food stamps were reporting cash expenditures over and above the value of their stamps, 82 percent of the one-adult households in which the head claimed that AFDC was her only source of income had total expenditures that exceeded her income. If we assume that all respondents' estimates of their grocery expenditures included the value of their food stamps, 73 percent of one-adult households reporting only AFDC income spent more than they received from AFDC.

28. Oscar Lewis, "The Culture of Poverty," in Daniel Patrick Moynihan, ed.,

On Understanding Poverty (New York: Basic Books, 1968), pp. 187–200.

29. William Julius Wilson, *The Truly Disadvantaged* (Chicago: University of Chicago Press, 1987).

30. Counting the homeless is difficult, and the numbers are surrounded by political controversy. Nonetheless, most experts agree that families with children almost always spend the night either in a regular household or in a shelter, not on the streets. This makes counting homeless families with children much easier than counting homeless individuals. The Department of Housing and Urban Development estimates that there were 60,000 homeless families living in shelters at any given time during 1988 ("A Report on the 1988 Survey of Shelters for the Homeless," Washington, 1989). This count may have missed some shelters, but the true count for 1988 is unlikely to have exceeded 80,000. All observers also agree that more than 90 percent of all families in shelters are receiving AFDC. Since the number of families receiving AFDC averaged 3.752 million in 1988 (*Statistical Abstract, 1990,* table 607), something like 2 percent must have been in shelters on any given night. Expanding the definition of homelessness to include welfare families living on sufferance in someone else's home would raise the count, but we have no way of knowing how large the increase would be.

31. Mental illness, alcohol abuse, and drug abuse not only make it harder for recipients to live on a small budget but also make it harder to earn money with which to supplement an inadequate check and harder to share an apartment with someone else.

32. These estimates do not include children living in institutions.

33. The Census Bureau issues an annual report on "Marital Status and Living Arrangements" (*Current Population Reports,* Series P-20). Table 4 of that report has always estimated the percentage of children separated from both parents. Until 1983, however, the bureau erroneously classified most children who lived with both their mother and their grandmother as living only with the grandmother. In 1980 and 1981, prior to correcting its classification procedures, the bureau classified an average of 11.8 percent of black children as living with neither parent and 2.4 percent as living with their mother and grandmother. In 1983 and 1984, after making the correction, it classified an average of 5.8 percent of black children as living with neither parent and 8.6 percent as living with their mother and grandmother. The decline in the estimated number of children separated from both parents is, therefore, almost entirely accounted for by the increase in the estimated number living with their mother and grandmother. It seems to follow that there was little real change in children's living arrangements between 1980–81 and 1983–84. If so, the data suggest that half the black children classified as living with neither parent in 1980–81 were ac-

tually living with their mother and grandmother. The estimates in the text assume that this was true throughout the years 1968–1980. Analogous calculations for whites and Hispanics show little change between 1980–81 and 1983–84, so we assume that the pre-1983 figures were roughly correct for these groups.

34. Estimates of welfare recipients' purchasing power appear in Table 5.5 of Chapter 5.

35. We estimated the number of single mothers with different amounts of schooling using a 1/1000 public-use sample of 1980 census records. To see if the figure had changed since 1980, we compared our 1980 results with Current Population Survey data on the educational attainment of mothers who headed households with children in 1987 ("Marital Status and Living Arrangements, March 1987," table 9). The CPS data differ from the census data in that the results are weighted by the number of children. Nonetheless, the 1987 CPS results are very close to those from the 1980 Census.

36. These estimates are for white mothers with no other income and two children under six, living in a metropolitan area of a western state with 6 percent unemployment. Rural mothers earned 13 percent less than urban mothers. A mother's age, the number and ages of her children, and her state's unemployment rate had little impact on her hourly earnings, though her children's ages did affect her chances of working. All these estimates are from Charles Michalopoulos' and Irwin Garfinkel's OLS results, reported in "Reducing Welfare Dependence and Poverty of Single Mothers by Means of Earnings and Child Support: Wishful Thinking and Realistic Possibilities," Institute for Research on Poverty, Discussion paper 882-89, University of Wisconsin, 1989, table 1. All have been converted from 1987 to 1989 dollars using the Consumer Price Index. As the authors emphasize, welfare mothers who do not currently report paid employment might earn either more or less than single mothers with the same demographic characteristics who currently report working for pay. We would need experimental data to determine the size and direction of this difference.

37. The finding that black and white women with the same education earn the same amount is at odds with Table 1.3 of Chapter 1. The difference could reflect the fact that Table 1.3 does not control age. Among women aged twenty-five to thirty-four who worked 35 or more hours per week in 1979, for example, high-school dropouts earned an average of $176 per week, regardless of their race. Among high-school graduates, the average was $208 for whites and $204 for blacks. The results for women under twenty-five and women aged thirty-five to forty-four follow the same pattern. See *1980 Census of Population, Vol. 1: Detailed Population Characteristics, United States Summary,* PC80-1-D1-A (Government Printing Office, 1981), table 296.

38. *Economic Report of the President* (Government Printing Office, 1990), p. 344.

39. Ibid., p. 338. This estimate assumes that the unemployment rate among single mothers is identical to that for all women who maintain families. The unemployment rate for women who maintained families ranged from a high of 12 percent in 1983 to a low of 8 percent in 1988 and 1989.

40. The figure would be somewhat higher if single mothers collected unemployment compensation whenever they were not working, but only a third of the unemployed get such compensation. The figure would be lower if, as seems likely, welfare mothers who entered the labor market were unemployed more than 10 percent of the time.

41. Gary Burtless, "The Effect of Reform on Employment, Earnings, and Income," in Phoebe Cottingham and David Ellwood, eds., *Welfare Policy for the 1990s* (Cambridge: Harvard University Press, 1989), pp. 103–140.

42. Another reason why training has not moved many mothers off welfare may be that those who gain the most usually seem to be those without much work experience. If a welfare mother was previously unemployable, raising her potential earnings to, say, $4000 a year would be an important accomplishment, but it would not get her off welfare. If she had previously earned $8000, the kind of training we have traditionally provided seldom seems to raise her potential earnings to $10,000.

43. This estimate is based on our analysis of the CES, which showed that nonwelfare single mothers paid an average of $761 a year for medical care (exclusive of nonprescription drugs) in 1984–85, while welfare mothers paid an average of $94. We inflated the difference to 1987 prices using the CPI's medical-care price index and rounded to the nearest $100. If welfare recipients have more medical problems than nonrecipients, as seems likely, losing their Medicaid coverage would increase their expenses more than $800. In addition, since single mothers who are not on welfare often have no medical insurance, they are likely to use fewer medical services than welfare mothers with identical problems. Nonwelfare mothers will experience this as a cost, even though it is not a budgetary cost.

44. To estimate the effect of employment in Table 6.2 we regressed clothing expenditures on household income and whether a mother worked in our sample of 1984–85 CES mothers. Assuming a $3000 increase in after-tax income, the income effect is $138 and the employment effect is $123, for a total of $261. Inflating to 1987 dollars and rounding yielded $300.

45. Both the finding that half of all working mothers pay for childcare and the dollar amounts in Table 6.2 are taken from Michalopoulos and Garfinkel, "Reducing Welfare Dependence and Poverty of Single Mothers by Means of Earnings and Child Support." All else equal, access to free childcare probably increases the likelihood that a single mother will take a job. If so,

more than 48 percent of today's welfare mothers would have to pay for childcare if they worked. If all welfare mothers worked 35 hours a week, moreover, the supply of cheap childcare in poor communities would diminish considerably, since baby sitting is a common way of supplementing an AFDC check. In very poor areas, where welfare mothers constitute a sizable fraction of all baby sitters, putting them all to work might raise the price of childcare significantly.

Note that, unlike the Ways and Means Committee, we did not assume that work-related expenses increased with earnings. The committee's estimates of work-related expenses are set at 30 percent of earnings for earnings up to $15,000. Our estimates average about $2500, regardless of earnings.

46. Working is more rewarding for a single mother who gets child-support payments from the absent father, because she can keep the entire payment. If she is on welfare, she can in theory keep only the first $50 a month. In practice, welfare departments cannot monitor an absent father's under-the-table payments, so it is not clear how much more a working mother gets to keep.

47. This estimate ignores goods and services provided by parents, boyfriends, and other private parties but includes food stamps and housing subsidies, as well as cash transfers from private parties.

48. Notes 43 and 44 describe the sources of the estimates for medical care and clothing. The estimate for childcare assumes that 60 percent of welfare mothers would have to pay for childcare if they worked and would pay the same amount that working single mothers now pay (see Table 6.2). The estimate for transportation assumes that mothers use public transportation. Many must buy cars, but the cost of a car cannot be treated solely as a work-related expense.

49. The Committee on Ways and Means ("Background Material," 1989, p. 536) estimates the net tax burden on a single mother earning $15,000 at $1676.

50. *Economic Report of the President, 1990,* p. 344.

51. See Table 5.5, Chapter 5.

52. See Robert Moffitt, "Historical Growth in Participation in Aid to Families with Dependent Children: Was There a Structural Shift?" *Journal of Post-Keynesian Economics,* 9 (Spring 1987), 347–363. Because state-to-state variation in benefit levels had only a moderate impact on the proportion of single mothers collecting AFDC, Moffitt concludes that the increase in benefits during the late 1960s and early 1970s played a modest role in the growth of the welfare rolls. This conclusion is quite sensitive to his assumption that food stamps should not be treated as part of the welfare package. Moffitt bases this argument on the fact that food stamps are also

available to single mothers who work at low-wage jobs. Anecdotal evidence suggests that the takeup rate for food stamps is much higher among welfare families than among families with the same cash income who do not collect welfare, but we could not find any empirical work on this issue. If the takeup rate *is* substantially lower among nonwelfare families, treating food stamps as if they were a generalized form of income maintenance may be a mistake.

53. Most analysts report much larger declines in the real value of welfare benefits. Our calculation differs from the usual ones in two respects. First, we define welfare as including not just AFDC but food stamps, whose value has risen with the Consumer Price Index. Second, we measure inflation using the fixed-weight price index for Personal Consumption Expenditures from the National Income and Product Accounts rather than the CPI. Because of an error in the treatment of housing costs, the CPI overstated inflation during the 1970s. It therefore exaggerates the decline in real welfare benefits.

54. See Table 5.5, Chapter 5.

55. The best single state-to-state comparison is David Ellwood and Mary Jo Bane, "The Impact of AFDC on Family Structure and Living Arrangements," *Research in Labor Economics,* 7 (1985), 137–207. For a review of other studies, see Irwin Garfinkel and Sara McLanahan, *Single Mothers and Their Children* (Washington: Urban Institute Press, 1986). All else equal, higher benefits are associated with a small increase in the proportion of families with children headed by single mothers. The effect seems to derive primarily from the fact that high benefits make mothers who already receive welfare less likely to marry (or remarry). High benefits also make single mothers more likely to establish their own households rather than live with their parents. High benefits do not appear to encourage out-of-wedlock births.

56. For a review of this literature, see Cheryl Hayes and Sheila Kamerman, eds., *Children of Working Parents: Experiences and Outcomes* (Washington: National Academy Press, 1983).

57. See Michalopoulos and Garfinkel, "Reducing Welfare Dependence and Poverty of Single Mothers by Means of Earnings and Child Support," table 1. The "Wisconsin standard" sets the absent father's obligation at 17 percent of his gross income for one child, 25 percent for two children, 29 percent for three, and 31 percent for four.

58. In 1988 there were 12.9 million children under eighteen living in female-headed families. Of the 7.33 million children receiving AFDC, roughly 88.6 percent or 6.49 million lived in single-parent families (Committee on Ways and Means, "Background Material," 1989, pp. 559, 563). Making all children in female-headed families eligible for AFDC would, therefore,

raise the number of children on the rolls by roughly $(12.9-6.5)/7.33 =$ 87 percent.

We expected to spend about $15.2 billion on AFDC for single mothers and their children in fiscal 1990. Had all female-headed families been eligible, and had the new recipients been distributed among states in the same way as existing recipients, costs would have risen by about $13.7 billion. The actual figure would probably be lower than this rough estimate, because the takeup rate among single mothers is currently lower in low-benefit states, so growth would be concentrated in those states. Making AFDC taxable, as we should if we made it available to all single mothers, would slightly reduce its cost. Allowing AFDC recipients to keep their earnings would also raise their money incomes, reducing their food-stamp entitlements somewhat. In theory, making eligibility depend entirely on marital status should also lower administrative costs.

59. Congress took a significant step in this direction as part of the deficit-reduction package passed in October 1990.

Index

Adams, Terry, 148
Affirmative action, 12–13, 16, 24–27, 66, 67–69, 93; economic differences and, 27–32; black family and income statistics, 32–34; racial differences in employment, 34–36; education effects, 36–40; economic discrimination and, 40–49; economic effects of, 49–58; Reagan policies and, 50, 51; employment and wage rates and, 56, 57; political costs of, 58–64; goals and quotas, 64–67
Aid to Dependent Children (ADC), 2–3, 20
Aid to Families with Dependent Children (AFDC), 2, 8, 13, 88, 214–215; family structure and, 11, 12, 195, 221; supplemental income and, 19–20, 78, 82, 83, 88–89, 207, 208, 212, 213, 217–226; benefit levels, 78, 79, 82, 84, 89, 90, 205, 206, 223, 226–228; "man in the house" rule, 80–81, 82, 83, 87; divorce rate and, 83–84; city comparison, 212–213; state comparison, 213–214, 219–220, 226; reforms, 232–235
Armed Forces Qualification Test (AFQT), 37–38
Auletta, Ken, 143

Bane, Mary Jo, 82, 83
Binet, Alfred, 104
Blau, Judith, 114–115
Blau, Peter, 4–5, 6–7, 114–115
Bound, John, 52
Bureau of Justice Statistics (BJS), 181, 183, 186–187
Burt, Sir Cyril, 106

Burtless, Gary, 222
Bush, George, 64

Carter, Jimmie, 127
Chicago. *See* Illinois welfare system
Civil Rights Act (1964), 3–4; Title VII, 49, 50, 53, 54, 57, 58, 59, 63–64
Coleman, James/Coleman Report, 4–5, 6
Confronting Crime (Currie), 14, 112
Consumer Expenditure Survey (CES), 214–215
Consumer Price Index (CPI), 72, 126, 147
Cook County. *See* Illinois welfare system
Crime and Human Nature (Wilson and Herrnstein), 14, 95–96, 99, 100, 109
Crime rates, 92–94; IQ and, 99, 103, 104–105, 108–109; city/nation comparison, 102, 113, 114–116, 118; historic overview, 116–119; underclass, 181–189
Current Population Survey (CPS), 152, 157
Currie, Elliott, 14, 112, 114, 116–117, 118

Denmark, study of adopted children, 100, 101
Duncan, Greg, 148
Duncan, Otis Dudley, 4–5, 6–7

Earned Income Tax Credit, 20, 223, 233
Eastern Europe, 22
Economic Opportunity Act, 3
Edin, Kathryn, 19, 206–207, 208, 209, 211, 213, 215, 217, 219, 225, 226
Ellwood, David, 82, 83
Equal Employment Opportunity Commission (EEOC), 50, 51, 57, 60, 69

Equal opportunity, 12, 13, 61. *See also* Affirmative action
Ethnic America (Sowell), 25
Ethnicity and income, 27–32
Executive Order 11246, 49

Family Assistance Plan, 9
Family Support Act (1988), 204, 222
Federal Bureau of Investigation (FBI), 181, 183, 185–186, 187
Federal Reserve Board, 125, 128
Food stamps, 24, 73, 74, 76, 86; eligibility for, 9, 25, 79, 130; allowances, 20, 205, 207, 208, 214, 215; poverty line and, 147, 205; family structure and, 195
Ford, Gerald, 9
France, 103, 104
Freeman, Richard, 52
Friedman, Milton

Garfinkel, Irwin, 222
General Education Development (GED) certificates, 171–173
General Social Survey (GSS), 27–29, 175
Ghetto culture, 16, 120–122, 215; black male joblessness, 122–120; neighborhood effects, 122, 136–138; single-parent families, 122, 130–136; discrimination and, 138–142
Great Depression, 1
Great Society programs, 3, 9–10
Griggs v. Duke Power Company, 50, 66, 67, 69

Harvard Educational Review, 105
Heredity, 13–14, 105–107; politics of, 94–96; environment and, 96–100; IQ and, 99, 104–105, 108–109; genetic effects of, 100–104; genetic theories, 109–111
Herrnstein, Richard, 14, 95, 97, 98, 100, 101, 102–103, 106, 109, 111, 112, 114, 118
Housing subsidies, 147; Section 8 certificates, 9, 10, 20, 219
Hughes, Mark, 159–160, 170, 177

Illinois welfare system, 205–214, 218–219
Inequality: A Reassessment of the Effect of Family and Schooling in America (Jencks et al.), 7–8, 9, 13
Institute for Policy Studies, 5
IQ, 13, 95; crime rates and, 99, 103, 104–105, 108–109

Japan, 103
Jensen, Arthur, 105–106
Johnson, Lyndon B., 3, 4, 9
Johnstone, John, 137
Jones, Lyle, 179–180
Juhn, Chinhui, 157, 158, 161

Kain, John, 123, 124
Kamin, Leon, 101, 106
Kennedy, John F., 3

Lane, Roger, 117
La Vida (Lewis), 120
Lewis, Oscar, 120, 215
Liebow, Elliot, 120
Losing Ground (Murray), 13, 70, 79, 85, 88, 91

Mare, Robert, 163–164
Markets and Minorities (Sowell), 25, 36
Marx, Karl, 128
Massachusetts, 125
McGovern, George, 9
Medicaid, 9, 20, 24, 72, 73–74, 75, 76, 147, 205, 223; eligibility, 25, 228
Medicare, 72, 73–74, 75, 147
Michalopoulos, Charles, 222
Moynihan, Daniel Patrick, 233
Murray, Charles, 13, 70–71, 72, 74, 75, 79–81, 82, 84, 85–86, 87, 88, 89, 90, 91

National Academy of Sciences, 189
National Assessment of Educational Progress (NAEP), 177–179
National Bureau of Economic Research, 127
National Center for Health Statistics (NCHS), 181, 183, 185

National Crime Survey (NCS), 183–185, 186, 187, 189

National Longitudinal Survey of Youth, 127

National Opinion Research Center, 27

Neighborhoods, 122; and behavior, 136–138; and crime, 137, 187; and education, 177, 179–180; and employment, 123–124, 159–160; and welfare, 170, 217

New Deal, 1, 3, 12

New York welfare system, 212, 227

Nixon, Richard, 9, 233

Nozick, Robert, 11

Office of Federal Contract Compliance (OFCC), 49, 50, 51

Office of Federal Contract Compliance Program (OFCCP), 50, 53, 57

Old Age and Survivors Insurance (OASI), 2

Personal Consumption Expenditure (PCE), 72

Phelps, Edmund, 42

Poverty line, 147, 205, 209–210

Poverty rates, 72–79, 147–151; latent, 85–86

Race: and affirmative action, 49–58, 64–69; and crime, 98–100, 182–185; and culture, 16–18, 128–130, 134–136, 138–142; defining, 27–29; and education, 171–179; and earnings, 36–40; and economic discrimination, 40–49, 58–63; and income, 27–32; and employment, 34–36, 122–130, 154, 160–165; and poverty, 149, 154–155; and underclass, 145, 149, 160–164; and welfare, 215–218

Reagan, Ronald/Reagan administration, 12, 14, 24, 52, 89; affirmative action program, 50, 51; military budget, 125

Reforms. *See* Welfare reform

Rise of the Meritocracy (Young), 13

Rogers, Willard, 148

Safety-net concept, 13, 70–72, 87–91; poverty rate and, 72–79; social policy

and single mothers, 79–85; welfare programs and, 85–87

Scarr, Sandra, 99

Seattle-Denver income-maintenance experiments, 83

Section 8 housing certificates and subsidies, 9, 10, 20, 219

Sharff, Jagna, 212

Smith, James, 51

Smith, Marshall, 7

Social Darwinism, 70

Social Security Act, 1–2

Soviet Union, 22

Sowell, Thomas, 12, 25–26, 27, 29, 30, 36, 39, 51, 52, 57, 58, 63

Supplemental Security Income (SSI), 9, 86

Sweden, 11, 23, 100, 110

Tally's Corner (Liebow), 120

"Thirty and a third" rule, 88–89

Title VII, Civil Rights Act, 49, 50, 53, 54, 57, 58, 59, 63–64

Truly Disadvantaged, The (Wilson), 16, 121, 130, 143

Underclass, 15–16, 18–19, 120, 136, 143–145, 198–203; impoverished, 145–151; jobless male, 152–166; jobless female, 166–170; educational, 170–181; violent, 181–189; reproductive, 189–198; mothers, 215–218

Unemployment Insurance (UI), 1–2, 8

Ward's Cove Packing Co. v. Frank Atonio, 64, 67

Weber, Max, 30

Wechsler Intelligence Scale for Children (WISC), 104–105

Welch, Finis, 51

Welfare reform, 204–205; Illinois study, 205–214; national surveys, 214–215; underclass vs. mainstream mothers, 215–218; benefits vs. supplemental income, 218–226; benefit levels, 226–230; working mothers and, 230–235

Wilson, James Q., 14, 94, 95, 97, 98,

Wilson, James Q. (*continued*)
    100, 101, 102–103, 104, 106, 109,
    111, 112, 114, 118
Wilson, William Julius, 16, 121–124,
    129–132, 136, 137, 140–143, 152,
    215

Winship, Christopher, 163–164
Wolfgang, Marvin, 113

Young, Michael, 13